# EDUCATORS GUIDE TO FREE HEALTH, PHYSICAL EDUCATION & RECREATION MATERIALS

*

Edited by
Staff Editors

*

Educational Consultant
Michael Belongie, B. S.
Curriculum Manager, Randolph Public Schools

*

## FIFTY-FIRST ANNUAL EDITION
## 2018-2019

**(For use during school year 2018-2019)**

## EDUCATORS PROGRESS SERVICE, INC.
### 214 Center Street
### Randolph, Wisconsin 53956

T0377936

Published by

Educators Progress Service, Inc.

Randolph, Wisconsin 53956

Library of Congress Catalog Card Number 68-57948

Printed and Bound in the United States of America

International Standard Book Number 978-0-87708-609-3

# TABLE OF CONTENTS

**III**

**IV**

# FROM THE PUBLISHER'S DESK

As always, health topics dominate the news. Sometimes you'll find that there's a cure for a previously fatal disease, and yes, sometimes you'll find that the health habits you practice might actually cause illness. The information about how to maintain proper health changes constantly. School textbooks would be hard pressed to keep up with this ever changing news. Thus, supplementary teaching aids have become a necessity for the health educator. However, as school budgets decrease everywhere, finding money to acquire these additional resources is difficult, if not impossible. That's the philosophy behind the series of EDUCATORS GUIDES TO FREE MATERIALS we have been publishing for more than 85 years. Money for supplementary teaching aids was next to impossible to find in 1934 and really hasn't changed in all these years.

This 51st annual edition of EDUCATORS GUIDE TO FREE HPER MATERIALS tells you where to find these teaching aids for your classroom, free of charge. As you might imagine, the process of revising the annual editions of the EDUCATORS GUIDES is a time consuming process (there are now sixteen titles in the series). In our efforts to find new materials every year, we write thousands of letters to companies inquiring about materials they are willing to offer free to educators and others. Each and every year these letters are written. If no response is received, no materials from that source are included. **No materials are included if we have not received permission from the sponsor to tell you about their availability**. All addresses are verified as well. Your requests for FREE educational aids WILL BE ANSWERED.

It's a lot of work but it is very rewarding. It really is a pleasure to be able to point educators to teaching aids that not only **save tight budgets** but **add to the educational environment**. We like to find materials that "help teachers teach," not only to make their jobs easier but to help students learn more.

It is fortunate, for students and educators alike, that the availability and quality of free supplementary teaching aids increases annually. It is imperative that teachers are able to "handle what's thrown at them" in a timely manner–these materials provide the ability to help you do so. Any comments you may have regarding this GUIDE are welcomed–we like to learn from you, too.

Kathy Nehmer

P. S. **Be sure to use only the 2018-2019 GUIDE for the current school year**, as hundreds of titles available last year are no longer available!

# HOW TO USE THE EDUCATORS GUIDE TO FREE HEALTH, PHYSICAL EDUCATION & RECREATION MATERIALS

The 2018-2019 GUIDE provides busy (and cash-strapped) educators with information about 601 free videotapes, lesson plans, slides, teacher's guides, print materials, and web resources to help save money and enrich the classroom. Finding the materials you desire, and requesting them, is easy.

The **BODY** of the GUIDE (white pages) gives you full information on each of the titles, **ALL of which are new in this edition**. These 601 new titles dramatically illustrate one reason that it is so important to use only the most current edition of the GUIDE.

The **TITLE INDEX** (blue pages) is an alphabetical listing of all items appearing in the body of the GUIDE, with page references. This enables readers to locate any item whose title is known. The TITLE INDEX guides you directly to any specific item in the GUIDE, where you can read the description of the material and find all ordering information.

In the **SUBJECT INDEX** (yellow pages) all materials relating to topics of a more specific nature than the general subject headings in the body of the GUIDE are categorized. These "yellow pages" work like the familiar "yellow pages" of a telephone directory.

The **SOURCE INDEX** (green pages) provides an alphabetical list of the names of the 165 organizations from which materials can be obtained. Also included in each entry are page numbers which indicate where the materials from that particular source appear in the body of the GUIDE. Use of this feature facilitates the ordering, with one letter, of more than one selection if a source offers several.

# ANALYSIS OF EDUCATORS GUIDE TO FREE
# HPER MATERIALS–2018

|  | TOTAL ITEMS |
|---|---|
| **HEALTH** | |
| Alcohol, Tobacco, and Other Drugs | 32 |
| Diseases | 109 |
| Family Life Education | 31 |
| Food and Nutrition | 220 |
| Mental Health | 20 |
| Personal Health and Hygiene | 33 |
| Public Health and Environment | 28 |
| Safety and First Aid | 38 |
| **PHYSICAL EDUCATION** | 46 |
| **RECREATION** | 44 |
| **TOTAL** | **601** |

# YOUR LETTERS OF REQUEST

When requesting materials, please make your letter of request clear. Identify yourself and your organization. Be sure to use any identifying numbers provided and **observe any restrictions** on distribution as indicated in the GUIDE.

Do not be alarmed if everything you request does not come. The list of materials changes; materials go out of date and are replaced by new items. We cannot tell at the time of printing how long each item will last. Sponsors are asked to assure us, with reasonable certainty, that their materials will be available for approximately one year. It is to meet this need that the GUIDE is revised annually.

There are 165 sources of free materials listed in the **2018-2019 EDUCATORS GUIDE TO FREE HEALTH, PHYSICAL EDUCATION & RECREATION MATERIALS.** Please make certain that the request you are making is to the proper company.

In writing for materials, the following form is suggested. The listing used as an example is selected from page 6.

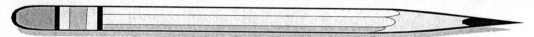

REGIONAL SCHOOL #7
Central Avenue
Randolph, WI 53956

August 25, 2018

National Cancer Institute
Publications Ordering Service
P. O. Box 24128
Baltimore, MD 21227

Dear Sponsor:

We would like to receive a copy of the following booklet as listed in the 2018 EDUCATORS GUIDE TO FREE HEALTH, PHYSICAL EDUCATION & RECREATION MATERIALS:

Biological Therapy: Treatments That Use Your Immune System to Fight Cancer

Thank you for your cooperation in assisting us to enrich the curriculum of our school.

Sincerely,

Debbie Stiemsma
8th Grade Health Educator

# HOW TO COOPERATE WITH THE SPONSORS

Subscribers to EPS services have frequently asked us for guidelines to follow in requesting sponsored materials. The following 14 questions are quoted from an address given by Thomas J. Sinclair, Ph.D., formerly Manager of Educational and Group Relations for the Association of American Railroads, at a convention of the National Science Teachers Association.

1. Poor handwriting, which you strive to correct in your pupils, often makes coupons and other requests useless. Is your handwriting distinct on requests?

2. Neither industry nor the U. S. Postal Service is omniscient. Do you include complete and accurate details of your address, including zip number?

3. Postcards, small social stationery, or slips of paper present filing problems and can easily be lost. Do you use standard sized stationery?

4. Remember that in big companies thousands of pieces of mail go in and out every day. Do you allow sufficient time for handling your request.

5. Most students advise businesses that they are studing a topic. Do you check your spelling?

6. If you were on the receiving end, you'd have a different view of mass classroom letter-writing projects to the same business organization. Do you make certain that only one request goes to a particular source from your classroom?

7. Instructions on a coupon, in a guide, or on an order form are there for a purpose. Do you read and follow these instructions?

8. Some organizations have dozens—sometimes hundreds—of different teaching aids. Specific needs should be outlined. Do you say "Send me everything you've got" or its equivalent?

9. Source lists and guides get out of date. Do you check to see if the list you are consulting is a recent one?

10. Sometimes aids are in limited supply or available only to teachers in single copies. Do you keep requests reasonable and show some respect for the costs of materials?

11. Sample copies are for examination, with the privilege of ordering quantities subsequently. Do you order classroom quantities blind—without first examining an item for suitability for your purpose?

12. Companies keep records and files. They frequently like to know precisely where their materials are going. Are you careful to mention your school connection?

13. Do you make a real effort to make certain the organization you are writing to is the correct one, and that it could reasonably have the material you are seeking?

14. Duplications and unnecessary correspondence only slow good service to the teaching profession. Do you consult your associates to see whether needed materials have already been supplied to your school?

These questions provide specific suggestions that should, in the long run, make for happier sponsors and better service to educators.

# EVALUATION OF INDUSTRY-SPONSORED EDUCATIONAL MATERIALS

The business community has long recognized its obligation to support the agencies of the community that contribute to its security and well-being. In partial fulfillment of this obligation, industry trade associations and non-profit organizations have been producing supplementary materials for use in our nation's schools for some time. Properly planned, sponsored educational resources serve a valuable role and are particularly effective in giving information to students in an area where the sponsoring organization has achieved a high degree of specialization. When properly designed, sponsored materials can be used to motivate students and direct their energies into productive channels of growth.

Educational systems can respond more effectively to changes in technology, job structure, income, population, and manpower requirements with close support and involvement of industry. Both sectors have a common goal of strengthening the institutional programs at all levels in our schools. Operationally, this requires a strong industry-education alliance, particularly at the local level in preparing people for a productive role in the marketplace.

The National Association for Industry-Education Cooperation (NAIEC) was established in 1964 as a logical development out of the Business Industry Section of the National Science Teachers Association. Its purposes were (and still are) to bring about a better understanding between Education and the Business community and to mobilize the resources of education and industry to improve the relevance and quality of educational programs at all levels.

NAIEC members represent a variety of private and public organizations. Major trade associations, corporations, schools, and school districts are members. School superintendents, college presidents, curriculum and other education coordinators, business executives, industry-education coordinators, deans, department chairpersons, career education and job placement specialists, and faculty participate in the Association's programs.

The membership works together to identify problems of mutual interest, formulate plans and procedures, develop acceptable business-sponsored instructional materials, and communicate the advantages of industry-education cooperation.

The NAIEC membership has determined that the set of guiding principles (see below) for the preparation of materials for distribution to schools established by a study financed by American Iron and Steel Institute and carried out by the George Peabody Teachers College are valid and has found that materials embracing these criteria have usually found acceptance and use in the nation's schools and classrooms.

1. Work with a representative group of teachers and administrators to ensure meeting a curricular need.

2. Provide factual material desired by the schools. Include only that information which is significant to the study of particular problems or topics of concern to the teacher and student.

3. Exclude all advertising. A credit line naming the sponsor is enough; indeed schools need to know the publisher and the date of the material.

4. Materials must be written to the particular age level, reading level, interests, and maturity of the group for whom they are intended.

5. Keep the materials free of persuasion; avoid special pleading of the interests of any one point of view or group.

6. Make the materials available to educators only upon request.

X

In 1976 members of the NAIEC developed "A Guide for Evaluating Industry-Sponsored Educational Materials" which embodies the above listed criteria from the educator's viewpoint. This guide is an effort by the National Association for Industry-Education Cooperation (NAIEC) to present teachers with an instrument for evaluating sponsored education resources. These supplemental materials may take the form of teacher guides, filmstrips, games actually designed for the classroom, or pamphlets, reprinted articles, annual reports which may provide valuable background information but are not developed specifically for the teacher's use. (It is suggested that the Guide is more effective with the items actually designed for the classroom.)

If, after completing your evaluation of those items designed for the classroom, you have no further use for the instrument, the sponsoring organization providing the item would appreciate your evaluation with any comments you might have for guidance in the development of future materials. Hopefully this will foster closer industry-education cooperation.

## A GUIDE FOR EVALUATING INDUSTRY-SPONSORED EDUCATIONAL MATERIALS

Title of material _____ Date produced, if available _____

Sponsor (name of organization)_____

Type of material:  Audio _____ Audiovisual _____ Printed _____ Other _____

Type of instruction suitable for this material:  Individual _____ Group _____

This evaluation is based on usage in _____ (grade level)

Evaluator _____ Date _____

Subject area/School _____

Address _____

_____

INSTRUCTIONS FOR USE:

Use the following scale by evaluating the material as it relates to your situation.  Each of the descriptive statements is followed by a scale of (1), (2), (3), (4), (5).  Indicate your assessment of the material by circling the appropriate number in the scale:

(1) Definitely yes          (4) Definitely no
(2) Yes                     (5) Material cannot be evaluated on this concept
(3) No

## OBJECTIVES

Identified outcomes may be obtained through use of the material.

1 2 3 4 5

The materials are representative of the curriculum involved; that is, they help further the objectives of the curriculum.

1 2 3 4 5

## ABILITY RANGE

The materials provide for the range of abilities and aptitudes of all pupils.

1 2 3 4 5

## CONTENT

The material is contemporary.

1 2 3 4 5

The material is controversial.

1 2 3 4 5

The material presents alternative views.

1 2 3 4 5

The material does not present a bias for a product, organization, or social cause.

1 2 3 4 5

The material does present a bias for a product, organization, or social cause.

1 2 3 4 5

If such a bias exists, it does not invalidate the material for my purposes.

1 2 3 4 5

The nature and scope of the material content is adequate to meet curriculum objectives.

1 2 3 4 5

The material is supplementary to the curriculum.

1 2 3 4 5

The material offers opportunity for integration of the subject within the existing curriculum.

1 2 3 4 5

The material correlates with a specific discipline area.

1 2 3 4 5

The material introduces experiences that would not otherwise be available in the classroom.

1 2 3 4 5

The material suggests other resources, supplementary and/or instructional.

1 2 3 4 5

## UTILIZATION CHARACTERISTICS

|  | SCALE |
|---|---|
| The anticipated time utilization is commensurate with anticipated value of outcome. | 1 2 3 4 5 |
| The material demands special conditions for use. | 1 2 3 4 5 |
| The material is appropriate for student's reading level. | 1 2 3 4 5 |
| The material is appropriate for student's interest level. | 1 2 3 4 5 |
| The material is attractive to students. | 1 2 3 4 5 |
| The material provides motivation for students. | 1 2 3 4 5 |

## PRESENTATION OF MATERIALS

| Provisions are made for evaluating the material as it is used within the educational program. | 1 2 3 4 5 |
|---|---|
| Instructional procedures are outlined. | 1 2 3 4 5 |
| The style of the presentation is likely to lead students toward accomplishing basic goals. | 1 2 3 4 5 |
| Sample student activities and questions are included. | 1 2 3 4 5 |
| The instructions to teachers are clearly stated. | 1 2 3 4 5 |
| The intended use is easily understood. | 1 2 3 4 5 |
| The production quality of the materials is acceptable. | 1 2 3 4 5 |

## EVALUATION

| The material provides for feedback to the user. | 1 2 3 4 5 |
|---|---|
| The material provides for self-evaluation. | 1 2 3 4 5 |

# HEALTH--ALCOHOL, TOBACCO, AND OTHER DRUGS

## Alcohol--A Potent Drug

Provides the history of alcohol and discusses the effect it has on the body--both temporary and permanent.

Availability: Single copies to schools, libraries, and homeschoolers world-wide. A stamped, self-addressed envelope is appreciated.
Suggested Grade: 2-12
Order Number: order by title
Format: Flyer

**Source: Narcotic Educational Foundation of America**
**28245 Avenue Crocker, Suite 230**
**Santa Clarita, CA 91355-1201**
**Phone: 1-661-775-6968**
**Fax: 1-661-775-1648**
**World Wide Web URL: http://www.cnoa.org**
**Email Address: lwhite@cnoa.org**

## Alcohol, Peer Pressure and Underage Drinking Info for Young Teens

Offers valuable information about underage drinking, alcohol addiction, and more.

Availability: All requesters
Suggested Grade: 5-8
Order Number: not applicable
Format: Web Site

**Source: National Institute on Alcohol Abuse and Alcoholism**
**World Wide Web URL: http://www.thecoolspot.gov/**

## Charting a Healthier Course for the Adolescent "At Risk" of Substance Abuse

Assists the health educator in teaching students the benefits of good health versus the harmful effects of alcohol and drugs on their mental and physical health.

Availability: Staff at schools with NET, WIC, CSFP, FDPIR, CACFP, UMD or Child Nutrition Program food programs in the United States. Those not having such an affiliation should contact their library to place an interlibrary loan request.
Suggested Grade: Teacher Reference
Order Number: NAL HV4999.Y68C4
Format: VHS videotape
Special Notes: Includes supplementary materials.
Terms: Borrower pays return postage. RETURN the day after scheduled use. Book at least 4 weeks in advance. Requests must include your name, phone, mail address, eligibility program, title, NAL number, show date, and a statement, "I have read the warning on copyright restrictions and accept full responsibility for compliance." One title per request.

**Source: National Agricultural Library**
**Document Delivery Services Branch**
**4th Floor, Photo Lab**
**10301 Baltimore Avenue**
**Beltsville, MD 20705-2351**
**Phone: 1-301-504-5994**
**Fax: 1-301-504-5675**
**World Wide Web URL: http://www.nal.usda.gov/fnic**
**Email Address: lending@nal.usda.gov**

## Cigars: No Such Thing as a Safe Smoke

Discusses the misconception that cigars are safer to smoke than cigarettes.

Availability: Limit of 49 copies to schools, libraries, and homeschoolers world-wide.
Suggested Grade: 6-Adult
Order Number: order by title
Format: Brochure
Special Notes: May also be downloaded from the Web site. Quantities in excess of 50 are available from Federal Trade Commission, Distribution Office, 600 Pennsylvania Avenue, NW, Washington, D. C. 20580-0001 or fax to: 1-703-739-0991.

**Source: Federal Trade Commission**
**Consumer Response Center**
**600 Pennsylvania, N. W., Room H-130**
**Washington, DC 20580**
**World Wide Web URL:**
**http://www.ftc.gov/bcp/consumer.shtm**

## Clearing the Air: Quit Smoking Today

Offers a variety of approaches to quitting smoking; for the motivated person.

Availability:
Suggested Grade: 6-Adult
Order Number: not applicable
Production Date: 2010
Format: Downloadable Booklet
Special Notes: May also be downloaded from the web site.

**Source: National Cancer Institute**
**World Wide Web URL: http://cancer.gov/publications**

## Club Drugs

This site discusses the types of drugs that are commonly used at dance clubs and raves. It explains the dangers of these drugs.

Availability: All requesters
Suggested Grade: 9-Adult
Order Number: not applicable
Format: Web Site

**Source: National Criminal Justice Reference Service**
**World Wide Web URL:**
**http://www.whitehousedrugpolicy.gov/drugfact/**
**club/index.html**

## College Drinking: Changing the Culture

Includes section for parents, high school counselors, and students that give the latest statistics and information about drinking and this age group.

Availability: All requesters
Suggested Grade: 9-Adult
Order Number: not applicable
Format: Web Site

**Source: National Institute on Alcohol Abuse and Alcoholism**
**World Wide Web URL:**
**http://www.collegedrinkingprevention.gov/**

# HEALTH--ALCOHOL, TOBACCO, AND OTHER DRUGS

## Creating Safe and Drug-Free Schools: An Action Guide
A complete guide to schools, students, parents, and community and business groups for creating schools that are safe.

Availability:        All requesters
Suggested Grade:  Teacher Reference
Order Number:     not applicable
Format:              Online Book
**Source: United States Department of Education**
**World Wide Web URL:**
**http://www.ed.gov/offices/OSDFS/actguid/index.html**

## Drug Abuse Resistance Education Web Site
For those schools that use the D.A.R.E. program, here is more material that reinforces the message. Also useful to others independent of the program.

Availability:        All requesters
Suggested Grade:  5-7
Order Number:     not applicable
Format:              Web Site
**Source: Drug Abuse Resistance Education**
**World Wide Web URL: http://www.dare.com/**

## Drugs, Trafficking, and Social Implications
Compilation of TV programs on the drug problem.

Availability:        Schools, libraries, and nursing homes in the United States.
Suggested Grade:  6-12
Order Number:     SILA7-video
Production Date:  1989
Format:              VHS videotape
Terms:              Borrowers must have a User's Agreement on file with this source--available by mail or via the Internet. Return postage is paid by borrower; return 12 days after showing. Book at least three weeks in advance. All borrowers are limited to a total of ten items per semester.
**Source: Latin American Resource Center**
**Stone Center for Latin American Studies**
**Tulane University**
**100 Jones Hall**
**New Orleans, LA  70118**
**Phone: 1-504-862-3143**
**Fax: 1-504-865-6719**
**World Wide Web URL:**
**http://stonecenter.tulane.edu/pages/detail/48/**
**Lending-Library**
**Email Address: crcrts@tulane.edu**

## Factline
Here are a number of facts sheets about various drugs of abuse as well as tobacco.

Availability:        All requesters
Suggested Grade:  6-Adult
Order Number:     not applicable
Format:              Online Fact Sheets
**Source: Indiana Prevention Resource Center**
**World Wide Web URL:**
**http://www.drugs.indiana.edu/library-factline.html**

## Fetal Alcohol Syndrome:  Prenatal Drug and Alcohol Use and Its Effects
Discusses the effects of drugs, alcohol, and smoking on the fetus.

Availability:        Staff at schools with NET, WIC, CSFP, FDPIR, CACFP, UMD or Child Nutrition Program food programs in the United States. Those not having such an affiliation should contact their library to place an interlibrary loan request.
Suggested Grade:  7-Adult
Languages:         English; Spanish
Order Number:     English Video 3251; Spanish Video 2352
Production Date:  1999
Format:              VHS videotape
Terms:              Borrower pays return postage.  RETURN the day after scheduled use.  Book at least 4 weeks in advance. Requests must include your name, phone, mail address, eligibility program, title, NAL number, show date, and a statement, "I have read the warning on copyright restrictions and accept full responsibility for compliance."  One title per request.
**Source: National Agricultural Library**
**Document Delivery Services Branch**
**4th Floor, Photo Lab**
**10301 Baltimore Avenue**
**Beltsville, MD  20705-2351**
**Phone: 1-301-504-5994**
**Fax: 1-301-504-5675**
**World Wide Web URL:  http://www.nal.usda.gov/fnic**
**Email Address:  lending@nal.usda.gov**

## First Grade Plus
A program to help educate young children about the dangers of drugs.

Availability:        All requesters
Suggested Grade:  1
Order Number:     not applicable
Format:              Downloadable Curriculum
**Source: First Grade Plus**
**World Wide Web URL: http://www.firstgradeplus.com**

## How to Avoid Weight Gain When You Stop Smoking
Discusses eating as the end result of a series of linked events and shows ex-smokers how to break those links to break the chain.

Availability:        Staff at schools with NET, WIC, CSFP, FDPIR, CACFP, UMD or Child Nutrition Program food programs in the United States. Those not having such an affiliation should contact their library to place an interlibrary loan request.
Suggested Grade:  7-12
Order Number:     NAL Video 1696
Production Date:  1992
Format:              VHS videotape
Terms:              Borrower pays return postage.  RETURN the day after scheduled use.  Book at least 4 weeks in advance. Requests must include your name, phone, mail address,

*All materials listed in this 2018-2019 edition are BRAND NEW!*

eligibility program, title, NAL number, show date, and a statement, "I have read the warning on copyright restrictions and accept full responsibility for compliance." One title per request.

**Source: National Agricultural Library**
**Document Delivery Services Branch**
**4th Floor, Photo Lab**
**10301 Baltimore Avenue**
**Beltsville, MD 20705-2351**
**Phone: 1-301-504-5994**
**Fax: 1-301-504-5675**
**World Wide Web URL: http://www.nal.usda.gov/fnic**
**Email Address: lending@nal.usda.gov**

## Joe Chemo
Designed to reduce teen smoking, this site is a takeoff on the Joe Camel advertisements.
Availability: All requesters
Suggested Grade: 6-12
Order Number: not applicable
Format: Web Site
**Source: Professor Scott Plous**
**World Wide Web URL: http://www.joechemo.org/**

## Making Healthy Choices
Designed to help the parents or caregivers of children with disabilities who are in middle school. Subject emphasizes being alcohol and drug free.
Availability: Librarians in the United States.
Suggested Grade: Adult
Order Number: Audiocassette No. 376
Production Date: 1995
Format: Set of 2 Audiotapes
Special Notes: Produced by Learning Systems Group.
Terms: Borrower pays return postage. RETURN the day after scheduled use. Book at least 4 weeks in advance. Requests must include your name, phone, mail address, eligibility program, title, NAL number, show date, and a statement, "I have read the warning on copyright restrictions and accept full responsibility for compliance." One title per request.
**Source: National Agricultural Library**
**Document Delivery Services Branch**
**4th Floor, Photo Lab**
**10301 Baltimore Avenue**
**Beltsville, MD 20705-2351**
**Phone: 1-301-504-5994**
**Fax: 1-301-504-5675**
**World Wide Web URL: http://www.nal.usda.gov/fnic**
**Email Address: lending@nal.usda.gov**

## Marijuana: Facts for Teens
Defines and explores the effects of marijuana on adolescents.
Availability: All requesters
Suggested Grade: 6-12
Order Number: not applicable
Format: Online Article
**Source: National Institute on Drug Abuse**
**World Wide Web URL:**
**http://www.nida.nih.gov/MarijBroch/MarijIntro.html**

## Marijuana: Facts Parents Need to Know
Informs parents about the effects of this drug and presents statistics concerning its use.
Availability: All requesters
Suggested Grade: Adult
Order Number: not applicable
Format: Online Article
**Source: National Institute on Drug Abuse**
**World Wide Web URL:**
**http://www.nida.nih.gov/MarijBroch/**
**MarijIntro.htmlParents**

## Mind Over Matter Series
A series of brochures, including a teacher's guide, about the brain's response to various drugs.
Availability: All requesters
Suggested Grade: 5-9
Order Number: not applicable
Format: Online Articles
**Source: National Institute on Drug Abuse**
**World Wide Web URL:**
**http://www.nida.nih.gov/MOM/MOMIndex.html**

## Real Scoop on Tobacco
You've been hired to convince a young man to stop smoking--how do you do it?
Availability: All requesters
Suggested Grade: 5-9
Order Number: not applicable
Format: WebQuest
**Source: Ginger Nehls**
**World Wide Web URL:**
**http://www.flagstaff.k12.az.us/demiguel/real.htm**

## Reconstructors, The
Online games to help students learn about drugs and how to make informed decisions about avoiding them.
Availability: All requesters
Suggested Grade: 6-8
Order Number: not applicable
Format: Web Site
**Source: Center for Technology in Teaching and Learning**
**World Wide Web URL: http://reconstructors.rice.edu/**

## Smoking Danger Demonstration
Demonstrate the potential harmful effects of smoking with this simple experiment
Availability: All requesters
Suggested Grade: All ages
Order Number: not applicable
Format: Online Lesson Plan
**Source: Gary Hopkins**
**World Wide Web URL:**
**http://www.educationworld.com/a_lesson/00-2/lp2192.shtml**

# HEALTH--ALCOHOL, TOBACCO, AND OTHER DRUGS

**Smoking Prevention Strategies for Urban and Minority Youth**

Explores how to get this particular audience to avoid smoking.

Availability:         All requesters
Suggested Grade:  Teacher Reference
Order Number:     not applicable
Production Date:  1997
Format:               Online Article
**Source: Wendy Schwartz**
**World Wide Web URL:**
**http://www.ericdigests.org/1998-1/smoking.htm**

**Speed--Amphetamines**

Explains what amphetamines are and their effect on the body.

Availability:         Single copies to schools, libraries, and homeschoolers world-wide. A stamped, self-addressed envelope is appreciated.
Suggested Grade:  2-12
Order Number:     order by title
Format:               Flyer
**Source: Narcotic Educational Foundation of America**
**28245 Avenue Crocker, Suite 230**
**Santa Clarita, CA 91355-1201**
**Phone: 1-661-775-6968**
**Fax: 1-661-775-1648**
**World Wide Web URL: http://www.cnoa.org**
**Email Address: lwhite@cnoa.org**

**Spit Tobacco: A Guide for Quitting**

Information to tell you how and why to quit.

Availability:         Limit of 50 copies to schools, libraries, and homeschoolers in the United States and Canada.
Suggested Grade:  6-12
Order Number:     NIH Pub. No. 06-3270
Production Date:  2006
Format:               Booklet
**Source: National Institute of Dental and Craniofacial Research**
**National Oral Health Information Clearinghouse**
**1 NOHIC Way**
**Bethesda, MD 20892-3500**
**Phone: 1-301-232-4528**
**Fax: 1-301-480-4098**
**World Wide Web URL: http://www.nidcr.nih.gov**
**Email Address: nidcrinfo@mail.nih.gov**

**Substance Abuse Fact Sheets**

The fact sheets discuss alcohol, marijuana, tobacco, and many other drugs.

Availability:         All requesters
Suggested Grade:  6-12
Order Number:     not applicable
Format:               Downloadable Fact Sheets
**Source: Oakland County Michigan Health Division**
**World Wide Web URL:**
**http://www.oakgov.com/health/info_pub/fs_index.html**

**Truth About Alcohol, The**

Designed to provide middle school students with facts about alcohol such as what alcohol is, how it acts on the body, and why young people are so vulnerable to its dangers. It focuses on situations adolescents can relate to in their own lives: peer pressure to drink, problems caused by drinking and driving, and the emotional trauma of living with a parent who abuses alcohol.

Availability:         Staff at schools with NET, WIC, CSFP, FDPIR, CACFP, UMD or Child Nutrition Program food programs in the United States. Those not having such an affiliation should contact their library to place an interlibrary loan request.
Suggested Grade:  5-8
Order Number:     NAL Video 1148
Production Date:  1991
Format:               VHS videotape
Terms:     Borrower pays return postage. RETURN the day after scheduled use. Book at least 4 weeks in advance. Requests must include your name, phone, mail address, eligibility program, title, NAL number, show date, and a statement, "I have read the warning on copyright restrictions and accept full responsibility for compliance." One title per request.
**Source: National Agricultural Library**
**Document Delivery Services Branch**
**4th Floor, Photo Lab**
**10301 Baltimore Avenue**
**Beltsville, MD 20705-2351**
**Phone: 1-301-504-5994**
**Fax: 1-301-504-5675**
**World Wide Web URL: http://www.nal.usda.gov/fnic**
**Email Address: lending@nal.usda.gov**

**Understanding Anabolic Steroids**

Explains these drugs which were originally developed to treat diseases, but are now being abused.

Availability:         Single copies to schools, libraries, and homeschoolers world-wide. A stamped, self-addressed envelope is appreciated.
Suggested Grade:  2-12
Order Number:     order by title
Format:               Flyer
**Source: Narcotic Educational Foundation of America**
**28245 Avenue Crocker, Suite 230**
**Santa Clarita, CA 91355-1201**
**Phone: 1-661-775-6968**
**Fax: 1-661-775-1648**
**World Wide Web URL: http://www.cnoa.org**
**Email Address: lwhite@cnoa.org**

**Up in Smoke: The Truth About Tar and Nicotine Ratings**

Explains the misleading ratings found on smoking materials.

Availability:         Limit of 49 copies to schools, libraries, and homeschoolers world-wide.
Suggested Grade:  6-Adult
Order Number:     order by title

**4**

# HEALTH--ALCOHOL, TOBACCO, AND OTHER DRUGS

Format:          Brochure
Special Notes:   May also be downloaded from the Web site. Quantities in excess of 50 are available from Federal Trade Commission, Distribution Office, 600 Pennsylvania Avenue, NW, Washington, D. C. 20580-0001 or fax to: 1-703-739-0991.

**Source:  Federal Trade Commission**
**Consumer Response Center**
**600 Pennsylvania, N. W., Room H-130**
**Washington, DC  20580**
**World Wide Web URL:**
**http://www.ftc.gov/bcp/consumer.shtm**

**You Can Control Your Weight As You Quit Smoking**
Offers help on how to avoid weight gain and adopt a healthier lifestyle when quitting smoking.

Availability:      All requesters
Suggested Grade:   4-Adult
Order Number:      not applicable
Production Date:   1998
Format:            Online Article; 10 pages
Special Notes:     Use the on-site search engine to easily find this title.  You may request a printed copy mailed to you for a fee.

**Source:  Federal Citizen Information Center**
**World Wide Web URL:  http://www.pueblo.gsa.gov/**

## Acute Lymphocytic Leukemia
Very complete information about this disease.

| | |
|---|---|
| Availability: | Limit of 25 copies to schools, libraries, and homeschoolers in the United States. |
| Suggested Grade: | 6-Adult |
| Order Number: | PS33 |
| Format: | Booklet; 48 pages |
| Special Notes: | Order via web site only. May also be downloaded from the web site. |

**Source: Leukemia & Lymphoma Society, The**
**World Wide Web URL: http://www.lls.org//resourcecenter/**
**freeeducationmaterials/leukemia/**

## Age-Related Macular Degeneration
Discusses macular degeneration and low vision resources.

| | |
|---|---|
| Availability: | All requesters |
| Suggested Grade: | 7-Adult |
| Order Number: | not applicable |
| Format: | Downloadable Article |

**Source: American Academy of Ophthalmology**
**World Wide Web URL:**
**http://www.geteyesmart.org/eyesmart/**

## Ah Choo!
Students use the Internet to find and compare illnesses that they have had or that they have heard about in the media.

| | |
|---|---|
| Availability: | All requesters |
| Suggested Grade: | 5-8 |
| Order Number: | not applicable |
| Format: | Online Lesson Plan |

**Source: Jerry Citron**
**World Wide Web URL:**
**http://www.thirteen.org/edonline/lessons/achoo/index.html**

## Asthma & Allergy Medications
Provides information on antihistamines, decongestants, and more.

| | |
|---|---|
| Availability: | Limit of one copy to non-profit schools, libraries, and homeschoolers world-wide. |
| Suggested Grade: | 7-Adult |
| Languages: | English; Spanish |
| Order Number: | order by title |
| Format: | Brochure |
| Special Notes: | Requests must be made via web site or email ONLY. |

**Source: American Academy of Allergy, Asthma &**
**Immunology**
**Attn: Membership Assistant**
**555 East Wells Street, Suite 1100**
**Milwaukee, WI 53202**
**World Wide Web URL: http://www.aaaai.org**
**Email Address: info@aaaai.org**

## Asthma and Physical Activity in the School
This easy-to-read booklet is a perfect companion for teachers and coaches who want to help students with asthma participate in sports and physical activities.

| | |
|---|---|
| Availability: | One copy is free to schools, libraries, and homeschoolers world-wide. Shipping charges will apply if more than one publication is requested. |
| Suggested Grade: | 4-12 |
| Order Number: | 05-3651 |
| Format: | Booklet |

**Source: National Heart, Lung, and Blood Institute**
**Information Center**
**P. O. Box 30105**
**Bethesda, MD 20824-0105**
**Phone: 1-301-592-8573**
**Fax: 1-240-629-3246**
**World Wide Web URL: http://www.nhlbi.nih.gov/**
**Email Address: nhlbiinfo@nhlbi.nih.gov**

## Battle Against Disease, The
Looks at the efforts of the Japanese government and the Japan Medical Association in their battle against infectious disease.

| | |
|---|---|
| Availability: | Schools, libraries, homeschoolers, and nursing homes in Arizona and California (zipcodes beginning 900-931 and 935). |
| Suggested Grade: | 6-Adult |
| Order Number: | 084 |
| Production Date: | 1982 |
| Format: | VHS videotape |
| Terms: | Borrower pays postage both ways; you may call the number below to learn how much postage costs. Return within two weeks of date borrowed. An individual may borrow 2 items at one time. For non-profit and educational use only. |

**Source: Consulate General of Japan, Los Angeles**
**350 South Grand Avenue, Suite 1700**
**Los Angeles, CA 90071-3459**
**Phone: 1-213-617-6700**
**Fax: 1-213-617-6727**
**World Wide Web URL: http://www.la.us.emb-japan.go.jp**

## Biological Therapy: Treatments That Use Your Immune System to Fight Cancer
Describes biological therapy, a type of cancer treatment that works with the patient's immune system.

| | |
|---|---|
| Availability: | Limit of 20 copies TOTAL, in any combination, to schools, libraries, homeschoolers and others world-wide. |
| Suggested Grade: | 9-Adult |
| Order Number: | P992 |
| Production Date: | 2004 |
| Format: | Booklet |
| Special Notes: | May also be downloaded from the web site. |

**Source: National Cancer Institute**
**Publications Ordering Service**
**P. O. Box 24128**
**Baltimore, MD 21227**
**Phone: 1-800-4-CANCER**
**Fax: 1-301-330-7968**
**World Wide Web URL: http://cancer.gov/publications**

**Bone Marrow Transplantation and Peripheral Blood Stem Cell Transplantation Questions and Answers**
A fact sheet that explains the step-by-step procedures of two types of transplantations used with high-dose chemotherapy, including their risks and benefits

| | |
|---|---|
| Availability: | All requesters |
| Suggested Grade: | 9-Adult |
| Order Number: | not applicable |
| Format: | Downloadable Fact Sheet |

**Source: National Cancer Institute**
**World Wide Web URL:**
**http://www.cancer.gov/cancertopics/factsheet/**
**Therapy/bone-marrow-transplant**

**Cancer and the Environment: What You Need to Know, What You Can Do**
Focuses on the agents in the environment that cause cancer and what we can do to lower our cancer risk.

| | |
|---|---|
| Availability: | |
| Suggested Grade: | Adult |
| Order Number: | P011 |
| Production Date: | 2003 |
| Format: | Downloadable Booklet |

**Source: National Cancer Institute**
**World Wide Web URL: http://cancer.gov/publications**

**Cancer Information Center**
Background information on all types of cancer.

| | |
|---|---|
| Availability: | All requesters |
| Suggested Grade: | 7-Adult |
| Order Number: | not applicable |
| Format: | Online Articles |

**Source: Cancer Group Institute**
**World Wide Web URL: http://www.cancergroup.com/**

**Catch the Wellness Bug! Elementary Level Wellness Promotion Activities**
Children are shown exercising, saying "no" to drugs and alcohol, and more.

| | |
|---|---|
| Availability: | Staff at schools with NET, WIC, CSFP, FDPIR, CACFP, UMD or Child Nutrition Program food programs in the United States. Those not having such an affiliation should contact their library to place an interlibrary loan request. |
| Suggested Grade: | 2-6 |
| Order Number: | NAL Kit 183 |
| Production Date: | 1993 |
| Format: | VHS videotape |
| Special Notes: | Includes supplementary teaching materials. |
| Terms: | Borrower pays return postage. RETURN the day after scheduled use. Book at least 4 weeks in advance. Requests must include your name, phone, mail address, eligibility program, title, NAL number, show date, and a statement, "I have read the warning on copyright restrictions and accept full responsibility for compliance." One title per request. |

**Source: National Agricultural Library**
**Document Delivery Services Branch**
**4th Floor, Photo Lab**
**10301 Baltimore Avenue**
**Beltsville, MD 20705-2351**
**Phone: 1-301-504-5994**
**Fax: 1-301-504-5675**
**World Wide Web URL: http://www.nal.usda.gov/fnic**
**Email Address: lending@nal.usda.gov**

**Childhood Asthma**
Includes tips for parents, caregivers, and school personnel.

| | |
|---|---|
| Availability: | Limit of one copy to non-profit schools, libraries, and homeschoolers world-wide. |
| Suggested Grade: | Teacher Reference |
| Languages: | English; Spanish |
| Order Number: | order by title |
| Format: | Brochure |
| Special Notes: | Requests must be made via web site or email ONLY. |

**Source: American Academy of Allergy, Asthma & Immunology**
**Attn: Membership Assistant**
**555 East Wells Street, Suite 1100**
**Milwaukee, WI 53202**
**World Wide Web URL: http://www.aaaai.org**
**Email Address: info@aaaai.org**

**Chronic Disease Fact Sheets**
Diseases discussed range from breast cancer to diabetes and other diseases.

| | |
|---|---|
| Availability: | All requesters |
| Suggested Grade: | 6-12 |
| Order Number: | not applicable |
| Format: | Downloadable Fact Sheets |

**Source: Oakland County Michigan Health Division**
**World Wide Web URL:**
**http://www.oakgov.com/health/info_pub/fs_index.html**

**Chronic Myelogenous Leukemia**
Very complete information about this disease.

| | |
|---|---|
| Availability: | Limit of 25 copies to schools, libraries, and homeschoolers in the United States. |
| Suggested Grade: | 6-Adult |
| Order Number: | CML |
| Format: | Booklet |
| Special Notes: | Order via web site only. May also be downloaded from the web site. |

**Source: Leukemia & Lymphoma Society, The**
**World Wide Web URL:**
**http://www.lls.org//resourcecenter/freeeducationmaterials/**
**leukemia/**

**Communicable Diseases Fact Sheets**
From anthrax to VRSA and all sorts of communicable diseases in between.

| | |
|---|---|
| Availability: | All requesters |
| Suggested Grade: | 6-12 |
| Order Number: | not applicable |

Format:                Downloadable Fact Sheets
         **Source: Oakland County Michigan Health Division**
               **World Wide Web URL:**
     **http://www.oakgov.com/health/info_pub/fs_index.html**

## Communicable Disease Fact Sheets

Lots of fact sheets about communicable diseases--from amebiasis to zoonoses.

Availability:        All requesters
Suggested Grade:  6-Adult
Languages:         English; Spanish
Order Number:     not applicable
Format:               Downloadable Fact Sheets
         **Source: New York Department of Health**
               **World Wide Web URL:**
    **http://www.health.state.ny.us/diseases/communicable/**

## Diet, Nutrition and Prostate Cancer

Discusses the connection between diet, nutrition, and cancer of this male gland.

Availability:        Limit of 1 copy to schools, libraries, and homeschoolers in the United States and Canada.
Suggested Grade:  10-Adult
Order Number:     order by title
Format:               Booklet
     **Source: American Institute for Cancer Research**
               **Publication Orders**
               **1759 R Street, N. W.**
             **Washington, DC 20009**
            **Phone: 1-800-843-8114**
             **Fax: 1-202-328-7226**
   **World Wide Web URL: http://www.aicr.org**
      **Email Address: aicrweb@aicr.org**

## Dry Mouth

Discusses the causes of dry mouth, the importance of saliva to oral health, and steps to follow to relieve dryness.

Availability:        Limit of 50 copies to schools, libraries, and homeschoolers in the United States and Canada.
Suggested Grade:  6-Adult
Languages:         English; Spanish
Order Number:     English NIH Pub. No. 08-3174; Spanish NIH Pub. No. 08-3174S
Production Date:  2008
Format:               Booklet
     **Source: National Institute of Dental and Craniofacial Research**
    **National Oral Health Information Clearinghouse**
                 **1 NOHIC Way**
           **Bethesda, MD 20892-3500**
           **Phone: 1-301-232-4528**
             **Fax: 1-301-480-4098**
  **World Wide Web URL: http://www.nidcr.nih.gov**
     **Email Address: nidcrinfo@mail.nih.gov**

## Environmental Health Fact Sheets

Fact sheets covering many environmental health issues.

Availability:        All requesters
Suggested Grade:  6-12
Order Number:     not applicable
Format:               Downloadable Fact Sheets
         **Source: Oakland County Michigan Health Division**
               **World Wide Web URL:**
     **http://www.oakgov.com/health/info_pub/fs_index.html**

## Epidemic Africa

Demonstrates the problem of HIV/AIDS in Africa and shows some positive response programs. Includes an introduction and conclusion from Archbishop Desmond Tutu.

Availability:        Schools, libraries, homeschoolers, and nursing homes in the United States.
Suggested Grade:  9-Adult
Order Number:     order by title
Production Date:  2000
Format:               VHS videotape
Terms:          Borrower pays return postage. Return the day after scheduled showing, via UPS or Priority Mail, insured for $100.00. Book 4 weeks in advance and include an alternate date. Order should include name of person responsible for handling the video, and complete mailing address. Please mention this Guide when ordering. Tapes may not be duplicated, edited or exhibited for a fee.
          **Source: Church World Service**
              **Film & Video Library**
    **28606 Phillips Street, P. O. Box 968**
            **Elkhart, IN 46515**
      **Phone: 1-800-297-1516, ext. 338**
           **Fax: 1-574-262-0966**
**World Wide Web URL: http://www.churchworldservice.org**
   **Email Address: videos@churchworldservice.org**

## Everybody's Different--Nobody's Perfect

Offered--for use in whole or in part--as one approach that may prove of value for parental guidance or for educators offering disability awareness curriculums.

Availability:        Single copies to schools, libraries, and homeschoolers in the United States; single copies to Canada.
Suggested Grade:  K-4
Languages:         English; Spanish
Order Number:     P-108
Format:               Booklet
Special Notes:    May also be downloaded from the web site.
       **Source: Muscular Dystrophy Association**
           **Publications Department**
           **3300 E. Sunrise Drive**
         **Tucson, AZ 85718-3208**
           **Phone: 1-800-572-1717**
            **Fax: 1-520-529-5300**
         **World Wide Web URL:**
**http://www.mdausa.org/publications/puborder.aspx**
       **Email Address: mda@mdausa.org**

## Everything Doesn't Cause Cancer

Worry a little less. Puts major, minor and unproven risk factors for cancer in perspective.

Availability: Limit of 1 copy to schools, libraries, and homeschoolers in the United States and Canada.
Suggested Grade: 10-Adult
Order Number: order by title
Format: Brochure
Special Notes: May also be downloaded from the web site.
Source: **American Institute for Cancer Research**
**Publication Orders**
**1759 R Street, N. W.**
**Washington, DC 20009**
**Phone: 1-800-843-8114**
**Fax: 1-202-328-7226**
**World Wide Web URL: http://www.aicr.org**
**Email Address: aicrweb@aicr.org**

## Everything You Need to Know About...Asthma & Food

Discusses what foods can trigger an asthma attack.

Availability: All requesters
Suggested Grade: 4-12
Order Number: not applicable
Production Date: 1997
Format: Downloadable Leaflet
Source: **International Food Information Council Foundation**
**World Wide Web URL:**
**http://ific.org/publications/brochures/index.cfm**

## Facts About Angina

Describes how this disease affects the body and includes information on symptoms, causes, diagnoses, and treatments. Reproducible.

Availability: One copy is free to schools, libraries, and homeschoolers world-wide. Shipping charges will apply if more than one publication is requested.
Suggested Grade: 4-12
Order Number: 04-5685
Format: Fact Sheet
Special Notes: May also be downloaded from the web site.
Source: **National Heart, Lung, and Blood Institute**
**Information Center**
**P. O. Box 30105**
**Bethesda, MD 20824-0105**
**Phone: 1-301-592-8573**
**Fax: 1-240-629-3246**
**World Wide Web URL: http://www.nhlbi.nih.gov/**
**Email Address: nhlbiinfo@nhlbi.nih.gov**

## Facts About Arrhythmias/Rhythm Disorders

Describes how this disease affects the body and includes information on symptoms, causes, diagnoses, and treatments. Reproducible.

Availability: One copy is free to schools, libraries, and homeschoolers world-wide. Shipping charges will apply if more than one publication is requested.
Suggested Grade: 4-12
Order Number: 07-5826
Format: Fact Sheet
Special Notes: May also be downloaded from the web site.
Source: **National Heart, Lung, and Blood Institute**
**Information Center**
**P. O. Box 30105**
**Bethesda, MD 20824-0105**
**Phone: 1-301-592-8573**
**Fax: 1-240-629-3246**
**World Wide Web URL: http://www.nhlbi.nih.gov/**
**Email Address: nhlbiinfo@nhlbi.nih.gov**

## Facts About Cardiomyopathy

Describes how this disease affects the body and includes information on symptoms, causes, diagnoses, and treatments. Reproducible.

Availability: One copy is free to schools, libraries, and homeschoolers world-wide. Shipping charges will apply if more than one publication is requested.
Suggested Grade: 4-12
Order Number: 06-5805
Format: Fact Sheet
Special Notes: May also be downloaded from the web site.
Source: **National Heart, Lung, and Blood Institute**
**Information Center**
**P. O. Box 30105**
**Bethesda, MD 20824-0105**
**Phone: 1-301-592-8573**
**Fax: 1-240-629-3246**
**World Wide Web URL: http://www.nhlbi.nih.gov/**
**Email Address: nhlbiinfo@nhlbi.nih.gov**

## Facts About Cystic Fibrosis

Information about this lung disease.

Availability: One copy is free to schools, libraries, and homeschoolers world-wide. Shipping charges will apply if more than one publication is requested.
Suggested Grade: 4-12
Order Number: 06-5803
Format: Leaflet
Special Notes: May also be downloaded from the web site.
Source: **National Heart, Lung, and Blood Institute**
**Information Center**
**P. O. Box 30105**
**Bethesda, MD 20824-0105**
**Phone: 1-301-592-8573**
**Fax: 1-240-629-3246**
**World Wide Web URL: http://www.nhlbi.nih.gov/**
**Email Address: nhlbiinfo@nhlbi.nih.gov**

## Facts About Heart Failure

Discusses this affliction and how it can be diagnosed.

Availability: One copy is free to schools, libraries, and homeschoolers world-wide. Shipping charges will apply if more than one publication is requested.

# HEALTH--DISEASES

Suggested Grade:   4-12
Order Number:   04-5694
Format:   Fact Sheet
Special Notes:   May also be downloaded from the web site.
    **Source: National Heart, Lung, and Blood Institute**
      **Information Center**
      **P. O. Box 30105**
      **Bethesda, MD 20824-0105**
      **Phone: 1-301-592-8573**
      **Fax: 1-240-629-3246**
    **World Wide Web URL: http://www.nhlbi.nih.gov/**
      **Email Address: nhlbiinfo@nhlbi.nih.gov**

## Facts About Heart Transplant
Facts about this life-saving procedure.

Availability:   One copy is free to schools, libraries, and homeschoolers world-wide. Shipping charges will apply if more than one publication is requested.
Suggested Grade:   4-12
Order Number:   08-6169
Format:   Fact Sheet
Special Notes:   May also be downloaded from the web site.
    **Source: National Heart, Lung, and Blood Institute**
      **Information Center**
      **P. O. Box 30105**
      **Bethesda, MD 20824-0105**
      **Phone: 1-301-592-8573**
      **Fax: 1-240-629-3246**
    **World Wide Web URL: http://www.nhlbi.nih.gov/**
      **Email Address: nhlbiinfo@nhlbi.nih.gov**

## Facts About Insomnia
Explains this sleep disorder.

Availability:   One copy is free to schools, libraries, and homeschoolers world-wide. Shipping charges will apply if more than one publication is requested.
Suggested Grade:   4-12
Order Number:   07-5824
Format:   Leaflet
Special Notes:   May also be downloaded from the web site.
    **Source: National Heart, Lung, and Blood Institute**
      **Information Center**
      **P. O. Box 30105**
      **Bethesda, MD 20824-0105**
      **Phone: 1-301-592-8573**
      **Fax: 1-240-629-3246**
    **World Wide Web URL: http://www.nhlbi.nih.gov/**
      **Email Address: nhlbiinfo@nhlbi.nih.gov**

## Facts About Narcolepsy
Explains this potentially deadly sleep disorder.

Availability:   One copy is free to schools, libraries, and homeschoolers world-wide. Shipping charges will apply if more than one publication is requested.
Suggested Grade:   4-12
Order Number:   06-5825

---

Format:   Leaflet
Special Notes:   May also be downloaded from the web site.
    **Source: National Heart, Lung, and Blood Institute**
      **Information Center**
      **P. O. Box 30105**
      **Bethesda, MD 20824-0105**
      **Phone: 1-301-592-8573**
      **Fax: 1-240-629-3246**
    **World Wide Web URL: http://www.nhlbi.nih.gov/**
      **Email Address: nhlbiinfo@nhlbi.nih.gov**

## Facts About Pesticides and Food Additives, The
There is no convincing evidence that foods with pesticide residues or additives increase cancer risk--here is more information.

Availability:   Limit of 1 copy to schools, libraries, and homeschoolers in the United States and Canada.
Suggested Grade:   10-Adult
Order Number:   order by title
Format:   Brochure
    **Source: American Institute for Cancer Research**
      **Publication Orders**
      **1759 R Street, N. W.**
      **Washington, DC 20009**
      **Phone: 1-800-843-8114**
      **Fax: 1-202-328-7226**
    **World Wide Web URL: http://www.aicr.org**
      **Email Address: aicrweb@aicr.org**

## Facts About Problem Sleepiness
Explains this sleep disorder.

Availability:   One copy is free to schools, libraries, and homeschoolers world-wide. Shipping charges will apply if more than one publication is requested.
Suggested Grade:   4-12
Order Number:   97-4071
Format:   Leaflet
Special Notes:   May also be downloaded from the web site.
    **Source: National Heart, Lung, and Blood Institute**
      **Information Center**
      **P. O. Box 30105**
      **Bethesda, MD 20824-0105**
      **Phone: 1-301-592-8573**
      **Fax: 1-240-629-3246**
    **World Wide Web URL: http://www.nhlbi.nih.gov/**
      **Email Address: nhlbiinfo@nhlbi.nih.gov**

## Facts About Raynaud's Phenomenon
Discusses this disorder of the small blood vessels that feed the skin.

Availability:   One copy is free to schools, libraries, and homeschoolers world-wide. Shipping charges will apply if more than one publication is requested.
Suggested Grade:   4-12
Order Number:   06-5814
Production Date:   1993

*All materials listed in this 2018-2019 edition are BRAND NEW!*

Format:             Article
Special Notes:      May also be downloaded from the web site.
Source:  National Heart, Lung, and Blood Institute
            Information Center
            P. O. Box 30105
            Bethesda, MD  20824-0105
            Phone: 1-301-592-8573
            Fax: 1-240-629-3246
World Wide Web URL:  http://www.nhlbi.nih.gov/
            Email Address:  nhlbiinfo@nhlbi.nih.gov

## Facts About Restless Legs Syndrome
Explains this sleep disorder.
Availability:        One copy is free to schools, libraries, and
                     homeschoolers world-wide. Shipping charges
                     will apply if more than one publication is
                     requested.
Suggested Grade:  4-12
Order Number:     06-5822
Format:           Leaflet
Special Notes:    May also be downloaded from the web site.
Source:  National Heart, Lung, and Blood Institute
            Information Center
            P. O. Box 30105
            Bethesda, MD  20824-0105
            Phone: 1-301-592-8573
            Fax: 1-240-629-3246
World Wide Web URL:  http://www.nhlbi.nih.gov/
            Email Address:  nhlbiinfo@nhlbi.nih.gov

## Facts About Sickle Cell Anemia
Concise, accurate information about this disease.
Availability:        One copy is free to schools, libraries, and
                     homeschoolers world-wide. Shipping charges
                     will apply if more than one publication is
                     requested.
Suggested Grade:  4-12
Order Number:     05-5681
Format:           Fact Sheet
Special Notes:    May also be downloaded from the web site.
Source:  National Heart, Lung, and Blood Institute
            Information Center
            P. O. Box 30105
            Bethesda, MD  20824-0105
            Phone: 1-301-592-8573
            Fax: 1-240-629-3246
World Wide Web URL:  http://www.nhlbi.nih.gov/
            Email Address:  nhlbiinfo@nhlbi.nih.gov

## Facts About Sleep Apnea
Explains this potentially deadly sleep disorder.
Availability:        One copy is free to schools, libraries, and
                     homeschoolers world-wide. Shipping charges
                     will apply if more than one publication is
                     requested.
Suggested Grade:  4-12
Order Number:     05-5680
Format:           Leaflet
Special Notes:    May also be downloaded from the web site.

Source:  National Heart, Lung, and Blood Institute
            Information Center
            P. O. Box 30105
            Bethesda, MD  20824-0105
            Phone: 1-301-592-8573
            Fax: 1-240-629-3246
World Wide Web URL:  http://www.nhlbi.nih.gov/
            Email Address:  nhlbiinfo@nhlbi.nih.gov

## Fibromyalgia--Questions and Answers
A collection of articles about this condition.
Availability:        Single copies to schools, libraries, and
                     homeschoolers in the United States and
                     Canada.
Suggested Grade:  6-Adult
Order Number:     AR-91QA
Production Date:  2004
Format:           Booklet
Special Notes:    May also be downloaded from the web site.
Source:  National Institute of Arthritis and Musculoskeletal
       and Skin Diseases Information Clearinghouse
            National Institutes of Health
            1 AMS Circle
            Bethesda, MD  20892-3675
            Phone: 1-877-226-4267
            Fax: 1-301-718-6366
World Wide Web URL:  http://www.niams.nih.gov
            Email Address:  NIAMSInfo@mail.nih.gov

## For Goodness Sake!  Prevent Anemia
Emphasizes ways to prevent anemia in children and adults.
Illustrates simple iron-rich recipes and demonstrates label
reading to choose foods high in iron.
Availability:        Staff at schools with NET, WIC, CSFP,
                     FDPIR, CACFP, UMD or Child Nutrition
                     Program food programs in the United States.
                     Those not having such an affiliation should
                     contact their library to place an interlibrary
                     loan request.
Suggested Grade:  7-12
Languages:        English and Spanish together
Order Number:     NAL Video 2809
Production Date:  1997
Format:           VHS videotape
Terms:            Borrower pays return postage.  RETURN the day after
                  scheduled use.  Book at least 4 weeks in advance.
                  Requests must include your name, phone, mail address,
                  eligibility program, title, NAL number, show date, and
                  a statement, "I have read the warning on copyright
                  restrictions and accept full responsibility for
                  compliance."  One title per request.
Source:  National Agricultural Library
       Document Delivery Services Branch
            4th Floor, Photo Lab
            10301 Baltimore Avenue
            Beltsville, MD  20705-2351
            Phone: 1-301-504-5994
            Fax: 1-301-504-5675
World Wide Web URL:  http://www.nal.usda.gov/fnic
            Email Address:  lending@nal.usda.gov

## General Health & Wellness Fact Sheets
Information on how to stay well.

Availability:        All requesters
Suggested Grade:   6-12
Order Number:       not applicable
Format:              Downloadable Fact Sheets
> **Source: Oakland County Michigan Health Division**
> **World Wide Web URL:**
> **http://www.oakgov.com/health/info_pub/fs_index.html**

## Genetic Testing for Breast Cancer Risk
Answers women's questions about the complex and profound issues of genetic testing for breast and ovarian cancers, including how it is done, what the results mean, and what effects the results may have on them and their families.

Availability:        All requesters through interlibrary loan.
Suggested Grade:   9-Adult
Order Number:       065.4 G4637 1997 VIDEOC
Production Date:    1997
Format:              VHS videotape
Terms:    These videotapes are available through interlibrary loan only. Simply request the specific video by name and number at your local public library, university library, or company library. The librarian will submit your request using an ALA interlibrary loan form, and the videos will be mailed to your library for your use. Interlibrary loans are limited to two videos at a time. The address listed below is for the ALA loan form only--your librarian must submit requests to this address.
> **Source: U. S. Geological Survey Library**
> **345 Middlefield Road, MS 955**
> **Menlo Park, CA   94025**

## Health at Home:  Controlling Asthma
Explains how you can do some simple things at home to help prevent an asthma attack from occurring. Tips on how to reduce exposure to asthma triggers are included.

Availability:        Schools, libraries, and homeschoolers in Connecticut, Maine, Massachusetts, New Hampshire, Rhode Island, and Vermont.
Suggested Grade:   All ages
Order Number:       VID 393
Format:              VHS videotape
Terms:    Borrower pays return postage. Return within three weeks of receipt. If the tape you request is available, it will be mailed within 5 business days. If not, you will be notified that this video is already out on loan. No more than three titles may be borrowed by one requestor at a time. No reservations for a specific date will be accepted. It is most efficient to order via the web site.
> **Source: U. S. Environmental Protection Agency, Region 1**
> **Customer Service Center**
> **One Congress Street, Suite 1100**
> **Boston, MA   02214**
> **World Wide Web URL:**
> **http://yosemite.epa.gov/r1/videolen.nsf/**

## Health Beat Fact Sheets
Lots of informational fact sheets about many health issues.

Availability:        All requesters
Suggested Grade:   6-Adult
Order Number:       not applicable
Format:              Downloadable Fact Sheets
> **Source: Illinois Department of Public Health**
> **World Wide Web URL:**
> **http://www.idph.state.il.us/public/hbhome.htm**

## Health Fact Sheets
A large number of fact sheets with information of particular interest to the Hispanic community.

Availability:        All requesters
Suggested Grade:   6-Adult
Order Number:       not applicable
Format:              Downloadable Fact Sheets
> **Source: National Alliance for Hispanic Health**
> **World Wide Web URL:**
> **http://www.hispanichealth.org/resource/healthfact.aspx**

## Health Fact Sheets
A large number of assorted fact sheet to help you learn more about important issues that can affect your health.

Availability:        All requesters
Suggested Grade:   6-Adult
Order Number:       not applicable
Format:              Downloadable Fact Sheets
> **Source: Tennessee Department of Health**
> **World Wide Web URL:**
> **http://health.state.tn.us/FactSheets/index.htm**

## Hepatitis C
Explains how this serious blood-borne infection is spread, diagnosed, and treated.

Availability:        All requesters
Suggested Grade:   6-Adult
Order Number:       not applicable
Production Date:    1999
Format:              Online Article; 6 pages
Special Notes:       Use the on-site search engine to easily find this title. You may request a printed copy mailed to you for a fee.
> **Source: Federal Citizen Information Center**
> **World Wide Web URL:  http://www.pueblo.gsa.gov/**

## How Asthma-Friendly Is Your School?
Parents and school staff will find this resource useful for determining how well their school accommodates children with asthma.

Availability:        One copy is free to schools, libraries, and homeschoolers world-wide. Shipping charges will apply if more than one publication is requested.
Suggested Grade:   4-12
Order Number:       55-830
Production Date:    1997
Format:              Leaflet

Special Notes:      May also be downloaded from the web site.
**Source:  National Heart, Lung, and Blood Institute**
**Information Center**
**P. O. Box 30105**
**Bethesda, MD   20824-0105**
**Phone:  1-301-592-8573**
**Fax:  1-240-629-3246**
**World Wide Web URL:  http://www.nhlbi.nih.gov/**
**Email Address:  nhlbiinfo@nhlbi.nih.gov**

## Infection, Detection, Protection
Through the use of interactive stories and games, students will learn about what causes infection, how to detect if you have one, and how to prevent getting one.
Availability:         All requesters
Suggested Grade:   K-5
Order Number:      not applicable
Format:            Web Site
**Source:  American Museum of Natural History**
**World Wide Web URL:**
**http://www.amnh.org/nationalcenter/infection/**

## Kidney Disease of Diabetes Fact Sheet
Defines the stages of this progressive disease and describes the preventive measures that can forestall kidney failure for many years.
Availability:         Single copies to schools, libraries, and homeschoolers in the United States and Canada.
Suggested Grade:   5-12
Order Number:      KU-93
Production Date:   1995
Format:            Fact Sheet
Special Notes:      May also be downloaded from the web site.
**Source:  National Institute of Diabetes and Digestive and**
**Kidney Diseases**
**5 Information Way**
**Bethesda, MD   20892-3568**
**Phone:  1-800-891-5390**
**Fax:  1-703-738-4929**
**World Wide Web URL:  http://www.niddk.nih.gov/**
**Email Address:  nkudic@info.niddk.nih.gov**

## Latex Allergy
Tells about the prevalence of this allergy as well as discussing reactions, evaluation, and treatment.
Availability:         Limit of one copy to non-profit schools, libraries, and homeschoolers world-wide.
Suggested Grade:   7-Adult
Languages:          English; Spanish
Order Number:      order by title
Format:            Brochure
Special Notes:      Requests must be made via web site or email ONLY.
**Source:  American Academy of Allergy, Asthma &**
**Immunology**
**Attn:  Membership Assistant**
**555 East Wells Street, Suite 1100**
**Milwaukee, WI   53202**

orld Wide Web URL:  http://www.aaaai.org
**Email Address:  info@aaaai.org**

## Lowe Syndrome Association
Provides brief information about this genetic condition that affects only males.
Availability:         One copy to schools, libraries, and homeschoolers world-wide.
Suggested Grade:   8-Adult
Order Number:      order by title
Format:            Brochure
Special Notes:      May also be downloaded from the web site.
**Source:  Lowe Syndrome Association, Inc.**
**P. O. Box 864346**
**Plano, TX   75086-4346**
**Phone:  1-972-733-1338**
**World Wide Web URL:  http://www.lowesyndrome.org**

## My Father, My Brother, and Me
A journalist set off on a personal journey to understand Parkinson's disease as it has taken a large toll on his family.
Availability:         All requesters
Suggested Grade:   All ages
Order Number:      not applicable
Format:            Streaming Video
**Source:  PBS**
**World Wide Web URL:**
**http://www.pbs.org/wgbh/pages/frontline/parkinsons/view/**

## Occupational Asthma
Find out if you are at risk for asthma that is triggered by your job.
Availability:         Limit of one copy to non-profit schools, libraries, and homeschoolers world-wide.
Suggested Grade:   7-Adult
Languages:          English; Spanish
Order Number:      order by title
Format:            Brochure
Special Notes:      Requests must be made via web site or email ONLY.
**Source:  American Academy of Allergy, Asthma &**
**Immunology**
**Attn:  Membership Assistant**
**555 East Wells Street, Suite 1100**
**Milwaukee, WI   53202**
**World Wide Web URL:  http://www.aaaai.org**
**Email Address:  info@aaaai.org**

## Oral Cancer Pamphlet
Presents possible signs and symptoms of this disease.
Availability:         Limit of 50 copies to schools, libraries, and homeschoolers in the United States and Canada.
Suggested Grade:   6-12
Order Number:      NIH Pub. No. 08-5032
Production Date:   2008
Format:            Card

**Source:  National Institute of Dental and Craniofacial Research**
**National Oral Health Information Clearinghouse**
**1 NOHIC Way**
**Bethesda, MD  20892-3500**
**Phone:  1-301-232-4528**
**Fax:  1-301-480-4098**
**World Wide Web URL:  http://www.nidcr.nih.gov**
**Email Address:  nidcrinfo@mail.nih.gov**

## Osteoporosis
A collection of articles about this condition.

| | |
|---|---|
| Availability: | Single copies to schools, libraries, and homeschoolers in the United States and Canada. |
| Suggested Grade: | 6-Adult |
| Order Number: | AR-28IP |
| Production Date: | 2000 |
| Format: | Packet of Materials |
| Special Notes: | May also be downloaded from the web site. |

**Source:  National Institute of Arthritis and Musculoskeletal and Skin Diseases Information Clearinghouse**
**National Institutes of Health**
**1 AMS Circle**
**Bethesda, MD  20892-3675**
**Phone:  1-877-226-4267**
**Fax:  1-301-718-6366**
**World Wide Web URL:  http://www.niams.nih.gov**
**Email Address:  NIAMSInfo@mail.nih.gov**

## Periodontal (Gum) Disease
Discusses the causes, risk factors, diagnosis, and treatment options.

| | |
|---|---|
| Availability: | Limit of 50 copies to schools, libraries, and homeschoolers in the United States and Canada. |
| Suggested Grade: | 6-Adult |
| Languages: | English; Spanish |
| Order Number: | English NIH Pub. No. 08-1142; Spanish NIH Pub. No. 08-1142S |
| Production Date: | 2008 |
| Format: | Brochure |

**Source:  National Institute of Dental and Craniofacial Research**
**National Oral Health Information Clearinghouse**
**1 NOHIC Way**
**Bethesda, MD  20892-3500**
**Phone:  1-301-232-4528**
**Fax:  1-301-480-4098**
**World Wide Web URL:  http://www.nidcr.nih.gov**
**Email Address:  nidcrinfo@mail.nih.gov**

## Plague Upon the Land, A
"River blindness" is spread by black flies that breed in rivers in west Africa.  An international effort is required to eradicate this disease that causes blindness in many countries of that region.  In one community, 75% of the people are infected by this debilitating disease.

| | |
|---|---|
| Availability: | Schools, libraries, homeschoolers, and nursing homes in the United States. |
| Suggested Grade: | 5-Adult |
| Order Number: | order by title |
| Production Date: | 1984 |
| Format: | VHS videotape |
| Terms: | Borrower pays return postage.  Return the day after scheduled showing, via UPS or Priority Mail, insured for $100.00.  Book 4 weeks in advance and include an alternate date.  Order should include name of person responsible for handling the video, and complete mailing address.  Please mention this Guide when ordering.  Tapes may not be duplicated, edited or exhibited for a fee. |

**Source:  Church World Service**
**Film & Video Library**
**28606 Phillips Street, P. O. Box 968**
**Elkhart, IN  46515**
**Phone:  1-800-297-1516, ext. 338**
**Fax:  1-574-262-0966**
**World Wide Web URL:  http://www.churchworldservice.org**
**Email Address:  videos@churchworldservice.org**

## Prevention of Allergies and Asthma in Children
Describes how some allergies are preventable.

| | |
|---|---|
| Availability: | Limit of one copy to non-profit schools, libraries, and homeschoolers world-wide. |
| Suggested Grade: | 7-Adult |
| Languages: | English; Spanish |
| Order Number: | order by title |
| Format: | Brochure |
| Special Notes: | Requests must be made via web site or email ONLY. |

**Source:  American Academy of Allergy, Asthma & Immunology**
**Attn:  Membership Assistant**
**555 East Wells Street, Suite 1100**
**Milwaukee, WI  53202**
**World Wide Web URL:  http://www.aaaai.org**
**Email Address:  info@aaaai.org**

## Protect Yourself from Testicular Cancer
Discusses the relationship of diet, physical activity and weight management to this type of cancer.

| | |
|---|---|
| Availability: | Limit of 1 copy to schools, libraries, and homeschoolers in the United States and Canada. |
| Suggested Grade: | 9-Adult |
| Order Number: | order by title |
| Format: | Brochure |
| Special Notes: | May also be downloaded from the web site. |

**Source:  American Institute for Cancer Research**
**Publication Orders**
**1759 R Street, N. W.**
**Washington, DC  20009**
**Phone:  1-800-843-8114**
**Fax:  1-202-328-7226**
**World Wide Web URL:  http://www.aicr.org**
**Email Address:  aicrweb@aicr.org**

## Psoriasis--Questions and Answers
Answers general questions about this skin condition.

| | |
|---|---|
| Availability: | Single copies to schools, libraries, and homeschoolers in the United States and Canada. |
| Suggested Grade: | 6-Adult |
| Order Number: | AR-97QA |
| Production Date: | 2003 |
| Format: | Booklet |
| Special Notes: | May also be downloaded from the web site. |

**Source: National Institute of Arthritis and Musculoskeletal and Skin Diseases Information Clearinghouse**
**National Institutes of Health**
**1 AMS Circle**
**Bethesda, MD 20892-3675**
**Phone: 1-877-226-4267**
**Fax: 1-301-718-6366**
**World Wide Web URL: http://www.niams.nih.gov**
**Email Address: NIAMSInfo@mail.nih.gov**

## Quick Start Diet Guide for Celiac Disease
A quick and simple overview of the Gluten-Free diet.

| | |
|---|---|
| Availability: | |
| Suggested Grade: | 5-12 |
| Languages: | English; Spanish |
| Order Number: | not applicable |
| Production Date: | 2004 |
| Format: | Downloadable Brochure |

**Source: Gluten Intolerance Group of North America**
**World Wide Web URL:**
**www.gluten.nethttp://www.gluten.net**

## Rabies
Describes rabies and outlines the role wildlife plays in its spread. It explains prevention and first-aid techniques and stresses the importance of vaccination. Excellent for use in rabies-awareness and prevention programs.

| | |
|---|---|
| Availability: | Teachers, librarians, and group leaders in the United States. |
| Suggested Grade: | 3-Adult |
| Order Number: | order by title |
| Format: | DVD |
| Special Notes: | May be retained permanently. |
| Terms: | It is asked that you complete a brief survey included with each program. Videos may not be duplicated--copies will be provided if you need them. Mail and FAX requests must be on school letterhead and contain a statement of total school enrollment, estimated number of student viewers, classes/subjects in which video is used and audience grade level (must match audience specified in description). Allow at least four weeks for delivery. |

**Source: American Veterinary Medical Association**
**Please forward all requests on official letterhead to:**
**Video Placement Worldwide**
**25 Second Street North**
**St. Petersburg, FL 33701**
**Fax: 1-813-823-2955**
**World Wide Web URL: http://www.vpw.com**

## Recurrent Infections
Discusses common types of chronic infections, diagnosis, and when to get treatment for immunodeficiency.

| | |
|---|---|
| Availability: | Limit of one copy to non-profit schools, libraries, and homeschoolers world-wide. |
| Suggested Grade: | 7-Adult |
| Languages: | English; Spanish |
| Order Number: | Tip 33 |
| Format: | Brochure |
| Special Notes: | Requests must be made via web site or email ONLY. |

**Source: American Academy of Allergy, Asthma & Immunology**
**Attn: Membership Assistant**
**555 East Wells Street, Suite 1100**
**Milwaukee, WI 53202**
**World Wide Web URL: http://www.aaaai.org**
**Email Address: info@aaaai.org**

## Reducing Your Risk of Breast Cancer
Helpful information for women.

| | |
|---|---|
| Availability: | Limit of 1 copy to schools, libraries, and homeschoolers in the United States and Canada. |
| Suggested Grade: | 10-Adult |
| Languages: | English; Spanish |
| Order Number: | order by title |
| Format: | Brochure |
| Special Notes: | May also be downloaded from the web site. |

**Source: American Institute for Cancer Research**
**Publication Orders**
**1759 R Street, N. W.**
**Washington, DC 20009**
**Phone: 1-800-843-8114**
**Fax: 1-202-328-7226**
**World Wide Web URL: http://www.aicr.org**
**Email Address: aicrweb@aicr.org**

## Reducing Your Risk of Colorectal Cancer
Clarifies the risk factors, warning signs and dietary changes that reduce risk of colorectal cancer.

| | |
|---|---|
| Availability: | Limit of 1 copy to schools, libraries, and homeschoolers in the United States and Canada. |
| Suggested Grade: | 10-Adult |
| Languages: | English; Spanish |
| Order Number: | order by title |
| Format: | Brochure |
| Special Notes: | May also be downloaded from the web site. |

**Source: American Institute for Cancer Research**
**Publication Orders**
**1759 R Street, N. W.**
**Washington, DC 20009**
**Phone: 1-800-843-8114**
**Fax: 1-202-328-7226**
**World Wide Web URL: http://www.aicr.org**
**Email Address: aicrweb@aicr.org**

## Reducing Your Risk of Prostate Cancer

Know what steps you can take to reduce your risk. Covers information on symptoms and screening.

| | |
|---|---|
| Availability: | Limit of 1 copy to schools, libraries, and homeschoolers in the United States and Canada. |
| Suggested Grade: | 10-Adult |
| Languages: | English; Spanish |
| Order Number: | order by title |
| Format: | Brochure |
| Special Notes: | May also be downloaded from the web site. |

**Source: American Institute for Cancer Research**
**Publication Orders**
**1759 R Street, N. W.**
**Washington, DC 20009**
**Phone: 1-800-843-8114**
**Fax: 1-202-328-7226**
**World Wide Web URL: http://www.aicr.org**
**Email Address: aicrweb@aicr.org**

## Reducing Your Risk of Skin Cancer

Explains how to reduce the chances you will get this most common type of cancer in the United States.

| | |
|---|---|
| Availability: | Limit of 1 copy to schools, libraries, and homeschoolers in the United States and Canada. |
| Suggested Grade: | 10-Adult |
| Languages: | English; Spanish |
| Order Number: | order by title |
| Format: | Brochure |
| Special Notes: | May also be downloaded from the web site. |

**Source: American Institute for Cancer Research**
**Publication Orders**
**1759 R Street, N. W.**
**Washington, DC 20009**
**Phone: 1-800-843-8114**
**Fax: 1-202-328-7226**
**World Wide Web URL: http://www.aicr.org**
**Email Address: aicrweb@aicr.org**

## Rhinitis

Describes what is also known as "hay fever."

| | |
|---|---|
| Availability: | Limit of one copy to non-profit schools, libraries, and homeschoolers world-wide. |
| Suggested Grade: | 7-Adult |
| Languages: | English; Spanish |
| Order Number: | order by title |
| Format: | Brochure |
| Special Notes: | Requests must be made via web site or email ONLY. |

**Source: American Academy of Allergy, Asthma &**
**Immunology**
**Attn: Membership Assistant**
**555 East Wells Street, Suite 1100**
**Milwaukee, WI 53202**
**World Wide Web URL: http://www.aaaai.org**
**Email Address: info@aaaai.org**

## Roxy to the Rescue

Young Roxy discovers what mysterious illness prevents her older cousin from playing ball. Viewer learns about the nature of asthma and myths and misconceptions about the disease. Also discusses warning signs, triggers, treatments, etc.

| | |
|---|---|
| Availability: | Schools, libraries, and homeschoolers in Connecticut, Maine, Massachusetts, New Hampshire, Rhode Island, and Vermont. |
| Suggested Grade: | 4-6 |
| Order Number: | VID 170 |
| Production Date: | 1995 |
| Format: | VHS videotape |
| Terms: | Borrower pays return postage. Return within three weeks of receipt. If the tape you request is available, it will be mailed within 5 business days. If not, you will be notified that this video is already out on loan. No more than three titles may be borrowed by one requestor at a time. No reservations for a specific date will be accepted. It is most efficient to order via the web site. |

**Source: U. S. Environmental Protection Agency, Region 1**
**Customer Service Center**
**One Congress Street, Suite 1100**
**Boston, MA 02214**
**World Wide Web URL:**
**http://yosemite.epa.gov/r1/videolen.nsf/**

## Sesame Street Childhood Asthma Awareness Project--A Is for Asthma

Dani, a brand-new Sesame Street friend, has asthma. Can he still play games with Rosita and Elmo? Yes, he can. With songs and a story video this film teaches children about asthma.

| | |
|---|---|
| Availability: | Schools, libraries, and homeschoolers in Connecticut, Maine, Massachusetts, New Hampshire, Rhode Island, and Vermont. |
| Suggested Grade: | preK |
| Order Number: | VID 350 |
| Production Date: | 1998 |
| Format: | VHS videotape |
| Terms: | Borrower pays return postage. Return within three weeks of receipt. If the tape you request is available, it will be mailed within 5 business days. If not, you will be notified that this video is already out on loan. No more than three titles may be borrowed by one requestor at a time. No reservations for a specific date will be accepted. It is most efficient to order via the web site. |

**Source: U. S. Environmental Protection Agency, Region 1**
**Customer Service Center**
**One Congress Street, Suite 1100**
**Boston, MA 02214**
**World Wide Web URL:**
**http://yosemite.epa.gov/r1/videolen.nsf/**

## Silent Spring Institute: Researching the Environment and Women's Health

Introduces the Silent Spring Institute, a joint effort between scientists and citizens concerned about breast cancer.

*All materials listed in this 2018-2019 edition are **BRAND NEW!***

Availability:     Schools, libraries, and homeschoolers in Connecticut, Maine, Massachusetts, New Hampshire, Rhode Island, and Vermont.
Suggested Grade:   9-Adult
Order Number:   VID 325
Format:   VHS videotape
Terms:   Borrower pays return postage. Return within three weeks of receipt. If the tape you request is available, it will be mailed within 5 business days. If not, you will be notified that this video is already out on loan. No more than three titles may be borrowed by one requestor at a time. No reservations for a specific date will be accepted. It is most efficient to order via the web site.

**Source: U. S. Environmental Protection Agency, Region 1**
**Customer Service Center**
**One Congress Street, Suite 1100**
**Boston, MA 02214**
**World Wide Web URL:**
**http://yosemite.epa.gov/r1/videolen.nsf/**

## Sinusitis

Explains the symptoms of this nasal problem.
Availability:   Limit of one copy to non-profit schools, libraries, and homeschoolers world-wide.
Suggested Grade:   7-Adult
Languages:   English; Spanish
Order Number:   order by title
Format:   Brochure
Special Notes:   Requests must be made via web site or email ONLY.

**Source: American Academy of Allergy, Asthma &**
**Immunology**
**Attn: Membership Assistant**
**555 East Wells Street, Suite 1100**
**Milwaukee, WI 53202**
**World Wide Web URL: http://www.aaaai.org**
**Email Address: info@aaaai.org**

## Stuttering and Tourette's Syndrome

Discusses the possible link between these two afflictions.
Availability:   Single copies to schools, libraries, and homeschoolers world-wide. May be copied.
Suggested Grade:   6-Adult
Order Number:   order by title
Production Date:   2004
Format:   Brochure

**Source: Stuttering Foundation of America**
**P. O. Box 11749**
**Memphis, TN 38111-0749**
**Phone: 1-800-992-9392**
**World Wide Web URL: http://www.stutteringhelp.org**
**Email Address: info@stutteringhelp.org**

## Sweating Disorders

A collection of articles about this condition.
Availability:   Single copies to schools, libraries, and homeschoolers in the United States and Canada.
Suggested Grade:   6-Adult

Order Number:   AR-77 IP
Production Date:   2004
Format:   Packet of Materials
Special Notes:   May also be downloaded from the web site.

**Source: National Institute of Arthritis and Musculoskeletal**
**and Skin Diseases Information Clearinghouse**
**National Institutes of Health**
**1 AMS Circle**
**Bethesda, MD 20892-3675**
**Phone: 1-877-226-4267**
**Fax: 1-301-718-6366**
**World Wide Web URL: http://www.niams.nih.gov**
**Email Address: NIAMSInfo@mail.nih.gov**

## Systemic Lupus Erythematosus--Handout on Health

A collection of articles about this condition.
Availability:   Single copies to schools, libraries, and homeschoolers in the United States and Canada.
Suggested Grade:   6-Adult
Order Number:   AR-96 HH
Production Date:   2000
Format:   Packet of Materials
Special Notes:   May also be downloaded from the web site.

**Source: National Institute of Arthritis and Musculoskeletal**
**and Skin Diseases Information Clearinghouse**
**National Institutes of Health**
**1 AMS Circle**
**Bethesda, MD 20892-3675**
**Phone: 1-877-226-4267**
**Fax: 1-301-718-6366**
**World Wide Web URL: http://www.niams.nih.gov**
**Email Address: NIAMSInfo@mail.nih.gov**

## Toxoplasmosis

Learn about a disease that pregnant women and immune-deficient people should be especially concerned about protecting themselves against.
Availability:   Single copies to schools, libraries, and homeschoolers in the United States and Canada.
Suggested Grade:   6-Adult
    English; Spanish
Order Number:   order by title
Format:   Brochure
Special Notes:   May also be downloaded from the web site.

**Source: American Veterinary Medical Association**
**Attn: Order Dept.**
**1931 North Meacham Road, Suite 100**
**Schaumburg, IL 60173-4360**
**Phone: 1-847-285-6655**
**Fax: 1-847-925-1329**
**World Wide Web URL: http://www.avma.org**
**Email Address: productorders@avma.org**

## Understanding Leukemia

Explains the four main types of leukemia, how leukemia is diagnosed, general methods of treatment, and how this organization can help.

| Availability: | One copy to schools, libraries, and homeschoolers world-wide. |
|---|---|
| Suggested Grade: | 6-Adult |
| Order Number: | PS70 |
| Format: | Booklet; 28 pages |
| Special Notes: | Order via web site only. May also be downloaded from the web site. |

**Source: Leukemia & Lymphoma Society, The**
**World Wide Web URL:**
**http://www.lls.org//resourcecenter/freeeducationmaterials/**
**leukemia/**

## What Are "Allergy Shots?"

Explains how allergy shots work to help patients live with severe allergies.

| Availability: | Limit of one copy to non-profit schools, libraries, and homeschoolers world-wide. |
|---|---|
| Suggested Grade: | 7-Adult |
| Languages: | English; Spanish |
| Order Number: | order by title |
| Format: | Brochure |
| Special Notes: | Requests must be made via web site or email ONLY. |

**Source: American Academy of Allergy, Asthma &**
**Immunology**
**Attn: Membership Assistant**
**555 East Wells Street, Suite 1100**
**Milwaukee, WI 53202**
**World Wide Web URL: http://www.aaaai.org**
**Email Address: info@aaaai.org**

## What I Need to Know About Eating and Diabetes

Reviews diabetes nutrition basics, including what, when, and how much a person with diabetes should eat.

| Availability: | Single copies to schools, libraries, and homeschoolers in the United States and Canada. |
|---|---|
| Suggested Grade: | 9-Adult |
| Languages: | English; Spanish |
| Order Number: | English DM-226; Spanish DM-233 |
| Format: | Booklet |
| Special Notes: | May also be downloaded from the web site. |

**Source: National Institute of Diabetes and Digestive and**
**Kidney Diseases**
**5 Information Way**
**Bethesda, MD 20892-3568**
**Phone: 1-800-891-5390**
**Fax: 1-703-738-4929**
**World Wide Web URL: http://www.niddk.nih.gov/**
**Email Address: nkudidc@info.niddk.nih.gov**

## What Is Allergy Testing?

Describes how these tests are conducted.

| Availability: | Limit of one copy to non-profit schools, libraries, and homeschoolers world-wide. |
|---|---|
| Suggested Grade: | 7-Adult |
| Languages: | English; Spanish |
| Order Number: | order by title |
| Format: | Brochure |

| Special Notes: | Requests must be made via web site or email ONLY. |
|---|---|

**Source: American Academy of Allergy, Asthma &**
**Immunology**
**Attn: Membership Assistant**
**555 East Wells Street, Suite 1100**
**Milwaukee, WI 53202**
**World Wide Web URL: http://www.aaaai.org**
**Email Address: info@aaaai.org**

## What Is Anaphylaxis?

Describes this medical emergency--an acute allergic reaction.

| Availability: | Limit of one copy to non-profit schools, libraries, and homeschoolers world-wide. |
|---|---|
| Suggested Grade: | 7-Adult |
| Languages: | English; Spanish |
| Order Number: | order by title |
| Format: | Brochure |
| Special Notes: | Requests must be made via web site or email ONLY. |

**Source: American Academy of Allergy, Asthma &**
**Immunology**
**Attn: Membership Assistant**
**555 East Wells Street, Suite 1100**
**Milwaukee, WI 53202**
**World Wide Web URL: http://www.aaaai.org**
**Email Address: info@aaaai.org**

## What Is a Peak Flow Meter?

Depicts how to use a peak flow meter to determine lung function and asthma severity.

| Availability: | Limit of one copy to non-profit schools, libraries, and homeschoolers world-wide. |
|---|---|
| Suggested Grade: | 7-Adult |
| Languages: | English; Spanish |
| Order Number: | order by title |
| Format: | Brochure |
| Special Notes: | Requests must be made via web site or email ONLY. |

**Source: American Academy of Allergy, Asthma &**
**Immunology**
**Attn: Membership Assistant**
**555 East Wells Street, Suite 1100**
**Milwaukee, WI 53202**
**World Wide Web URL: http://www.aaaai.org**
**Email Address: info@aaaai.org**

## What You Need to Know About Cancer

Discusses symptoms, diagnosis, treatment, emotional issues, and questions to ask the doctor.

| Availability: | Limit of 20 copies TOTAL, in any combination, to schools, libraries, homeschoolers and others world-wide. |
|---|---|
| Suggested Grade: | 7-Adult |
| Order Number: | P018 |
| Production Date: | 2006 |
| Format: | Pamphlet |
| Special Notes: | May also be downloaded from the web site. |

*All materials listed in this 2018-2019 edition are **BRAND NEW!***

Source: National Cancer Institute
Publications Ordering Service
P. O. Box 24128
Baltimore, MD  21227
Phone: 1-800-4-CANCER
Fax: 1-301-330-7968
World Wide Web URL: http://cancer.gov/publications

## What You Need to Know About Cancer--Bladder

Discusses symptoms, diagnosis, treatment, emotional issues, and questions to ask the doctor.

| | |
|---|---|
| Availability: | Limit of 20 copies TOTAL, in any combination, to schools, libraries, homeschoolers and others world-wide. |
| Suggested Grade: | 7-Adult |
| Order Number: | P014 |
| Production Date: | 2010 |
| Format: | Pamphlet |
| Special Notes: | May also be downloaded from the web site. |

Source: National Cancer Institute
Publications Ordering Service
P. O. Box 24128
Baltimore, MD  21227
Phone: 1-800-4-CANCER
Fax: 1-301-330-7968
World Wide Web URL: http://cancer.gov/publications

## What You Need to Know About Cancer--Brain Tumors

Discusses symptoms, diagnosis, treatment, emotional issues, and questions to ask the doctor.

| | |
|---|---|
| Availability: | Limit of 20 copies TOTAL, in any combination, to schools, libraries, homeschoolers and others world-wide. |
| Suggested Grade: | 7-Adult |
| Order Number: | P016 |
| Production Date: | 2009 |
| Format: | Pamphlet |
| Special Notes: | May also be downloaded from the web site. |

Source: National Cancer Institute
Publications Ordering Service
P. O. Box 24128
Baltimore, MD  21227
Phone: 1-800-4-CANCER
Fax: 1-301-330-7968
World Wide Web URL: http://cancer.gov/publications

## What You Need to Know About Cancer--Breast

Discusses symptoms, diagnosis, treatment, emotional issues, and questions to ask the doctor.

| | |
|---|---|
| Availability: | Limit of 20 copies TOTAL, in any combination, to schools, libraries, homeschoolers and others world-wide. |
| Suggested Grade: | 7-Adult |
| Order Number: | P017 |
| Production Date: | 2009 |
| Format: | Pamphlet |
| Special Notes: | May also be downloaded from the web site. |

Source: National Cancer Institute
Publications Ordering Service
P. O. Box 24128
Baltimore, MD  21227
Phone: 1-800-4-CANCER
Fax: 1-301-330-7968
World Wide Web URL: http://cancer.gov/publications

## What You Need to Know About Cancer--Cervical Cancer

Discusses symptoms, diagnosis, treatment, emotional issues, and questions to ask the doctor.

| | |
|---|---|
| Availability: | Limit of 20 copies TOTAL, in any combination, to schools, libraries, homeschoolers and others world-wide. |
| Suggested Grade: | 7-Adult |
| Order Number: | P019 |
| Production Date: | 2008 |
| Format: | Pamphlet |
| Special Notes: | May also be downloaded from the web site. |

Source: National Cancer Institute
Publications Ordering Service
P. O. Box 24128
Baltimore, MD  21227
Phone: 1-800-4-CANCER
Fax: 1-301-330-7968
World Wide Web URL: http://cancer.gov/publications

## What You Need to Know About Cancer--Colon & Rectum

Discusses symptoms, diagnosis, treatment, emotional issues, and questions to ask the doctor.

| | |
|---|---|
| Availability: | Limit of 20 copies TOTAL, in any combination, to schools, libraries, homeschoolers and others world-wide. |
| Suggested Grade: | 7-Adult |
| Order Number: | P020 |
| Production Date: | 2006 |
| Format: | Pamphlet |
| Special Notes: | May also be downloaded from the web site. |

Source: National Cancer Institute
Publications Ordering Service
P. O. Box 24128
Baltimore, MD  21227
Phone: 1-800-4-CANCER
Fax: 1-301-330-7968
World Wide Web URL: http://cancer.gov/publications

## What You Need to Know About Cancer--Esophagus

Discusses symptoms, diagnosis, treatment, emotional issues, and questions to ask the doctor.

| | |
|---|---|
| Availability: | Limit of 20 copies TOTAL, in any combination, to schools, libraries, homeschoolers and others world-wide. |
| Suggested Grade: | 7-Adult |
| Order Number: | P021 |
| Production Date: | 2008 |
| Format: | Pamphlet |
| Special Notes: | May also be downloaded from the web site. |

Source:  National Cancer Institute
Publications Ordering Service
P. O. Box 24128
Baltimore, MD  21227
Phone:  1-800-4-CANCER
Fax:  1-301-330-7968
World Wide Web URL:  http://cancer.gov/publications

### What You Need to Know About Cancer--Hodgkin's Disease
Discusses symptoms, diagnosis, treatment, emotional issues, and questions to ask the doctor.

Availability:    Limit of 20 copies TOTAL, in any combination, to schools, libraries, homeschoolers and others world-wide.
Suggested Grade:    7-Adult
Order Number:    P022
Production Date:    2007
Format:    Pamphlet
Special Notes:    May also be downloaded from the web site.

Source:  National Cancer Institute
Publications Ordering Service
P. O. Box 24128
Baltimore, MD  21227
Phone:  1-800-4-CANCER
Fax:  1-301-330-7968
World Wide Web URL:  http://cancer.gov/publications

### What You Need to Know About Cancer--Kidney
Discusses symptoms, diagnosis, treatment, emotional issues, and questions to ask the doctor.

Availability:    Limit of 20 copies TOTAL, in any combination, to schools, libraries, homeschoolers and others world-wide.
Suggested Grade:    7-Adult
Order Number:    P023
Production Date:    2010
Format:    Pamphlet
Special Notes:    May also be downloaded from the web site.

Source:  National Cancer Institute
Publications Ordering Service
P. O. Box 24128
Baltimore, MD  21227
Phone:  1-800-4-CANCER
Fax:  1-301-330-7968
World Wide Web URL:  http://cancer.gov/publications

### What You Need to Know About Cancer--Larynx
Discusses symptoms, diagnosis, treatment, emotional issues, and questions to ask the doctor.

Availability:    Limit of 20 copies TOTAL, in any combination, to schools, libraries, homeschoolers and others world-wide.
Suggested Grade:    7-Adult
Order Number:    P024
Production Date:    2010
Format:    Pamphlet
Special Notes:    May also be downloaded from the web site.

Source:  National Cancer Institute
Publications Ordering Service
P. O. Box 24128
Baltimore, MD  21227
Phone:  1-800-4-CANCER
Fax:  1-301-330-7968
World Wide Web URL:  http://cancer.gov/publications

### What You Need to Know About Cancer--Leukemia
Discusses symptoms, diagnosis, treatment, emotional issues, and questions to ask the doctor.

Availability:    Limit of 20 copies TOTAL, in any combination, to schools, libraries, homeschoolers and others world-wide.
Suggested Grade:    7-Adult
Order Number:    P832
Production Date:    2008
Format:    Pamphlet
Special Notes:    May also be downloaded from the web site.

Source:  National Cancer Institute
Publications Ordering Service
P. O. Box 24128
Baltimore, MD  21227
Phone:  1-800-4-CANCER
Fax:  1-301-330-7968
World Wide Web URL:  http://cancer.gov/publications

### What You Need to Know About Cancer--Liver
Discusses symptoms, diagnosis, treatment, emotional issues, and questions to ask the doctor.

Availability:    Limit of 20 copies TOTAL, in any combination, to schools, libraries, homeschoolers and others world-wide.
Suggested Grade:    7-Adult
Order Number:    P429
Production Date:    2009
Format:    Pamphlet
Special Notes:    May also be downloaded from the web site.

Source:  National Cancer Institute
Publications Ordering Service
P. O. Box 24128
Baltimore, MD  21227
Phone:  1-800-4-CANCER
Fax:  1-301-330-7968
World Wide Web URL:  http://cancer.gov/publications

### What You Need to Know About Cancer--Melanoma
Discusses symptoms, diagnosis, treatment, emotional issues, and questions to ask the doctor.

Availability:    Limit of 20 copies TOTAL, in any combination, to schools, libraries, homeschoolers and others world-wide.
Suggested Grade:    7-Adult
Order Number:    P027
Production Date:    2002
Format:    Pamphlet
Special Notes:    May also be downloaded from the web site.

*All materials listed in this 2018-2019 edition are **BRAND NEW!***

Source: National Cancer Institute
Publications Ordering Service
P. O. Box 24128
Baltimore, MD 21227
Phone: 1-800-4-CANCER
Fax: 1-301-330-7968
World Wide Web URL: http://cancer.gov/publications

## What You Need to Know About Cancer--Multiple Myeloma

Discusses symptoms, diagnosis, treatment, emotional issues, and questions to ask the doctor.

| | |
|---|---|
| Availability: | Limit of 20 copies TOTAL, in any combination, to schools, libraries, homeschoolers and others world-wide. |
| Suggested Grade: | 7-Adult |
| Order Number: | P030 |
| Production Date: | 2008 |
| Format: | Pamphlet |
| Special Notes: | May also be downloaded from the web site. |

Source: National Cancer Institute
Publications Ordering Service
P. O. Box 24128
Baltimore, MD 21227
Phone: 1-800-4-CANCER
Fax: 1-301-330-7968
World Wide Web URL: http://cancer.gov/publications

## What You Need to Know About Cancer--Non-Hodgkin's Lymphoma

Discusses symptoms, diagnosis, treatment, emotional issues, and questions to ask the doctor.

| | |
|---|---|
| Availability: | Limit of 20 copies TOTAL, in any combination, to schools, libraries, homeschoolers and others world-wide. |
| Suggested Grade: | 7-Adult |
| Order Number: | P031 |
| Production Date: | 2007 |
| Format: | Pamphlet |
| Special Notes: | May also be downloaded from the web site. |

Source: National Cancer Institute
Publications Ordering Service
P. O. Box 24128
Baltimore, MD 21227
Phone: 1-800-4-CANCER
Fax: 1-301-330-7968
World Wide Web URL: http://cancer.gov/publications

## What You Need to Know About Cancer--Oral Cancers

Discusses symptoms, diagnosis, treatment, emotional issues, and questions to ask the doctor.

| | |
|---|---|
| Availability: | Limit of 20 copies TOTAL, in any combination, to schools, libraries, homeschoolers and others world-wide. |
| Suggested Grade: | 7-Adult |
| Order Number: | P032 |
| Format: | Pamphlet |
| Special Notes: | May also be downloaded from the web site. |

Source: National Cancer Institute
Publications Ordering Service
P. O. Box 24128
Baltimore, MD 21227
Phone: 1-800-4-CANCER
Fax: 1-301-330-7968
World Wide Web URL: http://cancer.gov/publications

## What You Need to Know About Cancer--Ovary

Discusses symptoms, diagnosis, treatment, emotional issues, and questions to ask the doctor.

| | |
|---|---|
| Availability: | Limit of 20 copies TOTAL, in any combination, to schools, libraries, homeschoolers and others world-wide. |
| Suggested Grade: | 7-Adult |
| Order Number: | P033 |
| Production Date: | 2006 |
| Format: | Pamphlet |
| Special Notes: | May also be downloaded from the web site. |

Source: National Cancer Institute
Publications Ordering Service
P. O. Box 24128
Baltimore, MD 21227
Phone: 1-800-4-CANCER
Fax: 1-301-330-7968
World Wide Web URL: http://cancer.gov/publications

## What You Need to Know About Cancer--Pancreas

Discusses symptoms, diagnosis, treatment, emotional issues, and questions to ask the doctor.

| | |
|---|---|
| Availability: | Limit of 20 copies TOTAL, in any combination, to schools, libraries, homeschoolers and others world-wide. |
| Suggested Grade: | 7-Adult |
| Order Number: | P034 |
| Production Date: | 2010 |
| Format: | Pamphlet |
| Special Notes: | May also be downloaded from the web site. |

Source: National Cancer Institute
Publications Ordering Service
P. O. Box 24128
Baltimore, MD 21227
Phone: 1-800-4-CANCER
Fax: 1-301-330-7968
World Wide Web URL: http://cancer.gov/publications

## What You Need to Know About Cancer--Prostate

Discusses symptoms, diagnosis, treatment, emotional issues, and questions to ask the doctor.

| | |
|---|---|
| Availability: | Limit of 20 copies TOTAL, in any combination, to schools, libraries, homeschoolers and others world-wide. |
| Suggested Grade: | 7-Adult |
| Order Number: | P035 |
| Production Date: | 2008 |
| Format: | Pamphlet |
| Special Notes: | May also be downloaded from the web site. |

# HEALTH--DISEASES

Source:  National Cancer Institute
Publications Ordering Service
P. O. Box 24128
Baltimore, MD  21227
Phone:  1-800-4-CANCER
Fax:  1-301-330-7968
World Wide Web URL:  http://cancer.gov/publications

## What You Need to Know About Cancer--Stomach

Discusses symptoms, diagnosis, treatment, emotional issues, and questions to ask the doctor.

| | |
|---|---|
| Availability: | Limit of 20 copies TOTAL, in any combination, to schools, libraries, homeschoolers and others world-wide. |
| Suggested Grade: | 7-Adult |
| Order Number: | P037 |
| Production Date: | 2009 |
| Format: | Pamphlet |
| Special Notes: | May also be downloaded from the web site. |

Source:  National Cancer Institute
Publications Ordering Service
P. O. Box 24128
Baltimore, MD  21227
Phone:  1-800-4-CANCER
Fax:  1-301-330-7968
World Wide Web URL:  http://cancer.gov/publications

## What You Need to Know About Cancer--Thyroid

Discusses symptoms, diagnosis, treatment, emotional issues, and questions to ask the doctor.

| | |
|---|---|
| Availability: | Limit of 20 copies TOTAL, in any combination, to schools, libraries, homeschoolers and others world-wide. |
| Suggested Grade: | 7-Adult |
| Order Number: | P620 |
| Production Date: | 2007 |
| Format: | Pamphlet |
| Special Notes: | May also be downloaded from the web site. |

Source:  National Cancer Institute
Publications Ordering Service
P. O. Box 24128
Baltimore, MD  21227
Phone:  1-800-4-CANCER
Fax:  1-301-330-7968
World Wide Web URL:  http://cancer.gov/publications

## What You Need to Know About Cancer--Uterus

Discusses symptoms, diagnosis, treatment, emotional issues, and questions to ask the doctor.

| | |
|---|---|
| Availability: | Limit of 20 copies TOTAL, in any combination, to schools, libraries, homeschoolers and others world-wide. |
| Suggested Grade: | 7-Adult |
| Order Number: | P039 |
| Production Date: | 2010 |
| Format: | Pamphlet |
| Special Notes: | May also be downloaded from the web site. |

Source:  National Cancer Institute
Publications Ordering Service
P. O. Box 24128
Baltimore, MD  21227
Phone:  1-800-4-CANCER
Fax:  1-301-330-7968
World Wide Web URL:  http://cancer.gov/publications

## What You Need to Know About Oral Cancer

Discusses the cause and treatment of this disease.

| | |
|---|---|
| Availability: | Limit of 50 copies to schools, libraries, and homeschoolers in the United States and Canada. |
| Suggested Grade: | 6-Adult |
| Order Number: | NIH Pub. 03-1574 |
| Production Date: | 2003 |
| Format: | Booklet; 48 pages |

Source:  National Institute of Dental and Craniofacial Research
National Oral Health Information Clearinghouse
1 NOHIC Way
Bethesda, MD  20892-3500
Phone:  1-301-232-4528
Fax:  1-301-480-4098
World Wide Web URL:  http://www.nidcr.nih.gov
Email Address:  nidcrinfo@mail.nih.gov

## When Cancer Returns

Details the different types of recurrence, types of treatment, and coping with cancer's return.

| | |
|---|---|
| Availability: | Limit of 20 copies TOTAL, in any combination, to schools, libraries, homeschoolers and others world-wide. |
| Suggested Grade: | Adult |
| Order Number: | P129 |
| Production Date: | 2010 |
| Format: | Booklet |
| Special Notes: | May also be downloaded from the web site. |

## When Someone You Love Is Being Treated for Cancer

Provides care givers with coping strategies to help them deal with the stress and anxiety associated with caring for cancer patients. Discusses communication skills, ways to get support, feelings, helping with medical care, and the need for self-care.

| | |
|---|---|
| Availability: | Limit of 20 copies TOTAL, in any combination, to schools, libraries, homeschoolers and others world-wide. |
| Suggested Grade: | 5-Adult |
| Order Number: | P225 |
| Production Date: | 2010 |
| Format: | Booklet |

*All materials listed in this 2018-2019 edition are **BRAND NEW!***

Special Notes:　　May also be downloaded from the web site.
**Source: National Cancer Institute**
**Publications Ordering Service**
**P. O. Box 24128**
**Baltimore, MD 21227**
**Phone: 1-800-4-CANCER**
**Fax: 1-301-330-7968**
**World Wide Web URL: http://cancer.gov/publications**

### When Your Brother or Sister Has Cancer: A Guide for Teens

Describes how teens have dealt with finding out a sibling has cancer and shows ways teens can help themselves and their families.

Availability:　　Limit of 20 copies TOTAL, in any combination, to schools, libraries, homeschoolers and others world-wide.
Suggested Grade:　7-Adult
Order Number:　　P222
Production Date:　2005
Format:　　Booklet
Special Notes:　　May also be downloaded from the web site.
**Source: National Cancer Institute**
**Publications Ordering Service**
**P. O. Box 24128**
**Baltimore, MD 21227**
**Phone: 1-800-4-CANCER**
**Fax: 1-301-330-7968**
**World Wide Web URL: http://cancer.gov/publications**

### When Your Parent Has Cancer: A Guide for Teens

Read this booklet to hear how teens coped when they found out their mother or father had cancer. Provides information about treatments and more.

Availability:　　Limit of 20 copies TOTAL, in any combination, to schools, libraries, homeschoolers and others world-wide.
Suggested Grade:　7-Adult
Order Number:　　P223
Production Date:　2010
Format:　　Booklet
Special Notes:　　May also be downloaded from the web site.
**Source: National Cancer Institute**
**Publications Ordering Service**
**P. O. Box 24128**
**Baltimore, MD 21227**
**Phone: 1-800-4-CANCER**
**Fax: 1-301-330-7968**
**World Wide Web URL: http://cancer.gov/publications**

# HEALTH--FAMILY LIFE EDUCATION

**ABC's for Moms**

A guide through baby's first year.

| | |
|---|---|
| Availability: | Staff at schools with NET, WIC, CSFP, FDPIR, CACFP, UMD or Child Nutrition Program food programs in the United States. Those not having such an affiliation should contact their library to place an interlibrary loan request. |
| Suggested Grade: | 9-Adult |
| Languages: | English; Spanish |
| Order Number: | English Video 1504; Spanish Video 1505 |
| Production Date: | 1991 |
| Format: | VHS videotape |
| Terms: | Borrower pays return postage. RETURN the day after scheduled use. Book at least 4 weeks in advance. Requests must include your name, phone, mail address, eligibility program, title, NAL number, show date, and a statement, "I have read the warning on copyright restrictions and accept full responsibility for compliance." One title per request. |

**Source: National Agricultural Library**
**Document Delivery Services Branch**
**4th Floor, Photo Lab**
**10301 Baltimore Avenue**
**Beltsville, MD 20705-2351**
**Phone: 1-301-504-5994**
**Fax: 1-301-504-5675**
**World Wide Web URL: http://www.nal.usda.gov/fnic**
**Email Address: lending@nal.usda.gov**

**Asthma and Pregnancy**

Explains how the benefits of continuing to take asthma medications outweigh the risks in pregnant women.

| | |
|---|---|
| Availability: | Limit of one copy to non-profit schools, libraries, and homeschoolers world-wide. |
| Suggested Grade: | 7-Adult |
| Languages: | English; Spanish |
| Order Number: | order by title |
| Format: | Brochure |
| Special Notes: | Requests must be made via web site or email ONLY. |

**Source: American Academy of Allergy, Asthma &**
**Immunology**
**Attn: Membership Assistant**
**555 East Wells Street, Suite 1100**
**Milwaukee, WI 53202**
**World Wide Web URL: http://www.aaaai.org**
**Email Address: info@aaaai.org**

**Baby It's You!**

Tells how, when, and what to feed a baby. Breastfeeding is covered.

| | |
|---|---|
| Availability: | Staff at schools with NET, WIC, CSFP, FDPIR, CACFP, UMD or Child Nutrition Program food programs in the United States. Those not having such an affiliation should contact their library to place an interlibrary loan request. |
| Suggested Grade: | 9-Adult |

| | |
|---|---|
| Order Number: | NAL Video 2835 |
| Production Date: | 1998 |
| Format: | VHS videotape |
| Terms: | Borrower pays return postage. RETURN the day after scheduled use. Book at least 4 weeks in advance. Requests must include your name, phone, mail address, eligibility program, title, NAL number, show date, and a statement, "I have read the warning on copyright restrictions and accept full responsibility for compliance." One title per request. |

**Source: National Agricultural Library**
**Document Delivery Services Branch**
**4th Floor, Photo Lab**
**10301 Baltimore Avenue**
**Beltsville, MD 20705-2351**
**Phone: 1-301-504-5994**
**Fax: 1-301-504-5675**
**World Wide Web URL: http://www.nal.usda.gov/fnic**
**Email Address: lending@nal.usda.gov**

**Baby Shower for Betsy, A**

Betsy's friends try to convince her that breastfeeding is the best way to feed her baby.

| | |
|---|---|
| Availability: | Staff at schools with NET, WIC, CSFP, FDPIR, CACFP, UMD or Child Nutrition Program food programs in the United States. Those not having such an affiliation should contact their library to place an interlibrary loan request. |
| Suggested Grade: | 9-Adult |
| Order Number: | Videocassette No. 2351(E) |
| Production Date: | 1994 |
| Format: | VHS videotape |
| Terms: | Borrower pays return postage. RETURN the day after scheduled use. Book at least 4 weeks in advance. Requests must include your name, phone, mail address, eligibility program, title, NAL number, show date, and a statement, "I have read the warning on copyright restrictions and accept full responsibility for compliance." One title per request. |

**Source: National Agricultural Library**
**Document Delivery Services Branch**
**4th Floor, Photo Lab**
**10301 Baltimore Avenue**
**Beltsville, MD 20705-2351**
**Phone: 1-301-504-5994**
**Fax: 1-301-504-5675**
**World Wide Web URL: http://www.nal.usda.gov/fnic**
**Email Address: lending@nal.usda.gov**

**Baby-to-Be: The Video Guide to Pregnancy**

Covers many topics that will help a pregnant woman understand her pregnancy and how to take care of herself.

| | |
|---|---|
| Availability: | Staff at schools with NET, WIC, CSFP, FDPIR, CACFP, UMD or Child Nutrition Program food programs in the United States. Those not having such an affiliation should contact their library to place an interlibrary loan request. |
| Suggested Grade: | 9-Adult |

*All materials listed in this 2018-2019 edition are **BRAND NEW!***

Order Number:    Video 2748
Production Date:    1996
Format:    VHS videotape
Terms:    Borrower pays return postage. RETURN the day after scheduled use. Book at least 4 weeks in advance. Requests must include your name, phone, mail address, eligibility program, title, NAL number, show date, and a statement, "I have read the warning on copyright restrictions and accept full responsibility for compliance." One title per request.

    **Source: National Agricultural Library**
    **Document Delivery Services Branch**
    **4th Floor, Photo Lab**
    **10301 Baltimore Avenue**
    **Beltsville, MD 20705-2351**
    **Phone: 1-301-504-5994**
    **Fax: 1-301-504-5675**
    **World Wide Web URL: http://www.nal.usda.gov/fnic**
    **Email Address: lending@nal.usda.gov**

## Best Thing, The
Shows mothers relating their breastfeeding experiences.
Availability:    Staff at schools with NET, WIC, CSFP, FDPIR, CACFP, UMD or Child Nutrition Program food programs in the United States. Those not having such an affiliation should contact their library to place an interlibrary loan request.
Suggested Grade:    Adult
Languages:    English; Spanish
Order Number:    English Video 2971; Spanish Video 2970
Production Date:    1999
Format:    VHS videotape
Terms:    Borrower pays return postage. RETURN the day after scheduled use. Book at least 4 weeks in advance. Requests must include your name, phone, mail address, eligibility program, title, NAL number, show date, and a statement, "I have read the warning on copyright restrictions and accept full responsibility for compliance." One title per request.

    **Source: National Agricultural Library**
    **Document Delivery Services Branch**
    **4th Floor, Photo Lab**
    **10301 Baltimore Avenue**
    **Beltsville, MD 20705-2351**
    **Phone: 1-301-504-5994**
    **Fax: 1-301-504-5675**
    **World Wide Web URL: http://www.nal.usda.gov/fnic**
    **Email Address: lending@nal.usda.gov**

## Body Image for Boys
Discusses how young men see themselves and examines the growing phenomena of increasing gym memberships, exercise addiction, and more.
Availability:    Schools, libraries, and homeschoolers in the United States who serve the hearing impaired.
Suggested Grade:    6-12
Order Number:    11648
Production Date:    2002
Format:    DVD

Special Notes:    Also available as live streaming video over the Internet.
Terms:    Sponsor pays all transportation costs. Return one week after receipt. Participation is limited to deaf or hard of hearing Americans, their parents, families, teachers, counselors, or others whose use would benefit a deaf or hard of hearing person. Only one person in the audience needs to be hearing impaired. You must register--which is free. These videos are all open-captioned--no special equipment is required for viewing.

    **Source: Described and Captioned Media Program**
    **National Association of the Deaf**
    **4211 Church Street Ext.**
    **Roebuck, SC 29376**
    **Phone: 1-800-237-6213**
    **Fax: 1-800-538-5636**
    **World Wide Web URL: http://www.dcmp.org**

## Body, The: The Complete HIV/AIDS Resource
Find out about HIV and AIDS as well as information about symptoms, causes, treatments, and the demographics of the disease.
Availability:    All requesters
Suggested Grade:    9-Adult
Order Number:    not applicable
Format:    Web Site

    **Source: Body Health Resources Corporation**
    **World Wide Web URL:**
    **http://www.thebody.com/index.html**

## Breakfast: Lily Changes a Habit
A young mother learns the role that breakfast plays in starting the day off right for her family.
Availability:    Staff at schools with NET, WIC, CSFP, FDPIR, CACFP, UMD or Child Nutrition Program food programs in the United States. Those not having such an affiliation should contact their library to place an interlibrary loan request.
Suggested Grade:    9-Adult
Order Number:    Video 1626
Production Date:    1993
Format:    VHS videotape
Terms:    Borrower pays return postage. RETURN the day after scheduled use. Book at least 4 weeks in advance. Requests must include your name, phone, mail address, eligibility program, title, NAL number, show date, and a statement, "I have read the warning on copyright restrictions and accept full responsibility for compliance." One title per request.

    **Source: National Agricultural Library**
    **Document Delivery Services Branch**
    **4th Floor, Photo Lab**
    **10301 Baltimore Avenue**
    **Beltsville, MD 20705-2351**
    **Phone: 1-301-504-5994**
    **Fax: 1-301-504-5675**
    **World Wide Web URL: http://www.nal.usda.gov/fnic**
    **Email Address: lending@nal.usda.gov**

# HEALTH--FAMILY LIFE EDUCATION

## Breastfeeding Promotion
Discusses the benefits of breastfeeding to infants, mother, and society.

Availability: Schools, libraries, and nursing homes in the United States.
Suggested Grade: 9-Adult
Order Number: NAL Slide 548
Production Date: 1996
Format: Set of slides
Terms: Borrower pays return postage. RETURN the day after scheduled use. Book at least 4 weeks in advance. Requests must include your name, phone, mail address, eligibility program, title, NAL number, show date, and a statement, "I have read the warning on copyright restrictions and accept full responsibility for compliance." One title per request.

**Source: National Agricultural Library**
**Document Delivery Services Branch**
**4th Floor, Photo Lab**
**10301 Baltimore Avenue**
**Beltsville, MD 20705-2351**
**Phone: 1-301-504-5994**
**Fax: 1-301-504-5675**
**World Wide Web URL: http://www.nal.usda.gov/fnic**
**Email Address: lending@nal.usda.gov**

## Changes of Puberty
A complete lesson about the changes the body goes through in puberty.

Availability: All requesters
Suggested Grade: 6-8
Order Number: not applicable
Format: Online Lesson Plan

**Source: Marilyn Fenichel**
**World Wide Web URL:**
**http://www.discoveryeducation.com/teachers/**
**free-lesson-plans/changes-of-puberty.cfm**

## Choosing a Healthy Start: Nutrition for Pregnant Teens: Working Draft
Gives instructional suggestions for use in helping pregnant adolescents make healthy food choices. Material is ethnically appropriate for Hawaii's varied population.

Availability: Staff at schools with NET, WIC, CSFP, FDPIR, CACFP, UMD or Child Nutrition Program food programs in the United States. Those not having such an affiliation should contact their library to place an interlibrary loan request.
Suggested Grade: 7-12
Order Number: NAL Kit 153
Production Date: 1992
Format: VHS videotape
Special Notes: This is a Hawaii State Department of Health production.
Terms: Borrower pays return postage. RETURN the day after scheduled use. Book at least 4 weeks in advance. Requests must include your name, phone, mail address, eligibility program, title, NAL number, show date, and

a statement, "I have read the warning on copyright restrictions and accept full responsibility for compliance." One title per request.

**Source: National Agricultural Library**
**Document Delivery Services Branch**
**4th Floor, Photo Lab**
**10301 Baltimore Avenue**
**Beltsville, MD 20705-2351**
**Phone: 1-301-504-5994**
**Fax: 1-301-504-5675**
**World Wide Web URL: http://www.nal.usda.gov/fnic**
**Email Address: lending@nal.usda.gov**

## DNA Interactive
Explores the principles of genetic material and includes online teacher's guides, activities, video clips, and more.

Availability: All requesters
Suggested Grade: 6-Adult
Order Number: not applicable
Format: Web Site

**Source: Cold Spring Harbor Laboratory**
**World Wide Web URL: http://www.dnai.org/index.htm**

## Ear Infections and Language Development
Learn about symptoms and treatment, as well as signs of possible hearing damage.

Availability: All requesters
Suggested Grade: Parents
Order Number: not applicable
Production Date: 2000
Format: Online Article; 11 pages
Special Notes: Use the on-site search engine to easily find this title. You may request a printed copy mailed to you for a fee.

**Source: Federal Citizen Information Center**
**World Wide Web URL: http://www.pueblo.gsa.gov/**

## Expecting the Best
Encourages women to plan early for their pregnancy, exercise healthy behavior during pregnancy, and learn about caring for their babies after birth.

Availability: Staff at schools with NET, WIC, CSFP, FDPIR, CACFP, UMD or Child Nutrition Program food programs in the United States. Those not having such an affiliation should contact their library to place an interlibrary loan request.
Suggested Grade: 9-Adult
Order Number: Video 1508
Production Date: 1990
Format: VHS videotape
Terms: Borrower pays return postage. RETURN the day after scheduled use. Book at least 4 weeks in advance. Requests must include your name, phone, mail address, eligibility program, title, NAL number, show date, and a statement, "I have read the warning on copyright restrictions and accept full responsibility for compliance." One title per request.

*All materials listed in this 2018-2019 edition are **BRAND NEW!***

Source: National Agricultural Library
Document Delivery Services Branch
4th Floor, Photo Lab
10301 Baltimore Avenue
Beltsville, MD 20705-2351
Phone: 1-301-504-5994
Fax: 1-301-504-5675
World Wide Web URL: http://www.nal.usda.gov/fnic
Email Address: lending@nal.usda.gov

## 14 Steps to Better Breastfeeding

Provides information for new mothers on how to breastfeed successfully.

| | |
|---|---|
| Availability: | Staff at schools with NET, WIC, CSFP, FDPIR, CACFP, UMD or Child Nutrition Program food programs in the United States. Those not having such an affiliation should contact their library to place an interlibrary loan request. |
| Suggested Grade: | Adult |
| Languages: | English; Spanish |
| Order Number: | English NAL Video 2955; Spanish NAL Video 2956 |
| Production Date: | 2000 |
| Format: | VHS videotape |
| Terms: | Borrower pays return postage. RETURN the day after scheduled use. Book at least 4 weeks in advance. Requests must include your name, phone, mail address, eligibility program, title, NAL number, show date, and a statement, "I have read the warning on copyright restrictions and accept full responsibility for compliance." One title per request. |

Source: National Agricultural Library
Document Delivery Services Branch
4th Floor, Photo Lab
10301 Baltimore Avenue
Beltsville, MD 20705-2351
Phone: 1-301-504-5994
Fax: 1-301-504-5675
World Wide Web URL: http://www.nal.usda.gov/fnic
Email Address: lending@nal.usda.gov

## Genes: The Building Blocks of Life

Learn about genetics.

| | |
|---|---|
| Availability: | All requesters |
| Suggested Grade: | 9-12 |
| Order Number: | not applicable |
| Format: | WebQuest |

Source: Marc B. Sartori and Carrie L. Pogany
World Wide Web URL:
http://oncampus.richmond.edu/academics/education/
projects/webquests/genes/

## Genetic Science Learning Center

Activities and information about genetics.

| | |
|---|---|
| Availability: | All requesters |
| Suggested Grade: | 3-5 |
| Order Number: | not applicable |
| Format: | Web Site |

Source: Genetic Science Learning Center
World Wide Web URL: http://learn.genetics.utah.edu/

## Healthy Eating for a Healthy Baby

Expectant mothers are taught about proper weight gain and good nutrition practices using the food guide pyramid.

| | |
|---|---|
| Availability: | Staff at schools with NET, WIC, CSFP, FDPIR, CACFP, UMD or Child Nutrition Program food programs in the United States. Those not having such an affiliation should contact their library to place an interlibrary loan request. |
| Suggested Grade: | 9-Adult |
| Languages: | English; Spanish |
| Order Number: | English NAL Video 2765; Spanish NAL Video 2844 |
| Production Date: | 1995 |
| Format: | VHS videotape |
| Terms: | Borrower pays return postage. RETURN the day after scheduled use. Book at least 4 weeks in advance. Requests must include your name, phone, mail address, eligibility program, title, NAL number, show date, and a statement, "I have read the warning on copyright restrictions and accept full responsibility for compliance." One title per request. |

Source: National Agricultural Library
Document Delivery Services Branch
4th Floor, Photo Lab, 10301 Baltimore Avenue
Beltsville, MD 20705-2351
Phone: 1-301-504-5994
Fax: 1-301-504-5675
World Wide Web URL: http://www.nal.usda.gov/fnic
Email Address: lending@nal.usda.gov

## Healthy Foods, Healthy Baby

In a novella format, two young teens, one Black-American, one Hispanic, learn about good nutrition during pregnancy.

| | |
|---|---|
| Availability: | Staff at schools with NET, WIC, CSFP, FDPIR, CACFP, UMD or Child Nutrition Program food programs in the United States. Those not having such an affiliation should contact their library to place an interlibrary loan request. |
| Suggested Grade: | 6-Adult |
| Order Number: | NAL Video 1426 |
| Production Date: | 1992 |
| Format: | VHS videotape |
| Special Notes: | Produced by the Philadelphia Department of Health. |
| Terms: | Borrower pays return postage. RETURN the day after scheduled use. Book at least 4 weeks in advance. Requests must include your name, phone, mail address, eligibility program, title, NAL number, show date, and a statement, "I have read the warning on copyright restrictions and accept full responsibility for compliance." One title per request. |

Source: National Agricultural Library
Document Delivery Services Branch
4th Floor, Photo Lab, 10301 Baltimore Avenue
Beltsville, MD 20705-2351

# HEALTH--FAMILY LIFE EDUCATION

Phone: 1-301-504-5994
Fax: 1-301-504-5675
World Wide Web URL:  http://www.nal.usda.gov/fnic
Email Address:  lending@nal.usda.gov

## Human Anatomy Online

Here is a great reference for students studying human anatomy and for those who just want to know more about the medical descriptions commonly used by doctors and nurses.

| | |
|---|---|
| Availability: | All requesters |
| Suggested Grade: | 6-12 |
| Order Number: | not applicable |
| Format: | Online Tutorial |

Source: Inner Learning On-line
World Wide Web URL:
http://www.innerbody.com/http://www.innerbody.com/

## I Can Do That!

Learn about DNA, RNA, cells, protein, and cloning.

| | |
|---|---|
| Availability: | All requesters |
| Suggested Grade: | 6-12 |
| Order Number: | not applicable |
| Format: | Web Site |

Source: Eureka!Science
World Wide Web URL:
http://www.eurekascience.com/ICanDoThat/

## Inside My Mom

A cartoon fetus talks to his mom about how to feed him during pregnancy.

| | |
|---|---|
| Availability: | Staff at schools with NET, WIC, CSFP, FDPIR, CACFP, UMD or Child Nutrition Program food programs in the United States. Those not having such an affiliation should contact their library to place an interlibrary loan request. |
| Suggested Grade: | 9-Adult |
| Languages: | English; Spanish |
| Order Number: | NAL Video 933 |
| Production Date: | 1990 |
| Format: | VHS videotape |
| Special Notes: | Produced by the March of Dimes Birth Defects Foundation. |
| Terms: | Borrower pays return postage. RETURN the day after scheduled use. Book at least 4 weeks in advance. Requests must include your name, phone, mail address, eligibility program, title, NAL number, show date, and a statement, "I have read the warning on copyright restrictions and accept full responsibility for compliance." One title per request. |

Source: National Agricultural Library
Document Delivery Services Branch
4th Floor, Photo Lab, 10301 Baltimore Avenue
Beltsville, MD  20705-2351
Phone: 1-301-504-5994
Fax: 1-301-504-5675
World Wide Web URL:  http://www.nal.usda.gov/fnic
Email Address:  lending@nal.usda.gov

## Lead Poisoning Prevention:  A Parent's Guide

Focuses on the dangers of lead and the places where it is commonly found both in and outside of the home.

| | |
|---|---|
| Availability: | Schools, libraries, and homeschoolers in Connecticut, Maine, Massachusetts, New Hampshire, Rhode Island, and Vermont. |
| Suggested Grade: | Parents |
| Order Number: | VID 240 |
| Production Date: | 1994 |
| Format: | VHS videotape |
| Terms: | Borrower pays return postage. Return within three weeks of receipt. If the tape you request is available, it will be mailed within 5 business days. If not, you will be notified that this video is already out on loan. No more than three titles may be borrowed by one requestor at a time. No reservations for a specific date will be accepted. It is most efficient to order via the web site. |

Source: U. S. Environmental Protection Agency, Region 1
Customer Service Center
One Congress Street, Suite 1100
Boston, MA  02214
World Wide Web URL:
http://yosemite.epa.gov/r1/videolen.nsf/

## Life's Greatest Miracle

Lennart Nilsson's microphotography chronicles the growth of a baby from embryo to newborn.

| | |
|---|---|
| Availability: | All requesters |
| Suggested Grade: | 7-Adult |
| Order Number: | not applicable |
| Production Date: | 2001 |
| Format: | Streaming Video |

Source: NOVA
World Wide Web URL:
http://www.pbs.org/wgbh/nova/programs/index.html

## Lo Que Comes:  Por Ti Y Tu Bebe

This program uses the novella format to teach young pregnant women about healthy eating habits during pregnancy. It includes information about weight gain and WIC (Women, Infants & Children).

| | |
|---|---|
| Availability: | Staff at schools with NET, WIC, CSFP, FDPIR, CACFP, UMD or Child Nutrition Program food programs in the United States. Those not having such an affiliation should contact their library to place an interlibrary loan request. |
| Suggested Grade: | 6-Adult |
| Language: | Spanish |
| Order Number: | NAL Video 1797 |
| Production Date: | 1993 |
| Format: | VHS videotape |
| Special Notes: | This Philadelphia Department of Health and Ethnovision production includes a discussion guide and an English script. |
| Terms: | Borrower pays return postage. RETURN the day after scheduled use. Book at least 4 weeks in advance. Requests must include your name, phone, mail address, eligibility program, title, NAL number, show date, and |

*All materials listed in this 2018-2019 edition are BRAND NEW!*

a statement, "I have read the warning on copyright restrictions and accept full responsibility for compliance." One title per request.

**Source: National Agricultural Library**
**Document Delivery Services Branch**
**4th Floor, Photo Lab**
**10301 Baltimore Avenue**
**Beltsville, MD 20705-2351**
**Phone: 1-301-504-5994**
**Fax: 1-301-504-5675**
**World Wide Web URL: http://www.nal.usda.gov/fnic**
**Email Address: lending@nal.usda.gov**

## Pregnant Teens Taking Care

Discusses the importance of nutrition and early medical care during pregnancy, and describes the ways in which the mother's eating habits affect the fetus as well as the risk of "casual" use of drugs, alcohol and cigarettes during pregnancy.

Availability: Staff at schools with NET, WIC, CSFP, FDPIR, CACFP, UMD or Child Nutrition Program food programs in the United States. Those not having such an affiliation should contact their library to place an interlibrary loan request.
Suggested Grade: 9-Adult
Order Number: NAL Video 743
Format: VHS videotape
Terms: Borrower pays return postage. RETURN the day after scheduled use. Book at least 4 weeks in advance. Requests must include your name, phone, mail address, eligibility program, title, NAL number, show date, and a statement, "I have read the warning on copyright restrictions and accept full responsibility for compliance." One title per request.

**Source: National Agricultural Library**
**Document Delivery Services Branch**
**4th Floor, Photo Lab**
**10301 Baltimore Avenue**
**Beltsville, MD 20705-2351**
**Phone: 1-301-504-5994**
**Fax: 1-301-504-5675**
**World Wide Web URL: http://www.nal.usda.gov/fnic**
**Email Address: lending@nal.usda.gov**

## Teen Breastfeeding: The Natural Choice

A diverse group of breastfeeding teen mothers present their own experiences of fitting breastfeeding into an active teen lifestyle.

Availability: Staff at schools with NET, WIC, CSFP, FDPIR, CACFP, UMD or Child Nutrition Program food programs in the United States. Those not having such an affiliation should contact their library to place an interlibrary loan request.
Suggested Grade: 9-12
Order Number: Video 2758
Production Date: 1998
Format: VHS videotape

Special Notes: Includes a facilitator's guide. Two parts are included.
Terms: Borrower pays return postage. RETURN the day after scheduled use. Book at least 4 weeks in advance. Requests must include your name, phone, mail address, eligibility program, title, NAL number, show date, and a statement, "I have read the warning on copyright restrictions and accept full responsibility for compliance." One title per request.

**Source: National Agricultural Library**
**Document Delivery Services Branch**
**4th Floor, Photo Lab**
**10301 Baltimore Avenue**
**Beltsville, MD 20705-2351**
**Phone: 1-301-504-5994**
**Fax: 1-301-504-5675**
**World Wide Web URL: http://www.nal.usda.gov/fnic**
**Email Address: lending@nal.usda.gov**

## Wake Up Call

Young people being sexually harassed and exploited is a serious issue today, particularly if the relationship is with someone in a trusted role, such as a teacher or boss. Lizzie finds a flexible, well-paying job, but her boss makes inappropriate and unwanted sexual overtures and innuendoes. She must decide whether to compromise her values for the chance to earn money for college.

Availability: Schools, libraries, and homeschoolers in the United States who serve the hearing impaired.
Suggested Grade: 8-Adult
Order Number: 12401
Production Date: 1996
Format: DVD
Special Notes: Produced by Aims Multimedia.
Terms: Sponsor pays all transportation costs. Return one week after receipt. Participation is limited to deaf or hard of hearing Americans, their parents, families, teachers, counselors, or others whose use would benefit a deaf or hard of hearing person. Only one person in the audience needs to be hearing impaired. You must register--which is free. These videos are all open-captioned--no special equipment is required for viewing.

**Source: Described and Captioned Media Program**
**National Association of the Deaf**
**4211 Church Street Ext.**
**Roebuck, SC 29376**
**Phone: 1-800-237-6213**
**Fax: 1-800-538-5636**
**World Wide Web URL: http://www.dcmp.org**

## We're Growing Up!

Talks matter-of-factly about human growth and discusses the physical changes adolescents undergo. Reviews male and female anatomy and sexual development. Emphasizes and encourages emotional maturity and responsible choices.

Availability: Schools, libraries, and homeschoolers in the United States who serve the hearing impaired.
Suggested Grade: 5-8
Order Number: 12832

*All materials listed in this 2018-2019 edition are **BRAND NEW!***

# HEALTH--FAMILY LIFE EDUCATION

Production Date:     1995
Format:                   DVD
Special Notes:        Produced by Marsh Media.
Terms:    Sponsor pays all transportation costs. Return one week
             after receipt. Participation is limited to deaf or hard of
             hearing Americans, their parents, families, teachers,
             counselors, or others whose use would benefit a deaf or
             hard of hearing person. Only one person in the audience
             needs to be hearing impaired. You must register--which
             is free. These videos are all open-captioned--no special
             equipment is required for viewing.

**Source: Described and Captioned Media Program**
**National Association of the Deaf**
**4211 Church Street Ext.**
**Roebuck, SC  29376**
**Phone:  1-800-237-6213**
**Fax: 1-800-538-5636**
**World Wide Web URL:  http://www.dcmp.org**

## When Dating Turns Dangerous

Zach and Lucy have been dating, but his attention changes to jealousy, possessiveness, and ultimately, to physical violence and emotional abuse. Their relationship models the growing problem of dating violence, its patterns, and how abuse destroys the victim's self-esteem. Stresses the abuser is responsible for the violent behavior and that the victim is never to blame.

Availability:          Schools, libraries, and homeschoolers in the
                            United States who serve the hearing impaired.
Suggested Grade:  9-Adult
Order Number:      13035
Production Date:   1995
Format:                  DVD
Special Notes:       Produced by Sunburst Communications.
Terms:    Sponsor pays all transportation costs. Return one week
             after receipt. Participation is limited to deaf or hard of
             hearing Americans, their parents, families, teachers,
             counselors, or others whose use would benefit a deaf or
             hard of hearing person. Only one person in the audience
             needs to be hearing impaired. You must register--which
             is free. These videos are all open-captioned--no special
             equipment is required for viewing.

**Source: Described and Captioned Media Program**
**National Association of the Deaf**
**4211 Church Street Ext.**
**Roebuck, SC  29376**
**Phone: 1-800-237-6213**
**Fax: 1-800-538-5636**
**World Wide Web URL:  http://www.dcmp.org**

*All materials listed in this 2018-2019 edition are **BRAND NEW!***

## ABC's of Children's Nutrition, The
Examines the child's behavior and development of physically fit children. It looks at quick and easy ways to ensure a balanced diet for children during their growing years.

Availability: Staff at schools with NET, WIC, CSFP, FDPIR, CACFP, UMD or Child Nutrition Program food programs in the United States. Those not having such an affiliation should contact their library to place an interlibrary loan request.
Suggested Grade: preK-6
Order Number: NAL Video 1340
Production Date: 1992
Format: VHS videotape
Special Notes: This Turner Multimedia production includes a teacher's guide.
Terms: Borrower pays return postage. RETURN the day after scheduled use. Book at least 4 weeks in advance. Requests must include your name, phone, mail address, eligibility program, title, NAL number, show date, and a statement, "I have read the warning on copyright restrictions and accept full responsibility for compliance." One title per request.
**Source: National Agricultural Library**
**Document Delivery Services Branch**
**4th Floor, Photo Lab**
**10301 Baltimore Avenue**
**Beltsville, MD 20705-2351**
**Phone: 1-301-504-5994**
**Fax: 1-301-504-5675**
**World Wide Web URL: http://www.nal.usda.gov/fnic**
**Email Address: lending@nal.usda.gov**

## Action Guide for Healthy Eating
Gives helpful hints to help you include more low fat, high-fiber foods in your diet.

Availability: All requesters
Suggested Grade: 4-Adult
Order Number: not applicable
Format: Online Article; 17 pages
Special Notes: Use the on-site search engine to easily find this title. You may request a printed copy mailed to you for a fee.
**Source: Federal Citizen Information Center**
**World Wide Web URL: http://www.pueblo.gsa.gov/**

## Adjusting Recipes to Meet Dietary Guidelines
Take a step toward meeting your nutritional goals by learning how to adjust your favorite recipes in accordance with the Dietary Guidelines for Americans.

Availability: All requesters
Suggested Grade: 9-Adult
Order Number: not applicable
Format: Online Article
Special Notes: This is a PDF file which will open automatically on your computer.

**Source: Georgia Jones, Julie Albrecht, and Linda Boeckner**
**World Wide Web URL:**
**http://www.ianrpubs.unl.edu/epublic/live/ec442/build/ec442.pdf**

## Adventures of Buddy McNutty, The Volume II
The adventures of Buddy make learning about peanuts fun.

Availability: Single copies to schools, libraries, and homeschoolers in the United States.
Suggested Grade: K-3
Order Number: order by title
Format: Teacher's Kit
**Source: Peanut Education Service**
**Marianne Copelan**
**P. O. Box 8**
**Nashville, NC 27856**
**Phone: 1-252-459-9977**
**Fax: 1-252-459-7396**
**World Wide Web URL: http://www.aboutpeanuts.com**
**Email Address: info@aboutpeanuts.com**

## Aisles Have It, The!
This is a brief vignette about two teens whose school assignment leads to the grocery store. It includes tips on food packaging, labels and ingredients, unit pricing and how to get more nutrition for your food dollar.

Availability: Staff at schools with NET, WIC, CSFP, FDPIR, CACFP, UMD or Child Nutrition Program food programs in the United States. Those not having such an affiliation should contact their library to place an interlibrary loan request.
Suggested Grade: 7-12
Order Number: NAL Video 1767
Production Date: 1991
Format: VHS videotape
Terms: Borrower pays return postage. RETURN the day after scheduled use. Book at least 4 weeks in advance. Requests must include your name, phone, mail address, eligibility program, title, NAL number, show date, and a statement, "I have read the warning on copyright restrictions and accept full responsibility for compliance." One title per request.
**Source: National Agricultural Library**
**Document Delivery Services Branch**
**4th Floor, Photo Lab**
**10301 Baltimore Avenue**
**Beltsville, MD 20705-2351**
**Phone: 1-301-504-5994**
**Fax: 1-301-504-5675**
**World Wide Web URL: http://www.nal.usda.gov/fnic**
**Email Address: lending@nal.usda.gov**

## All About Peanuts & Peanut Butter
Activities, songs, recipes and more for teaching young children about peanuts and peanut butter.

Availability: Single copies to schools, libraries, and homeschoolers in the United States.
Suggested Grade: K-2

# HEALTH--FOOD AND NUTRITION

Order Number:       order by title
Format:             Teacher's Kit
Special Notes:      May also be downloaded from the web site.

**Source: Peanut Education Service**
**Marianne Copelan**
**P. O. Box 8**
**Nashville, NC  27856**
**Phone:  1-252-459-9977**
**Fax:  1-252-459-7396**
**World Wide Web URL:  http://www.aboutpeanuts.com**
**Email Address:  info@aboutpeanuts.com**

## Anemia:  The Silent Shadow
Discusses iron deficiency and folic acid, identifies groups at risk, provides nutrition guidelines for prevention, and offers recipes and cooking tips.

Availability:       Staff at schools with NET, WIC, CSFP, FDPIR, CACFP, UMD or Child Nutrition Program food programs in the United States. Those not having such an affiliation should contact their library to place an interlibrary loan request.
Suggested Grade:    7-12
Languages:          English; Spanish
Order Number:       English  NAL  Video 2295; Spanish NAL Video 3243
Production Date:    1995
Format:             VHS videotape
Terms:              Borrower pays return postage.  RETURN the day after scheduled use.  Book at least 4 weeks in advance. Requests must include your name, phone, mail address, eligibility program, title, NAL number, show date, and a statement, "I have read the warning on copyright restrictions and accept full responsibility for compliance."  One title per request.

**Source:  National Agricultural Library**
**Document Delivery Services Branch**
**4th Floor, Photo Lab**
**10301 Baltimore Avenue**
**Beltsville, MD  20705-2351**
**Phone:  1-301-504-5994**
**Fax:  1-301-504-5675**
**World Wide Web URL:  http://www.nal.usda.gov/fnic**
**Email Address:  lending@nal.usda.gov**

## Apples!  Apples!
Learn more about apples.

Availability:       All requesters
Suggested Grade:    2-5
Order Number:       not applicable
Format:             WebQuest

**Source:  Tricia Goodman**
**World Wide Web URL:**
**http://its.guilford.k12.nc.us/webquests/Apples/apples.htm**

## Ask Sofia About Food Safety
An advice columnist answers questions about food safety.

Availability:       Staff at schools with NET, WIC, CSFP, FDPIR, CACFP, UMD or Child Nutrition Program food programs in the United States. Those not having such an affiliation should contact their library to place an interlibrary loan request.
Suggested Grade:    6-12
Language:           Spanish
Order Number:       NAL Video 2296
Production Date:    1996
Format:             VHS videotape
Terms:              Borrower pays return postage.  RETURN the day after scheduled use.  Book at least 4 weeks in advance. Requests must include your name, phone, mail address, eligibility program, title, NAL number, show date, and a statement, "I have read the warning on copyright restrictions and accept full responsibility for compliance."  One title per request.

**Source:  National Agricultural Library**
**Document Delivery Services Branch**
**4th Floor, Photo Lab**
**10301 Baltimore Avenue**
**Beltsville, MD  20705-2351**
**Phone:  1-301-504-5994**
**Fax:  1-301-504-5675**
**World Wide Web URL:  http://www.nal.usda.gov/fnic**
**Email Address:  lending@nal.usda.gov**

## Ask the Dietitian
You can find the answers to an incredible number of questions about nutrition.  If you don't find the answer to your question, you can submit it.

Availability:       All requesters
Suggested Grade:    9-12
Order Number:       not applicable
Format:             Web Site

**Source:  Joanne Larsen**
**World Wide Web URL:  http://www.dietitian.com/**

## Awesome Body by Age 14, An
Two teens help you create your own eating plan, interpret food labels, provide grocery shopping tips, and more.

Availability:       Staff at schools with NET, WIC, CSFP, FDPIR, CACFP, UMD or Child Nutrition Program food programs in the United States. Those not having such an affiliation should contact their library to place an interlibrary loan request.
Suggested Grade:    5-12
Order Number:       NAL Video 2402
Production Date:    1994
Format:             VHS videotape
Terms:              Borrower pays return postage.  RETURN the day after scheduled use.  Book at least 4 weeks in advance. Requests must include your name, phone, mail address, eligibility program, title, NAL number, show date, and a statement, "I have read the warning on copyright restrictions and accept full responsibility for compliance."  One title per request.

Source: National Agricultural Library
Document Delivery Services Branch
4th Floor, Photo Lab
10301 Baltimore Avenue
Beltsville, MD 20705-2351
Phone: 1-301-504-5994
Fax: 1-301-504-5675
World Wide Web URL: http://www.nal.usda.gov/fnic
Email Address: lending@nal.usda.gov

## Bacterial Contamination of Foods

Includes two videotapes, "Mystery of the Poisoned Panther Picnic," and "Dirty Dining," along with other materials for teaching food safety.

Availability: Staff at schools with NET, WIC, CSFP, FDPIR, CACFP, UMD or Child Nutrition Program food programs in the United States. Those not having such an affiliation should contact their library to place an interlibrary loan request.

Suggested Grade: 7-10
Order Number: NAL Kit 376
Production Date: 1996
Format: VHS videotape
Terms: Borrower pays return postage. RETURN the day after scheduled use. Book at least 4 weeks in advance. Requests must include your name, phone, mail address, eligibility program, title, NAL number, show date, and a statement, "I have read the warning on copyright restrictions and accept full responsibility for compliance." One title per request.

Source: National Agricultural Library
Document Delivery Services Branch
4th Floor, Photo Lab, 10301 Baltimore Avenue
Beltsville, MD 20705-2351
Phone: 1-301-504-5994
Fax: 1-301-504-5675
World Wide Web URL: http://www.nal.usda.gov/fnic
Email Address: lending@nal.usda.gov

## Balancing Your Act!

Michael Jordan talks to kids about practicing good eating habits and exercise.

Availability: Staff at schools with NET, WIC, CSFP, FDPIR, CACFP, UMD or Child Nutrition Program food programs in the United States. Those not having such an affiliation should contact their library to place an interlibrary loan request.

Suggested Grade: 2-6
Order Number: NAL Video 2831
Format: VHS videotape
Terms: Borrower pays return postage. RETURN the day after scheduled use. Book at least 4 weeks in advance. Requests must include your name, phone, mail address, eligibility program, title, NAL number, show date, and a statement, "I have read the warning on copyright restrictions and accept full responsibility for compliance." One title per request.

Source: National Agricultural Library
Document Delivery Services Branch
4th Floor, Photo Lab
10301 Baltimore Avenue
Beltsville, MD 20705-2351
Phone: 1-301-504-5994
Fax: 1-301-504-5675
World Wide Web URL: http://www.nal.usda.gov/fnic
Email Address: lending@nal.usda.gov

## Barbecues, Picnics, and Potlucks

Consumers journey to a family barbecue to learn the principles of preparing and transporting food safely.

Availability: Staff at schools with NET, WIC, CSFP, FDPIR, CACFP, UMD or Child Nutrition Program food programs in the United States. Those not having such an affiliation should contact their library to place an interlibrary loan request.

Suggested Grade: 6-Adult
Order Number: NAL Video 2406
Production Date: 1996
Format: VHS videotape
Terms: Borrower pays return postage. RETURN the day after scheduled use. Book at least 4 weeks in advance. Requests must include your name, phone, mail address, eligibility program, title, NAL number, show date, and a statement, "I have read the warning on copyright restrictions and accept full responsibility for compliance." One title per request.

Source: National Agricultural Library
Document Delivery Services Branch
4th Floor, Photo Lab, 10301 Baltimore Avenue
Beltsville, MD 20705-2351
Phone: 1-301-504-5994
Fax: 1-301-504-5675
World Wide Web URL: http://www.nal.usda.gov/fnic
Email Address: lending@nal.usda.gov

## Barely Bear Learns About Good Nutrition

Designed to teach basic nutrition lessons.

Availability: Staff at schools with NET, WIC, CSFP, FDPIR, CACFP, UMD or Child Nutrition Program food programs in the United States. Those not having such an affiliation should contact their library to place an interlibrary loan request.

Suggested Grade: preK-3
Order Number: NAL Kit 193
Production Date: 1993
Format: Set of 2 VHS videotapes
Special Notes: Includes a storybook, a poster and an instructor's guide.
Terms: Borrower pays return postage. RETURN the day after scheduled use. Book at least 4 weeks in advance. Requests must include your name, phone, mail address, eligibility program, title, NAL number, show date, and a statement, "I have read the warning on copyright restrictions and accept full responsibility for compliance." One title per request.

Source:  National Agricultural Library
Document Delivery Services Branch
4th Floor, Photo Lab
10301 Baltimore Avenue
Beltsville, MD  20705-2351
Phone:  1-301-504-5994
Fax:  1-301-504-5675
World Wide Web URL:  http://www.nal.usda.gov/fnic
Email Address:  lending@nal.usda.gov

## Barnyard Basics of Good Nutrition with Sammy Chef
Teaches youngsters about the food guide pyramid and the source of many foods.

| | |
|---|---|
| Availability: | Staff at schools with NET, WIC, CSFP, FDPIR, CACFP, UMD or Child Nutrition Program food programs in the United States. Those not having such an affiliation should contact their library to place an interlibrary loan request. |
| Suggested Grade: | 1-2 |
| Order Number: | NAL Kit 514 |
| Production Date: | 1996 |
| Format: | VHS videotape |
| Special Notes: | Includes a teacher's guide. |
| Terms: | Borrower pays return postage.  RETURN the day after scheduled use.  Book at least 4 weeks in advance. Requests must include your name, phone, mail address, eligibility program, title, NAL number, show date, and a statement, "I have read the warning on copyright restrictions and accept full responsibility for compliance."  One title per request. |

Source:  National Agricultural Library
Document Delivery Services Branch
4th Floor, Photo Lab
10301 Baltimore Avenue
Beltsville, MD  20705-2351
Phone:  1-301-504-5994
Fax:  1-301-504-5675
World Wide Web URL:  http://www.nal.usda.gov/fnic
Email Address:  lending@nal.usda.gov

## Be a Food Groupie--And Care About Healthy Eating
Centers around five characters:  Orange, Broccoli, Bread, Milk, and Peanut Food Groupie.  Each character represents one of five food groups as established by USDA.  The characters explain where the foods they represent come from and how each food group helps children stay healthy. Children are advised to eat a variety of foods from all the food groups.

| | |
|---|---|
| Availability: | Staff at schools with NET, WIC, CSFP, FDPIR, CACFP, UMD or Child Nutrition Program food programs in the United States. Those not having such an affiliation should contact their library to place an interlibrary loan request. |
| Suggested Grade: | preK-6 |
| Order Number: | NAL Kit 141 |
| Production Date: | 1992 |
| Format: | Set of 3 VHS videotapes |

| | |
|---|---|
| Special Notes: | Includes 5 plush representations of food characters, hanging mobile, storybook, poster, sticker cards, parent letters, and a teacher's guide. |
| Terms: | Borrower pays return postage.  RETURN the day after scheduled use.  Book at least 4 weeks in advance. Requests must include your name, phone, mail address, eligibility program, title, NAL number, show date, and a statement, "I have read the warning on copyright restrictions and accept full responsibility for compliance."  One title per request. |

Source:  National Agricultural Library
Document Delivery Services Branch
4th Floor, Photo Lab
10301 Baltimore Avenue
Beltsville, MD  20705-2351
Phone:  1-301-504-5994
Fax:  1-301-504-5675
World Wide Web URL:  http://www.nal.usda.gov/fnic
Email Address:  lending@nal.usda.gov

## Best Breakfast, The
A healthy nutritious breakfast is described in this video as one which is low in fat and sodium, and consists of a variety of foods high in carbohydrates and vitamin C.  The most common breakfast foods eaten by Americans and other peoples around the  world are discussed.  To choose a nutritious cereal, one should select one that is low in sugar, fat and sodium, high in fiber and contains a short ingredient list.

| | |
|---|---|
| Availability: | Staff at schools with NET, WIC, CSFP, FDPIR, CACFP, UMD or Child Nutrition Program food programs in the United States. Those not having such an affiliation should contact their library to place an interlibrary loan request. |
| Suggested Grade: | 4-12 |
| Order Number: | NAL Video 375 |
| Production Date: | 1987 |
| Format: | VHS videotape |
| Terms: | Borrower pays return postage.  RETURN the day after scheduled use.  Book at least 4 weeks in advance. Requests must include your name, phone, mail address, eligibility program, title, NAL number, show date, and a statement, "I have read the warning on copyright restrictions and accept full responsibility for compliance."  One title per request. |

Source:  National Agricultural Library
Document Delivery Services Branch
4th Floor, Photo Lab, 10301 Baltimore Avenue
Beltsville, MD  20705-2351
Phone:  1-301-504-5994
Fax:  1-301-504-5675
World Wide Web URL:  http://www.nal.usda.gov/fnic
Email Address:  lending@nal.usda.gov

## Better Fitness Through Nutrition
Learn how the body regulates intake of fluids, through interactive calculators.

Availability:       All requesters
Suggested Grade:    6-12
Order Number:       not applicable
Format:             Web Site
Special Notes:      This URL will lead you to a subject page.
                    Then click on the appropriate subject heading.

**Source: ThinkQuest**
**World Wide Web URL:**
**http://www.thinkquest.org/pls/html/think.library**

## Breakfast Makes It Happen

Discusses how a school breakfast program can benefit the children who participate, their parents, and the community.

Availability:       Staff at schools with NET, WIC, CSFP, FDPIR, CACFP, UMD or Child Nutrition Program food programs in the United States. Those not having such an affiliation should contact their library to place an interlibrary loan request.
Suggested Grade:    Teacher Reference
Order Number:       NAL Video TX733.B73.B73
Production Date:    1995
Format:             VHS videotape
Special Notes:      Also available as NAL Video 2111, which is a National Dairy Council production with leader guide, 3 charts and a pamphlet.
Terms:      Borrower pays return postage. RETURN the day after scheduled use. Book at least 4 weeks in advance. Requests must include your name, phone, mail address, eligibility program, title, NAL number, show date, and a statement, "I have read the warning on copyright restrictions and accept full responsibility for compliance." One title per request.

**Source: National Agricultural Library**
**Document Delivery Services Branch**
**4th Floor, Photo Lab, 10301 Baltimore Avenue**
**Beltsville, MD 20705-2351**
**Phone: 1-301-504-5994**
**Fax: 1-301-504-5675**
**World Wide Web URL: http://www.nal.usda.gov/fnic**
**Email Address: lending@nal.usda.gov**

## Calcium Quiz

Take this quiz to see if you are getting enough of this important nutrient in your diet.

Availability:       All requesters
Suggested Grade:    9-Adult
Order Number:       not applicable
Format:             Online Quiz

**Source: Dairy Council of California**
**World Wide Web URL:**
**http://www.dairycouncilofca.org/activities/quiz/**
**acti_calc_main.htm**

## Cardiac Fitness: A Guide to Shopping Smart, Eating Healthy

Designed to educate about the new food labels and present nutrition facts that help patients shop and dine in a heart-smart way.

Availability:       Staff at schools with NET, WIC, CSFP, FDPIR, CACFP, UMD or Child Nutrition Program food programs in the United States. Those not having such an affiliation should contact their library to place an interlibrary loan request.
Suggested Grade:    7-12
Order Number:       NAL Video 257
Format:             VHS videotape
Special Notes:      Includes a slide program and other materials.
Terms:      Borrower pays return postage. RETURN the day after scheduled use. Book at least 4 weeks in advance. Requests must include your name, phone, mail address, eligibility program, title, NAL number, show date, and a statement, "I have read the warning on copyright restrictions and accept full responsibility for compliance." One title per request.

**Source: National Agricultural Library**
**Document Delivery Services Branch**
**4th Floor, Photo Lab**
**10301 Baltimore Avenue**
**Beltsville, MD 20705-2351**
**Phone: 1-301-504-5994**
**Fax: 1-301-504-5675**
**World Wide Web URL: http://www.nal.usda.gov/fnic**
**Email Address: lending@nal.usda.gov**

## Catchoo and Gesundheit

Designed to teach children about the importance of vitamins and minerals in the diet, this animated cartoon depicts the scrawny lifestyle of Catchoo, the alley cat and Gesundheit, the ally rat.

Availability:       Staff at schools with NET, WIC, CSFP, FDPIR, CACFP, UMD or Child Nutrition Program food programs in the United States. Those not having such an affiliation should contact their library to place an interlibrary loan request.
Suggested Grade:    preK-4
Order Number:       NAL Video 140
Production Date:    1986
Format:             VHS videotape
Terms:      Borrower pays return postage. RETURN the day after scheduled use. Book at least 4 weeks in advance. Requests must include your name, phone, mail address, eligibility program, title, NAL number, show date, and a statement, "I have read the warning on copyright restrictions and accept full responsibility for compliance." One title per request.

**Source: National Agricultural Library**
**Document Delivery Services Branch**
**4th Floor, Photo Lab**
**10301 Baltimore Avenue**
**Beltsville, MD 20705-2351**
**Phone: 1-301-504-5994**
**Fax: 1-301-504-5675**
**World Wide Web URL: http://www.nal.usda.gov/fnic**
**Email Address: lending@nal.usda.gov**

# HEALTH--FOOD AND NUTRITION

## Chances and Choices with Food
Includes lesson plans that encourage critical thinking. Concepts deal with food safety.

Availability: Staff at schools with NET, WIC, CSFP, FDPIR, CACFP, UMD or Child Nutrition Program food programs in the United States. Those not having such an affiliation should contact their library to place an interlibrary loan request.
Suggested Grade: 4-6
Order Number: NAL Video 2230
Production Date: 1992
Format: VHS videotape
Special Notes: Includes other supplementary material.
Terms: Borrower pays return postage. RETURN the day after scheduled use. Book at least 4 weeks in advance. Requests must include your name, phone, mail address, eligibility program, title, NAL number, show date, and a statement, "I have read the warning on copyright restrictions and accept full responsibility for compliance." One title per request.

**Source: National Agricultural Library
Document Delivery Services Branch
4th Floor, Photo Lab
10301 Baltimore Avenue
Beltsville, MD 20705-2351
Phone: 1-301-504-5994
Fax: 1-301-504-5675
World Wide Web URL: http://www.nal.usda.gov/fnic
Email Address: lending@nal.usda.gov**

## Chicken Fabrication by the Professional Chef
Teaches you how to cut chicken or other poultry into a variety of portion cuts.

Availability: Staff at schools with NET, WIC, CSFP, FDPIR, CACFP, UMD or Child Nutrition Program food programs in the United States. Those not having such an affiliation should contact their library to place an interlibrary loan request.
Suggested Grade: 6-12
Order Number: NAL Video 2408
Production Date: 1986
Format: VHS videotape
Terms: Borrower pays return postage. RETURN the day after scheduled use. Book at least 4 weeks in advance. Requests must include your name, phone, mail address, eligibility program, title, NAL number, show date, and a statement, "I have read the warning on copyright restrictions and accept full responsibility for compliance." One title per request.

**Source: National Agricultural Library
Document Delivery Services Branch
4th Floor, Photo Lab
10301 Baltimore Avenue
Beltsville, MD 20705-2351
Phone: 1-301-504-5994
Fax: 1-301-504-5675
World Wide Web URL: http://www.nal.usda.gov/fnic
Email Address: lending@nal.usda.gov**

## Chocolate Chip Cookies: To Eat or Not to Eat!
Students will learn if chocolate chips are nutritious (we know they are delicious).

Availability: All requesters
Suggested Grade: 3-5
Order Number: not applicable
Format: WebQuest

**Source: Grace M. Vaknin
World Wide Web URL:
http://collier.k12.fl.us/weblessons/cookiewq/index.htm**

## Choices: It's Time to Eat Right: Healthy Food Choices for Teens: Working Draft
This video presentation provides instructions to help adolescents make healthy food choices. This material is ethnically appropriate for Hawaii's populations, and features Hawaii's own students, athletes, and famous personalities with their nutrition messages.

Availability: Staff at schools with NET, WIC, CSFP, FDPIR, CACFP, UMD or Child Nutrition Program food programs in the United States. Those not having such an affiliation should contact their library to place an interlibrary loan request.
Suggested Grade: 7-12
Order Number: NAL Kit 154
Production Date: 1992
Format: VHS videotape
Special Notes: This Hawaii State Department of Health production includes an assortment of related teaching aids.
Terms: Borrower pays return postage. RETURN the day after scheduled use. Book at least 4 weeks in advance. Requests must include your name, phone, mail address, eligibility program, title, NAL number, show date, and a statement, "I have read the warning on copyright restrictions and accept full responsibility for compliance." One title per request.

**Source: National Agricultural Library
Document Delivery Services Branch
4th Floor, Photo Lab
10301 Baltimore Avenue
Beltsville, MD 20705-2351
Phone: 1-301-504-5994
Fax: 1-301-504-5675
World Wide Web URL: http://www.nal.usda.gov/fnic
Email Address: lending@nal.usda.gov**

## Cholesterol and Your Health
This video includes five programs, each giving practical, easy-to-remember tips for dealing with cholesterol on a daily basis. Discussed are which foods do and do not contain cholesterol and how to identify them. The program points out the best choices to pick when eating at home or dining out, and explains the relationship between cholesterol, triglycerides, and fats.

Availability: Staff at schools with NET, WIC, CSFP, FDPIR, CACFP, UMD or Child Nutrition Program food programs in the United States. Those not having such an affiliation should contact their library to place an interlibrary loan request.
Suggested Grade: 7-Adult
Order Number: NAL Video 1088
Production Date: 1990
Format: VHS videotape
Special Notes: The kit includes six fact sheets.
Terms: Borrower pays return postage. RETURN the day after scheduled use. Book at least 4 weeks in advance. Requests must include your name, phone, mail address, eligibility program, title, NAL number, show date, and a statement, "I have read the warning on copyright restrictions and accept full responsibility for compliance." One title per request.
**Source: National Agricultural Library**
**Document Delivery Services Branch**
**4th Floor, Photo Lab**
**10301 Baltimore Avenue**
**Beltsville, MD 20705-2351**
**Phone: 1-301-504-5994**
**Fax: 1-301-504-5675**
**World Wide Web URL: http://www.nal.usda.gov/fnic**
**Email Address: lending@nal.usda.gov**

## Cholesterol Control

Practical suggestions for controlling blood cholesterol levels are offered in this program and accompanying manual. Background information is provided on the definition, functions, and types (high density lipoprotein, low-density lipoprotein) of cholesterol.
Availability: Staff at schools with NET, WIC, CSFP, FDPIR, CACFP, UMD or Child Nutrition Program food programs in the United States. Those not having such an affiliation should contact their library to place an interlibrary loan request.
Suggested Grade: 6-12
Order Number: NAL Video 296
Production Date: 1989
Format: VHS videotape
Terms: Borrower pays return postage. RETURN the day after scheduled use. Book at least 4 weeks in advance. Requests must include your name, phone, mail address, eligibility program, title, NAL number, show date, and a statement, "I have read the warning on copyright restrictions and accept full responsibility for compliance." One title per request.
**Source: National Agricultural Library**
**Document Delivery Services Branch**
**4th Floor, Photo Lab**
**10301 Baltimore Avenue**
**Beltsville, MD 20705-2351**
**Phone: 1-301-504-5994**
**Fax: 1-301-504-5675**
**World Wide Web URL: http://www.nal.usda.gov/fnic**
**Email Address: lending@nal.usda.gov**

## Cholesterol Control: An Eater's Guide

This program demonstrates how to live and eat well on a low cholesterol diet. It offers a step-by-step approach to cooking and eating with a low cholesterol approach.
Availability: Staff at schools with NET, WIC, CSFP, FDPIR, CACFP, UMD or Child Nutrition Program food programs in the United States. Those not having such an affiliation should contact their library to place an interlibrary loan request.
Suggested Grade: All ages
Order Number: NAL Video 591
Production Date: 1989
Format: VHS videotape
Special Notes: Kit includes a recipe tips pamphlet.
Terms: Borrower pays return postage. RETURN the day after scheduled use. Book at least 4 weeks in advance. Requests must include your name, phone, mail address, eligibility program, title, NAL number, show date, and a statement, "I have read the warning on copyright restrictions and accept full responsibility for compliance." One title per request.
**Source: National Agricultural Library**
**Document Delivery Services Branch**
**4th Floor, Photo Lab**
**10301 Baltimore Avenue**
**Beltsville, MD 20705-2351**
**Phone: 1-301-504-5994**
**Fax: 1-301-504-5675**
**World Wide Web URL: http://www.nal.usda.gov/fnic**
**Email Address: lending@nal.usda.gov**

## Chow!: A Nutrition Curriculum for Grades 7-12

These activities provide useful nutrition information on which students can base their food choices.
Availability: Staff at schools with NET, WIC, CSFP, FDPIR, CACFP, UMD or Child Nutrition Program food programs in the United States. Those not having such an affiliation should contact their library to place an interlibrary loan request.
Suggested Grade: 7-12
Order Number: NAL Kit 304
Production Date: 1995
Format: VHS videotape
Special Notes: Includes supplemental teaching materials.
Terms: Borrower pays return postage. RETURN the day after scheduled use. Book at least 4 weeks in advance. Requests must include your name, phone, mail address, eligibility program, title, NAL number, show date, and a statement, "I have read the warning on copyright restrictions and accept full responsibility for compliance." One title per request.
**Source: National Agricultural Library**
**Document Delivery Services Branch**
**4th Floor, Photo Lab**
**10301 Baltimore Avenue**
**Beltsville, MD 20705-2351**
**Phone: 1-301-504-5994**
**Fax: 1-301-504-5675**

World Wide Web URL: http://www.nal.usda.gov/fnic
Email Address: lending@nal.usda.gov

## Closer Look at Antioxidants, A

Takes a closer look at the group of vitamins and minerals known as antioxidants and the role they play in the prevention of cancer.

Availability: Limit of 1 copy to schools, libraries, and homeschoolers in the United States and Canada.
Suggested Grade: 10-Adult
Order Number: order by title
Format: Brochure

Source: American Institute for Cancer Research
Publication Orders
1759 R Street, N. W.
Washington, DC 20009
Phone: 1-800-843-8114
Fax: 1-202-328-7226
World Wide Web URL: http://www.aicr.org
Email Address: aicrweb@aicr.org

## Closer Look at Phytochemicals, A

Explains what phytochemicals are (naturally occurring chemicals in plant-based foods), where they occur and why they help make plant-based foods such an important part of a healthy diet.

Availability: Limit of 1 copy to schools, libraries, and homeschoolers in the United States and Canada.
Suggested Grade: 10-Adult
Order Number: order by title
Format: Brochure
Special Notes: May also be downloaded from the web site.

Source: American Institute for Cancer Research
Publication Orders
1759 R Street, N. W.
Washington, DC 20009
Phone: 1-800-843-8114
Fax: 1-202-328-7226
World Wide Web URL: http://www.aicr.org
Email Address: aicrweb@aicr.org

## Comparison Food Shopping: Buying Groceries for Two People for One Week

This exercise helps students discover that nutritious food can be bought and prepared more cheaply than "fast food." They "shop" the newspaper buying groceries for two people for one week.

Availability: All requesters
Suggested Grade: 12
Order Number: not applicable
Format: Online Lesson Plan

Source: Kay B. Edwards
World Wide Web URL:
http://youth.net/cec/cecmisc/cecmisc.75.txt

## Complete Guide to Using Nutrition Food Labels, The

Discusses why the food labeling law is important, what it means to consumers, the kinds of nutrition information that are required on the label, and takes a close look at the nutrition facts panel.

Availability: Staff at schools with NET, WIC, CSFP, FDPIR, CACFP, UMD or Child Nutrition Program food programs in the United States. Those not having such an affiliation should contact their library to place an interlibrary loan request.
Suggested Grade: 7-12
Order Number: NAL Video 2548
Production Date: 1994
Format: VHS videotape
Special Notes: Includes a teacher's guide.
Terms: Borrower pays return postage. RETURN the day after scheduled use. Book at least 4 weeks in advance. Requests must include your name, phone, mail address, eligibility program, title, NAL number, show date, and a statement, "I have read the warning on copyright restrictions and accept full responsibility for compliance." One title per request.

Source: National Agricultural Library
Document Delivery Services Branch
4th Floor, Photo Lab, 10301 Baltimore Avenue
Beltsville, MD 20705-2351
Phone: 1-301-504-5994
Fax: 1-301-504-5675
World Wide Web URL: http://www.nal.usda.gov/fnic
Email Address: lending@nal.usda.gov

## Contemporary Nutrition: An Interactive Look at the Food Guide Pyramid

Provides basic guidelines on proper nutrition and diet. Using a four-level pyramid diagram, the program's menu explores the six food groups, their effects on our health, and how much we should consume from each group. Viewers answer varied questions within each segment. CC option. PC REQUIREMENTS: Windows 95 or higher, 16MB RAM, 40MB Free hard disk space, 2X CD-ROM drive, 256-color VGA display, SoundBlaster(tm) compatible sound card with speakers

Availability: Schools, libraries, and homeschoolers in the United States who serve the hearing impaired.
Suggested Grade: 8-12
Order Number: 9002
Production Date: 1997
Format: DVD
Special Notes: Produced by Cambridge Educational.
Terms: Sponsor pays all transportation costs. Return one week after receipt. Participation is limited to deaf or hard of hearing Americans, their parents, families, teachers, counselors, or others whose use would benefit a deaf or hard of hearing person. Only one person in the audience needs to be hearing impaired. You must register--which is free. These videos are all open-captioned--no special equipment is required for viewing.

Source: Described and Captioned Media Program
National Association of the Deaf
4211 Church Street Ext.
Roebuck, SC  29376
Phone:  1-800-237-6213
Fax:  1-800-538-5636
World Wide Web URL:  http://www.dcmp.org

## Controlling Cholesterol:  Through Diet and Nutrition

This video shows how to control cholesterol through diet. It offers substitutions that deliver maximum flavor with minimum cholesterol.

Availability:         Staff at schools with NET, WIC, CSFP, FDPIR, CACFP, UMD or Child Nutrition Program food programs in the United States. Those not having such an affiliation should contact their library to place an interlibrary loan request.
Suggested Grade:  6-Adult
Order Number:     NAL Video 1022
Production Date:  1989
Format:              VHS videotape
Terms:    Borrower pays return postage.  RETURN the day after scheduled use.  Book at least 4 weeks in advance. Requests must include your name, phone, mail address, eligibility program, title, NAL number, show date, and a statement, "I have read the warning on copyright restrictions and accept full responsibility for compliance."  One title per request.

Source:  National Agricultural Library
Document Delivery Services Branch
4th Floor, Photo Lab, 10301 Baltimore Avenue
Beltsville, MD  20705-2351
Phone:  1-301-504-5994
Fax:  1-301-504-5675
World Wide Web URL:  http://www.nal.usda.gov/fnic
Email Address:  lending@nal.usda.gov

## Cooking Basics:  Meat

Discusses what meat is (pork, veal, beef, and lamb), its nutritional value, and various cuts of meat. Details labeling information on meat before demonstrating ways to cook both tender and tough cuts.

Availability:         Schools, libraries, and homeschoolers in the United States who serve the hearing impaired.
Suggested Grade:  6-Adult
Order Number:     11427
Production Date:  2001
Format:              DVD
Special Notes:      Also available as live streaming video over the Internet.
Terms:    Sponsor pays all transportation costs.  Return one week after receipt.  Participation is limited to deaf or hard of hearing Americans, their parents, families, teachers, counselors, or others whose use would benefit a deaf or hard of hearing person.  Only one person in the audience needs to be hearing impaired.  You must register--which is free.  These videos are all open-captioned--no special equipment is required for viewing.

Source: Described and Captioned Media Program
National Association of the Deaf
4211 Church Street Ext.
Roebuck, SC  29376
Phone:  1-800-237-6213
Fax:  1-800-538-5636
World Wide Web URL:  http://www.dcmp.org

## Cooking for Your Heart's Delight

Shopping and cooking tips on ways to have a heart healthy diet are discussed in this video.  The concept that a healthy diet must be boring is dispelled in this program by demonstrating the variety of tasty foods that fit into such a diet.  Food preparation of various dishes is demonstrated.

Availability:         Staff at schools with NET, WIC, CSFP, FDPIR, CACFP, UMD or Child Nutrition Program food programs in the United States. Those not having such an affiliation should contact their library to place an interlibrary loan request.
Suggested Grade:  6-12
Order Number:     NAL Video 1096
Production Date:  1983
Format:              VHS videotape
Terms:    Borrower pays return postage.  RETURN the day after scheduled use.  Book at least 4 weeks in advance. Requests must include your name, phone, mail address, eligibility program, title, NAL number, show date, and a statement, "I have read the warning on copyright restrictions and accept full responsibility for compliance."  One title per request.

Source:  National Agricultural Library
Document Delivery Services Branch
4th Floor, Photo Lab
10301 Baltimore Avenue
Beltsville, MD  20705-2351
Phone:  1-301-504-5994
Fax:  1-301-504-5675
World Wide Web URL:  http://www.nal.usda.gov/fnic
Email Address:  lending@nal.usda.gov

## Cook's Choice

This program discusses how to provide students with food choices that lead to satisfied customers and less waste.  It shows how to manage these choices with menu development, physical setup, and self service.

Availability:         Staff at schools with NET, WIC, CSFP, FDPIR, CACFP, UMD or Child Nutrition Program food programs in the United States. Those not having such an affiliation should contact their library to place an interlibrary loan request.
Suggested Grade:  Adult
Order Number:     NAL Video 2283
Production Date:  1994
Format:              VHS videotape
Terms:    Borrower pays return postage.  RETURN the day after scheduled use.  Book at least 4 weeks in advance. Requests must include your name, phone, mail address,

eligibility program, title, NAL number, show date, and a statement, "I have read the warning on copyright restrictions and accept full responsibility for compliance." One title per request.

> Source: National Agricultural Library
> Document Delivery Services Branch
> 4th Floor, Photo Lab
> 10301 Baltimore Avenue
> Beltsville, MD 20705-2351
> Phone: 1-301-504-5994
> Fax: 1-301-504-5675
> World Wide Web URL: http://www.nal.usda.gov/fnic
> Email Address: lending@nal.usda.gov

## Crunchy Critter Club, The

The nutrition education goals of these videos for early childhood programs include: to develop a positive attitude about trying new foods; to identify a wide variety of foods and their important relationship to health; to participate in cooking activities which enhance physical and social development; reinforce curricular content area; follow sanitation and safety principles; and to make eating an enjoyable experience.

Availability: Staff at schools with NET, WIC, CSFP, FDPIR, CACFP, UMD or Child Nutrition Program food programs in the United States. Those not having such an affiliation should contact their library to place an interlibrary loan request.

Suggested Grade: preK-6
Order Number: NAL Video 460
Production Date: 1991
Format: Set of 2 VHS videotapes
Special Notes: This Georgia State production includes a teacher's guide and a guidebook.

Terms: Borrower pays return postage. RETURN the day after scheduled use. Book at least 4 weeks in advance. Requests must include your name, phone, mail address, eligibility program, title, NAL number, show date, and a statement, "I have read the warning on copyright restrictions and accept full responsibility for compliance." One title per request.

> Source: National Agricultural Library
> Document Delivery Services Branch
> 4th Floor, Photo Lab
> 10301 Baltimore Avenue
> Beltsville, MD 20705-2351
> Phone: 1-301-504-5994
> Fax: 1-301-504-5675
> World Wide Web URL: http://www.nal.usda.gov/fnic
> Email Address: lending@nal.usda.gov

## Cut the Fat in Your Diet: Following the Food Guide Pyramid

Explains the effects of dietary fats upon the body and gives practical tips on healthy eating and food preparation. Designed for school food preparation staff and students.

Availability: Staff at schools with NET, WIC, CSFP, FDPIR, CACFP, UMD or Child Nutrition Program food programs in the United States. Those not having such an affiliation should contact their library to place an interlibrary loan request.

Suggested Grade: 10-Adult
Order Number: NAL Video 2081
Production Date: 1994
Format: VHS videotape

Terms: Borrower pays return postage. RETURN the day after scheduled use. Book at least 4 weeks in advance. Requests must include your name, phone, mail address, eligibility program, title, NAL number, show date, and a statement, "I have read the warning on copyright restrictions and accept full responsibility for compliance." One title per request.

> Source: National Agricultural Library
> Document Delivery Services Branch
> 4th Floor, Photo Lab
> 10301 Baltimore Avenue
> Beltsville, MD 20705-2351
> Phone: 1-301-504-5994
> Fax: 1-301-504-5675
> World Wide Web URL: http://www.nal.usda.gov/fnic
> Email Address: lending@nal.usda.gov

## Daily Food Choices for Healthy Living

Explains and brings alive the very latest information on Dietary Guidelines. Designed for multi-grade interest levels, the program includes information and activities for the five food groups.

Availability: Staff at schools with NET, WIC, CSFP, FDPIR, CACFP, UMD or Child Nutrition Program food programs in the United States. Those not having such an affiliation should contact their library to place an interlibrary loan request.

Suggested Grade: 7-12
Order Number: NAL Video 1671
Production Date: 1992
Format: VHS videotape

Terms: Borrower pays return postage. RETURN the day after scheduled use. Book at least 4 weeks in advance. Requests must include your name, phone, mail address, eligibility program, title, NAL number, show date, and a statement, "I have read the warning on copyright restrictions and accept full responsibility for compliance." One title per request.

> Source: National Agricultural Library
> Document Delivery Services Branch
> 4th Floor, Photo Lab
> 10301 Baltimore Avenue
> Beltsville, MD 20705-2351
> Phone: 1-301-504-5994
> Fax: 1-301-504-5675
> World Wide Web URL: http://www.nal.usda.gov/fnic
> Email Address: lending@nal.usda.gov

## Diabetes Recipes

Five tasty and easy-to-follow recipes for people with diabetes.

Availability: All requesters
Suggested Grade: 4-Adult
Languages: English; Spanish
Order Number: not applicable
Production Date: 2005
Format: Online Article; 5 pages
Special Notes: Use the on-site search engine to easily find this title. You may request a printed copy mailed to you for a fee.

**Source: Federal Citizen Information Center**
**World Wide Web URL: http://www.pueblo.gsa.gov/**

## Diet and Behavior

Includes talks on the following subjects: nutrition and cognitive development and performance; food additives; the effects of nutritive sweeteners on the behavior of children; and non-nutritive sweeteners, including aspartame, cyclamates, and saccharin.

Availability: Librarians in the United States.
Suggested Grade: preK-6
Order Number: DNAL Audiocassette 255
Production Date: 1991
Format: Audiotape
Terms: Borrower pays return postage. RETURN the day after scheduled use. Book at least 4 weeks in advance. Requests must include your name, phone, mail address, eligibility program, title, NAL number, show date, and a statement, "I have read the warning on copyright restrictions and accept full responsibility for compliance." One title per request.

**Source: National Agricultural Library**
**Document Delivery Services Branch**
**4th Floor, Photo Lab**
**10301 Baltimore Avenue**
**Beltsville, MD 20705-2351**
**Phone: 1-301-504-5994**
**Fax: 1-301-504-5675**
**World Wide Web URL: http://www.nal.usda.gov/fnic**
**Email Address: lending@nal.usda.gov**

## Dietary Guidelines for Americans

Discusses how to choose a diet that will taste good, be nutritious, and reduce chronic disease risks.

Availability: All requesters
Suggested Grade: 4-Adult
Order Number: not applicable
Production Date: 2000
Format: Online Article; 44 pages
Special Notes: Use the on-site search engine to easily find this title. You may request a printed copy mailed to you for a fee.

**Source: Federal Citizen Information Center**
**World Wide Web URL: http://www.pueblo.gsa.gov/**

## Dietary Guidelines

Discusses dietary guidelines to follow for overall good health.

Availability: Staff at schools with NET, WIC, CSFP, FDPIR, CACFP, UMD or Child Nutrition Program food programs in the United States. Those not having such an affiliation should contact their library to place an interlibrary loan request.
Suggested Grade: 6-12
Order Number: NAL Video 2407
Format: VHS videotape
Terms: Borrower pays return postage. RETURN the day after scheduled use. Book at least 4 weeks in advance. Requests must include your name, phone, mail address, eligibility program, title, NAL number, show date, and a statement, "I have read the warning on copyright restrictions and accept full responsibility for compliance." One title per request.

**Source: National Agricultural Library**
**Document Delivery Services Branch**
**4th Floor, Photo Lab**
**10301 Baltimore Avenue**
**Beltsville, MD 20705-2351**
**Phone: 1-301-504-5994**
**Fax: 1-301-504-5675**
**World Wide Web URL: http://www.nal.usda.gov/fnic**
**Email Address: lending@nal.usda.gov**

## Dietary Guidelines for Americans

Tells what the nutrition requirements are for the average adult and child. It shows what foods to eat to meet the requirements and what to avoid. The requirements are based on the USDA nutrition requirements guidelines.

Availability: Staff at schools with NET, WIC, CSFP, FDPIR, CACFP, UMD or Child Nutrition Program food programs in the United States. Those not having such an affiliation should contact their library to place an interlibrary loan request.
Suggested Grade: 4-12
Order Number: NAL Video 735
Production Date: 1987
Format: VHS videotape
Terms: Borrower pays return postage. RETURN the day after scheduled use. Book at least 4 weeks in advance. Requests must include your name, phone, mail address, eligibility program, title, NAL number, show date, and a statement, "I have read the warning on copyright restrictions and accept full responsibility for compliance." One title per request.

**Source: National Agricultural Library**
**Document Delivery Services Branch**
**4th Floor, Photo Lab, 10301 Baltimore Avenue**
**Beltsville, MD 20705-2351**
**Phone: 1-301-504-5994**
**Fax: 1-301-504-5675**
**World Wide Web URL: http://www.nal.usda.gov/fnic**
**Email Address: lending@nal.usda.gov**

## Dietary Management of Fats and Cholesterol

Describes how one can lower their fat intake and blood cholesterol content and reduce the risk of heart disease. This may be done by eating plenty of fruits and vegetables, buying foods low in fat and cholesterol, and seasoning foods with onions and garlic.

Availability: Staff at schools with NET, WIC, CSFP, FDPIR, CACFP, UMD or Child Nutrition Program food programs in the United States. Those not having such an affiliation should contact their library to place an interlibrary loan request.

Suggested Grade: 6-12

Languages: English; Spanish

Order Number: English--NAL Video 388; Spanish--NAL Video 776

Production Date: 1987

Format: VHS videotape

Terms: Borrower pays return postage. RETURN the day after scheduled use. Book at least 4 weeks in advance. Requests must include your name, phone, mail address, eligibility program, title, NAL number, show date, and a statement, "I have read the warning on copyright restrictions and accept full responsibility for compliance." One title per request.

**Source: National Agricultural Library**
**Document Delivery Services Branch**
**4th Floor, Photo Lab, 10301 Baltimore Avenue**
**Beltsville, MD  20705-2351**
**Phone: 1-301-504-5994**
**Fax: 1-301-504-5675**
**World Wide Web URL: http://www.nal.usda.gov/fnic**
**Email Address: lending@nal.usda.gov**

## Digestion:  Food to Energy

Traces how food is digested into nutrients that are absorbed by the human body to keep it healthy.  Also, it discusses the key digestive organs and their functions, and presents some advice on proper nutrition and disease prevention.

Availability: Staff at schools with NET, WIC, CSFP, FDPIR, CACFP, UMD or Child Nutrition Program food programs in the United States. Those not having such an affiliation should contact their library to place an interlibrary loan request.

Suggested Grade: preK-6

Order Number: NAL Video 1020

Format: VHS videotape

Terms: Borrower pays return postage. RETURN the day after scheduled use. Book at least 4 weeks in advance. Requests must include your name, phone, mail address, eligibility program, title, NAL number, show date, and a statement, "I have read the warning on copyright restrictions and accept full responsibility for compliance." One title per request.

**Source: National Agricultural Library**
**Document Delivery Services Branch**
**4th Floor, Photo Lab, 10301 Baltimore Avenue**
**Beltsville, MD  20705-2351**

**Phone: 1-301-504-5994**
**Fax: 1-301-504-5675**
**World Wide Web URL: http://www.nal.usda.gov/fnic**
**Email Address: lending@nal.usda.gov**

## Dirty Little Secrets

Conveys basic home food safety lessons.

Availability: Staff at schools with NET, WIC, CSFP, FDPIR, CACFP, UMD or Child Nutrition Program food programs in the United States. Those not having such an affiliation should contact their library to place an interlibrary loan request.

Suggested Grade: 6-Adult

Order Number: NAL Video 2513

Production Date: 1996

Format: VHS videotape

Terms: Borrower pays return postage. RETURN the day after scheduled use. Book at least 4 weeks in advance. Requests must include your name, phone, mail address, eligibility program, title, NAL number, show date, and a statement, "I have read the warning on copyright restrictions and accept full responsibility for compliance." One title per request.

**Source: National Agricultural Library**
**Document Delivery Services Branch**
**4th Floor, Photo Lab**
**10301 Baltimore Avenue**
**Beltsville, MD  20705-2351**
**Phone: 1-301-504-5994**
**Fax: 1-301-504-5675**
**World Wide Web URL: http://www.nal.usda.gov/fnic**
**Email Address: lending@nal.usda.gov**

## Dudley and Dee Dee in Nutrition Land

Cartoon Characters Dudley, Dee Dee, and friend get to nutrition land and discover how eating foods from five food groups will keep your teeth healthy and your body strong.

Availability: Staff at schools with NET, WIC, CSFP, FDPIR, CACFP, UMD or Child Nutrition Program food programs in the United States. Those not having such an affiliation should contact their library to place an interlibrary loan request.

Suggested Grade: preK-6

Order Number: NAL Video 2288

Format: VHS videotape

Special Notes: This is a Startoons and American Dental Association production.

Terms: Borrower pays return postage. RETURN the day after scheduled use. Book at least 4 weeks in advance. Requests must include your name, phone, mail address, eligibility program, title, NAL number, show date, and a statement, "I have read the warning on copyright restrictions and accept full responsibility for compliance." One title per request.

**Source: National Agricultural Library**
**Document Delivery Services Branch**
**4th Floor, Photo Lab, 10301 Baltimore Avenue**
**Beltsville, MD  20705-2351**

*All materials listed in this 2018-2019 edition are BRAND NEW!*

Phone: 1-301-504-5994
Fax: 1-301-504-5675
World Wide Web URL: http://www.nal.usda.gov/fnic
Email Address: lending@nal.usda.gov

## Eat and Be Healthy
Uses the Food Guide Pyramid to explain the concepts of healthy eating and offers practical advice for making them a permanent part of any lifestyle.

| | |
|---|---|
| Availability: | Staff at schools with NET, WIC, CSFP, FDPIR, CACFP, UMD or Child Nutrition Program food programs in the United States. Those not having such an affiliation should contact their library to place an interlibrary loan request. |
| Suggested Grade: | 4-12 |
| Order Number: | NAL Video 2000 |
| Production Date: | 1994 |
| Format: | VHS videotape |
| Terms: | Borrower pays return postage. RETURN the day after scheduled use. Book at least 4 weeks in advance. Requests must include your name, phone, mail address, eligibility program, title, NAL number, show date, and a statement, "I have read the warning on copyright restrictions and accept full responsibility for compliance." One title per request. |

Source: National Agricultural Library
Document Delivery Services Branch
4th Floor, Photo Lab, 10301 Baltimore Avenue
Beltsville, MD 20705-2351
Phone: 1-301-504-5994
Fax: 1-301-504-5675
World Wide Web URL: http://www.nal.usda.gov/fnic
Email Address: lending@nal.usda.gov

## Eater's Digest: A Guide to Nutrition for Teenagers
A compilation of a comprehensive nutrition education curriculum covering 13 subject areas: digestion, energy providers, vitamins and minerals, comparative shopping, food preparation, nutrition during pregnancy, infant/child nutrition, adolescent nutrition, weight management and eating disorders, fat diets, nutrition and athletics, coronary heart disease, and dietary guidelines.

| | |
|---|---|
| Availability: | Staff at schools with NET, WIC, CSFP, FDPIR, CACFP, UMD or Child Nutrition Program food programs in the United States. Those not having such an affiliation should contact their library to place an interlibrary loan request. |
| Suggested Grade: | 6-12 |
| Order Number: | NAL Video 883 |
| Format: | VHS videotape |
| Terms: | Borrower pays return postage. RETURN the day after scheduled use. Book at least 4 weeks in advance. Requests must include your name, phone, mail address, eligibility program, title, NAL number, show date, and a statement, "I have read the warning on copyright restrictions and accept full responsibility for compliance." One title per request. |

Source: National Agricultural Library
Document Delivery Services Branch
4th Floor, Photo Lab, 10301 Baltimore Avenue
Beltsville, MD 20705-2351
Phone: 1-301-504-5994
Fax: 1-301-504-5675
World Wide Web URL: http://www.nal.usda.gov/fnic
Email Address: lending@nal.usda.gov

## Eating for Life
Covers healthy lifestyle changes that will improve health and help prevent heart disease, steps for changing eating habits, the value of vitamin and mineral supplements, and how to eat healthy in restaurants.

| | |
|---|---|
| Availability: | Schools, libraries, and homeschoolers in the United States who serve the hearing impaired. |
| Suggested Grade: | 9-Adult |
| Order Number: | 12907 |
| Production Date: | 2000 |
| Format: | DVD |
| Special Notes: | Also available as live streaming video over the Internet. |
| Terms: | Sponsor pays all transportation costs. Return one week after receipt. Participation is limited to deaf or hard of hearing Americans, their parents, families, teachers, counselors, or others whose use would benefit a deaf or hard of hearing person. Only one person in the audience needs to be hearing impaired. You must register--which is free. These videos are all open-captioned--no special equipment is required for viewing. |

Source: Described and Captioned Media Program
National Association of the Deaf
4211 Church Street Ext.
Roebuck, SC 29376
Phone: 1-800-237-6213
Fax: 1-800-538-5636
World Wide Web URL: http://www.dcmp.org

## Eating for Life: The Nutrition Pyramid
Learn how to construct a diet based on the Food Guide Pyramid.

| | |
|---|---|
| Availability: | Staff at schools with NET, WIC, CSFP, FDPIR, CACFP, UMD or Child Nutrition Program food programs in the United States. Those not having such an affiliation should contact their library to place an interlibrary loan request. |
| Suggested Grade: | 4-12 |
| Order Number: | NAL Video 2126 |
| Production Date: | 1994 |
| Format: | VHS videotape |
| Special Notes: | Includes a teacher's guide. |
| Terms: | Borrower pays return postage. RETURN the day after scheduled use. Book at least 4 weeks in advance. Requests must include your name, phone, mail address, eligibility program, title, NAL number, show date, and a statement, "I have read the warning on copyright restrictions and accept full responsibility for compliance." One title per request. |

# HEALTH--FOOD AND NUTRITION

Source: National Agricultural Library
Document Delivery Services Branch
4th Floor, Photo Lab
10301 Baltimore Avenue
Beltsville, MD 20705-2351
Phone: 1-301-504-5994
Fax: 1-301-504-5675
World Wide Web URL: http://www.nal.usda.gov/fnic
Email Address: lending@nal.usda.gov

## Eating Healthy for Heart Health

This program provides the latest nutritional information aimed at controlling dietary fat intake and reducing cholesterol.

Availability: Staff at schools with NET, WIC, CSFP, FDPIR, CACFP, UMD or Child Nutrition Program food programs in the United States. Those not having such an affiliation should contact their library to place an interlibrary loan request.
Suggested Grade: 6-12
Order Number: NAL Video 1035
Production Date: 1990
Format: VHS videotape
Terms: Borrower pays return postage. RETURN the day after scheduled use. Book at least 4 weeks in advance. Requests must include your name, phone, mail address, eligibility program, title, NAL number, show date, and a statement, "I have read the warning on copyright restrictions and accept full responsibility for compliance." One title per request.

Source: National Agricultural Library
Document Delivery Services Branch
4th Floor, Photo Lab
10301 Baltimore Avenue
Beltsville, MD 20705-2351
Phone: 1-301-504-5994
Fax: 1-301-504-5675
World Wide Web URL: http://www.nal.usda.gov/fnic
Email Address: lending@nal.usda.gov

## Eating Healthy for Life

This program explores various options for improving eating habits by examining ways to incorporate healthy food choices throughout the day.

Availability: Staff at schools with NET, WIC, CSFP, FDPIR, CACFP, UMD or Child Nutrition Program food programs in the United States. Those not having such an affiliation should contact their library to place an interlibrary loan request.
Suggested Grade: 6-12
Order Number: NAL Video 1033
Production Date: 1990
Format: VHS videotape
Terms: Borrower pays return postage. RETURN the day after scheduled use. Book at least 4 weeks in advance. Requests must include your name, phone, mail address, eligibility program, title, NAL number, show date, and

a statement, "I have read the warning on copyright restrictions and accept full responsibility for compliance." One title per request.

Source: National Agricultural Library
Document Delivery Services Branch
4th Floor, Photo Lab
10301 Baltimore Avenue
Beltsville, MD 20705-2351
Phone: 1-301-504-5994
Fax: 1-301-504-5675
World Wide Web URL: http://www.nal.usda.gov/fnic
Email Address: lending@nal.usda.gov

## Eating on the Run

Discusses the importance of good nutrition and contains suggestions on how to meet the body's nutritional requirements when time is short.

Availability: Librarians in the United States.
Suggested Grade: All ages
Order Number: NAL Slide 510
Production Date: 1994
Format: Set of 55 slides
Special Notes: Accompanied by a script.
Terms: Borrower pays return postage. RETURN the day after scheduled use. Book at least 4 weeks in advance. Requests must include your name, phone, mail address, eligibility program, title, NAL number, show date, and a statement, "I have read the warning on copyright restrictions and accept full responsibility for compliance." One title per request.

Source: National Agricultural Library
Document Delivery Services Branch
4th Floor, Photo Lab
10301 Baltimore Avenue
Beltsville, MD 20705-2351
Phone: 1-301-504-5994
Fax: 1-301-504-5675
World Wide Web URL: http://www.nal.usda.gov/fnic
Email Address: lending@nal.usda.gov

## Eating the Pyramid Way with Marv & Mary, 3rd Edition

Using humor and special effects, a narrator looks in on a group of children having a picnic at the park. He explains how the Food Group Pyramid can be used to help maintain a healthy diet. By eating more of those foods at the bottom of the Pyramid and fewer of those as you go up the Pyramid, the narrator shows a variety of foods to eat to grow strong and healthy.

Availability: Staff at schools with NET, WIC, CSFP, FDPIR, CACFP, UMD or Child Nutrition Program food programs in the United States. Those not having such an affiliation should contact their library to place an interlibrary loan request.
Suggested Grade: preK-6
Order Number: NAL Video 2054
Production Date: 1994
Format: VHS videotape

*All materials listed in this 2018-2019 edition are **BRAND NEW!***

Terms: Borrower pays return postage. RETURN the day after scheduled use. Book at least 4 weeks in advance. Requests must include your name, phone, mail address, eligibility program, title, NAL number, show date, and a statement, "I have read the warning on copyright restrictions and accept full responsibility for compliance." One title per request.
**Source: National Agricultural Library**
**Document Delivery Services Branch**
**4th Floor, Photo Lab**
**10301 Baltimore Avenue**
**Beltsville, MD 20705-2351**
**Phone: 1-301-504-5994**
**Fax: 1-301-504-5675**
**World Wide Web URL: http://www.nal.usda.gov/fnic**
**Email Address: lending@nal.usda.gov**

## Eating to the Beat

Contains seven children's songs presenting the importance of nutrition, table manners, and exercise.

Availability: Librarians in the United States.
Suggested Grade: preK-6
Order Number: 395
Production Date: 1995
Format: Audiotape
Special Notes: Includes a teacher's guide.
Terms: Borrower pays return postage. RETURN the day after scheduled use. Book at least 4 weeks in advance. Requests must include your name, phone, mail address, eligibility program, title, NAL number, show date, and a statement, "I have read the warning on copyright restrictions and accept full responsibility for compliance." One title per request.
**Source: National Agricultural Library**
**Document Delivery Services Branch**
**4th Floor, Photo Lab**
**10301 Baltimore Avenue**
**Beltsville, MD 20705-2351**
**Phone: 1-301-504-5994**
**Fax: 1-301-504-5675**
**World Wide Web URL: http://www.nal.usda.gov/fnic**
**Email Address: lending@nal.usda.gov**

## Eating Well, Increasing Fiber

This cooking program demonstrates how to prepare stir-fry and a high-fiber dessert. The cooks discuss the five fiber groups, their roles in a well-balanced diet, how much fiber is too much and examples of the categories of foods containing fiber.

Availability: Staff at schools with NET, WIC, CSFP, FDPIR, CACFP, UMD or Child Nutrition Program food programs in the United States. Those not having such an affiliation should contact their library to place an interlibrary loan request.
Suggested Grade: 6-12
Order Number: NAL Video 765
Production Date: 1989
Format: VHS videotape

Terms: Borrower pays return postage. RETURN the day after scheduled use. Book at least 4 weeks in advance. Requests must include your name, phone, mail address, eligibility program, title, NAL number, show date, and a statement, "I have read the warning on copyright restrictions and accept full responsibility for compliance." One title per request.
**Source: National Agricultural Library**
**Document Delivery Services Branch**
**4th Floor, Photo Lab**
**10301 Baltimore Avenue**
**Beltsville, MD 20705-2351**
**Phone: 1-301-504-5994**
**Fax: 1-301-504-5675**
**World Wide Web URL: http://www.nal.usda.gov/fnic**
**Email Address: lending@nal.usda.gov**

## Every Day, Lots of Ways: An Interdisciplinary Nutrition Curriculum for Kindergarten-Sixth Grade

This program uses core subjects to promote fresh, frozen and canned vegetables and fruits, vegetable and fruit juices, and dried fruits. It is part of a campaign to reduce the risk of cancer and other chronic diseases such as heart disease.

Availability: Staff at schools with NET, WIC, CSFP, FDPIR, CACFP, UMD or Child Nutrition Program food programs in the United States. Those not having such an affiliation should contact their library to place an interlibrary loan request.
Suggested Grade: preK-6
Order Number: NAL Kit 245
Production Date: 1993
Format: Set of 2 VHS videotapes
Special Notes: Includes teaching materials.
Terms: Borrower pays return postage. RETURN the day after scheduled use. Book at least 4 weeks in advance. Requests must include your name, phone, mail address, eligibility program, title, NAL number, show date, and a statement, "I have read the warning on copyright restrictions and accept full responsibility for compliance." One title per request.
**Source: National Agricultural Library**
**Document Delivery Services Branch**
**4th Floor, Photo Lab**
**10301 Baltimore Avenue**
**Beltsville, MD 20705-2351**
**Phone: 1-301-504-5994**
**Fax: 1-301-504-5675**
**World Wide Web URL: http://www.nal.usda.gov/fnic**
**Email Address: lending@nal.usda.gov**

## Experience: The Dietary Guidelines

This program consists primarily of interviews with food service staff, principals, students, and educators explaining successful ways to implement the Dietary Guidelines for Americans in schools. Designed for school food preparation staff and students.

Availability: Staff at schools with NET, WIC, CSFP, FDPIR, CACFP, UMD or Child Nutrition Program food programs in the United States. Those not having such an affiliation should contact their library to place an interlibrary loan request.

Suggested Grade: Teacher Reference
Order Number: NAL Video 2242
Production Date: 1995
Format: VHS videotape
Terms: Borrower pays return postage. RETURN the day after scheduled use. Book at least 4 weeks in advance. Requests must include your name, phone, mail address, eligibility program, title, NAL number, show date, and a statement, "I have read the warning on copyright restrictions and accept full responsibility for compliance." One title per request.

Source: National Agricultural Library
Document Delivery Services Branch
4th Floor, Photo Lab
10301 Baltimore Avenue
Beltsville, MD 20705-2351
Phone: 1-301-504-5994
Fax: 1-301-504-5675
World Wide Web URL: http://www.nal.usda.gov/fnic
Email Address: lending@nal.usda.gov

## Fabulous Fruits...Versatile Vegetables

Get tips on new ways to serve fruits and vegetables--you need 5 to 9 daily servings in your diet.

Availability: All requesters
Suggested Grade: 6-Adult
Order Number: not applicable
Production Date: 2003
Format: Online Article; 6 pages
Special Notes: Use the on-site search engine to easily find this title. You may request a printed copy mailed to you for a fee.

Source: Federal Citizen Information Center
World Wide Web URL: http://www.pueblo.gsa.gov/

## Facts About Fats, The

Explains good fat versus bad fat in your diet and how knowing these can lower your risk for cancer.

Availability: Limit of 1 copy to schools, libraries, and homeschoolers in the United States and Canada.
Suggested Grade: 10-Adult
Order Number: order by title
Format: Brochure

Source: American Institute for Cancer Research
Publication Orders
1759 R Street, N. W.
Washington, DC 20009
Phone: 1-800-843-8114
Fax: 1-202-328-7226
World Wide Web URL: http://www.aicr.org
Email Address: aicrweb@aicr.org

## Facts About Fiber, The

Explains why fiber is beneficial to your health and explains how to increase the amount of fiber in your diet.

Availability: Limit of 1 copy to schools, libraries, and homeschoolers in the United States and Canada.
Suggested Grade: 10-Adult
Order Number: order by title
Production Date: 2005
Format: Brochure
Special Notes: May also be downloaded from the web site.

Source: American Institute for Cancer Research
Publication Orders
1759 R Street, N. W.
Washington, DC 20009
Phone: 1-800-843-8114
Fax: 1-202-328-7226
World Wide Web URL: http://www.aicr.org
Email Address: aicrweb@aicr.org

## Fad Versus Fit: Your Lifetime Fight Against Fat

This program pits the long and short-term damaging effects of fad diets against the benefits of a healthy diet with exercise.

Availability: Staff at schools with NET, WIC, CSFP, FDPIR, CACFP, UMD or Child Nutrition Program food programs in the United States. Those not having such an affiliation should contact their library to place an interlibrary loan request.

Suggested Grade: 7-12
Order Number: NAL Video 2150
Production Date: 1992
Format: VHS videotape
Terms: Borrower pays return postage. RETURN the day after scheduled use. Book at least 4 weeks in advance. Requests must include your name, phone, mail address, eligibility program, title, NAL number, show date, and a statement, "I have read the warning on copyright restrictions and accept full responsibility for compliance." One title per request.

Source: National Agricultural Library
Document Delivery Services Branch
4th Floor, Photo Lab
10301 Baltimore Avenue
Beltsville, MD 20705-2351
Phone: 1-301-504-5994
Fax: 1-301-504-5675
World Wide Web URL: http://www.nal.usda.gov/fnic
Email Address: lending@nal.usda.gov

## Fast and Easy Teen Meals--Pasta

This program discusses what pasta is, different types that are available, what nutrients it provides, how it fits into the Food Guide Pyramid, how to cook it, toppings to put on it, etc.

Availability: Staff at schools with NET, WIC, CSFP, FDPIR, CACFP, UMD or Child Nutrition Program food programs in the United States.

Those not having such an affiliation should contact their library to place an interlibrary loan request.

Suggested Grade: 7-12
Order Number: NAL Video 2072
Production Date: 1994
Format: VHS videotape
Terms: Borrower pays return postage. RETURN the day after scheduled use. Book at least 4 weeks in advance. Requests must include your name, phone, mail address, eligibility program, title, NAL number, show date, and a statement, "I have read the warning on copyright restrictions and accept full responsibility for compliance." One title per request.

**Source: National Agricultural Library**
**Document Delivery Services Branch**
**4th Floor, Photo Lab**
**10301 Baltimore Avenue**
**Beltsville, MD 20705-2351**
**Phone: 1-301-504-5994**
**Fax: 1-301-504-5675**
**World Wide Web URL: http://www.nal.usda.gov/fnic**
**Email Address: lending@nal.usda.gov**

## Fast Food

This program teaches one how to maintain a balanced diet when selecting fast foods. The difference between junk and fast foods is discussed. Various types of fast foods are examined from a nutritional viewpoint and recommendations are made to assist one in selecting a balanced meal.

Availability: Staff at schools with NET, WIC, CSFP, FDPIR, CACFP, UMD or Child Nutrition Program food programs in the United States. Those not having such an affiliation should contact their library to place an interlibrary loan request.

Suggested Grade: 7-12
Order Number: NAL Video 378
Production Date: 1988
Format: VHS videotape
Special Notes: A teaching guide with script; a fast food quiz and answer sheet; review sheet; food calorie, fat, and sodium guide; background reading on hamburger vs. chicken; and an article on "Fast Food" are included.
Terms: Borrower pays return postage. RETURN the day after scheduled use. Book at least 4 weeks in advance. Requests must include your name, phone, mail address, eligibility program, title, NAL number, show date, and a statement, "I have read the warning on copyright restrictions and accept full responsibility for compliance." One title per request.

**Source: National Agricultural Library**
**Document Delivery Services Branch**
**4th Floor, Photo Lab**
**10301 Baltimore Avenue**
**Beltsville, MD 20705-2351**
**Phone: 1-301-504-5994**
**Fax: 1-301-504-5675**

World Wide Web URL: http://www.nal.usda.gov/fnic
Email Address: lending@nal.usda.gov

## Fat Stuff

Various types of sources of dietary fat and practical guidelines for moderating fat intake are reviewed in this video, that is part of the Bodywatch series hosted by Dr. James Duke and American Health Magazine. Normal fat and cholesterol metabolism, and the process of atherosclerosis are described. Characteristics and food sources of different types of fats (polyunsaturated, monounsaturated, saturated) are identified, such as "hidden fats" found in many snack foods, cereals, dairy products, and fast foods.

Availability: Staff at schools with NET, WIC, CSFP, FDPIR, CACFP, UMD or Child Nutrition Program food programs in the United States. Those not having such an affiliation should contact their library to place an interlibrary loan request.

Suggested Grade: 9-12
Order Number: NAL Video 231
Production Date: 1987
Format: VHS videotape
Terms: Borrower pays return postage. RETURN the day after scheduled use. Book at least 4 weeks in advance. Requests must include your name, phone, mail address, eligibility program, title, NAL number, show date, and a statement, "I have read the warning on copyright restrictions and accept full responsibility for compliance." One title per request.

**Source: National Agricultural Library**
**Document Delivery Services Branch**
**4th Floor, Photo Lab**
**10301 Baltimore Avenue**
**Beltsville, MD 20705-2351**
**Phone: 1-301-504-5994**
**Fax: 1-301-504-5675**
**World Wide Web URL: http://www.nal.usda.gov/fnic**
**Email Address: lending@nal.usda.gov**

## Feeding for the Future: Exceptional Nutrition in the I.E.P.

This video was created to help care givers of exceptional children build self feeding skills and improve the nutritional health of these children. Designed for school food preparation staff and students.

Availability: Staff at schools with NET, WIC, CSFP, FDPIR, CACFP, UMD or Child Nutrition Program food programs in the United States. Those not having such an affiliation should contact their library to place an interlibrary loan request.

Suggested Grade: 10-Adult
Order Number: NAL Video 2286
Production Date: 1993
Format: VHS videotape

Terms: Borrower pays return postage. RETURN the day after scheduled use. Book at least 4 weeks in advance. Requests must include your name, phone, mail address, eligibility program, title, NAL number, show date, and a statement, "I have read the warning on copyright restrictions and accept full responsibility for compliance." One title per request.

**Source: National Agricultural Library**
**Document Delivery Services Branch**
**4th Floor, Photo Lab**
**10301 Baltimore Avenue**
**Beltsville, MD 20705-2351**
**Phone: 1-301-504-5994**
**Fax: 1-301-504-5675**
**World Wide Web URL: http://www.nal.usda.gov/fnic**
**Email Address: lending@nal.usda.gov**

## Feeding Young Children

Discusses the USDA foodguide pyramid for young children.

Availability: Staff at schools with NET, WIC, CSFP, FDPIR, CACFP, UMD or Child Nutrition Program food programs in the United States. Those not having such an affiliation should contact their library to place an interlibrary loan request.
Suggested Grade: Adult
Order Number: NAL DVD 11
Production Date: 2003
Format: DVD
Terms: Borrower pays return postage. RETURN the day after scheduled use. Book at least 4 weeks in advance. Requests must include your name, phone, mail address, eligibility program, title, NAL number, show date, and a statement, "I have read the warning on copyright restrictions and accept full responsibility for compliance." One title per request.

**Source: National Agricultural Library**
**Document Delivery Services Branch**
**4th Floor, Photo Lab**
**10301 Baltimore Avenue**
**Beltsville, MD 20705-2351**
**Phone: 1-301-504-5994**
**Fax: 1-301-504-5675**
**World Wide Web URL: http://www.nal.usda.gov/fnic**
**Email Address: lending@nal.usda.gov**

## Fight BAC!: Four Simple Steps to Food Safety

Gives advice on how to handle food safely to avoid bacteria.

Availability: All requesters
Suggested Grade: 4-Adult
Order Number: not applicable
Production Date: 1998
Format: Online Article; 5 pages
Special Notes: Use the on-site search engine to easily find this title. You may request a printed copy mailed to you for a fee.

**Source: Federal Citizen Information Center**
**World Wide Web URL: http://www.pueblo.gsa.gov/**

## Food Allergy

Summarizes what is currently known about food allergy.

Availability: Limit of one copy to non-profit schools, libraries, and homeschoolers world-wide.
Suggested Grade: 7-Adult
Languages: English; Spanish
Order Number: order by title
Format: Brochure
Special Notes: Requests must be made via web site or email ONLY.

**Source: American Academy of Allergy, Asthma & Immunology**
**Attn: Membership Assistant**
**555 East Wells Street, Suite 1100**
**Milwaukee, WI 53202**
**World Wide Web URL: http://www.aaaai.org**
**Email Address: info@aaaai.org**

## Food for Thought

Suggests ways for parents of young children to cope with the dinner hour in a peaceful way. It presents helpful suggestions that encourage appropriate behavior, such as how to deal with picky eaters and how to keep one hungry child from disrupting the entire family meal.

Availability: Staff at schools with NET, WIC, CSFP, FDPIR, CACFP, UMD or Child Nutrition Program food programs in the United States. Those not having such an affiliation should contact their library to place an interlibrary loan request.
Suggested Grade: Adult
Order Number: NAL Video 2146
Format: VHS videotape
Terms: Borrower pays return postage. RETURN the day after scheduled use. Book at least 4 weeks in advance. Requests must include your name, phone, mail address, eligibility program, title, NAL number, show date, and a statement, "I have read the warning on copyright restrictions and accept full responsibility for compliance." One title per request.

**Source: National Agricultural Library**
**Document Delivery Services Branch**
**4th Floor, Photo Lab, 10301 Baltimore Avenue**
**Beltsville, MD 20705-2351**
**Phone: 1-301-504-5994**
**Fax: 1-301-504-5675**
**World Wide Web URL: http://www.nal.usda.gov/fnic**
**Email Address: lending@nal.usda.gov**

## Food Guide Pyramid, The: Building a Healthy Body

Presents information using the food guide pyramid in preparing meals and in building a leaner, healthier body. Shows fun, healthy food for the whole family.

Availability: Staff at schools with NET, WIC, CSFP, FDPIR, CACFP, UMD or Child Nutrition Program food programs in the United States. Those not having such an affiliation should contact their library to place an interlibrary loan request.

Suggested Grade: 7-Adult
Languages: English; Spanish
Order Number: English Video 2781; Spanish Video 2783
Production Date: 1994
Format: VHS videotape
Terms: Borrower pays return postage. RETURN the day after scheduled use. Book at least 4 weeks in advance. Requests must include your name, phone, mail address, eligibility program, title, NAL number, show date, and a statement, "I have read the warning on copyright restrictions and accept full responsibility for compliance." One title per request.

**Source: National Agricultural Library**
**Document Delivery Services Branch**
**4th Floor, Photo Lab, 10301 Baltimore Avenue**
**Beltsville, MD 20705-2351**
**Phone: 1-301-504-5994**
**Fax: 1-301-504-5675**
**World Wide Web URL: http://www.nal.usda.gov/fnic**
**Email Address: lending@nal.usda.gov**

## Food Guide Pyramid

This easy guide can help you select the nutrients you need (without too many calories) and reduce the fat, cholesterol, sugar, sodium, or alcohol in your diet.

Availability: All requesters
Suggested Grade: 4-Adult
Order Number: not applicable
Production Date: 1996
Format: Online Article; 29 pages
Special Notes: Use the on-site search engine to easily find this title. You may request a printed copy mailed to you for a fee.

**Source: Federal Citizen Information Center**
**World Wide Web URL: http://www.pueblo.gsa.gov/**

## Food Label & You, The

Explains how to read and interpret the nutrition facts panel on food items.

Availability: Staff at schools with NET, WIC, CSFP, FDPIR, CACFP, UMD or Child Nutrition Program food programs in the United States. Those not having such an affiliation should contact their library to place an interlibrary loan request.
Suggested Grade: 7-Adult
Order Number: NAL Video 2232
Format: VHS videotape
Terms: Borrower pays return postage. RETURN the day after scheduled use. Book at least 4 weeks in advance. Requests must include your name, phone, mail address, eligibility program, title, NAL number, show date, and a statement, "I have read the warning on copyright restrictions and accept full responsibility for compliance." One title per request.

**Source: National Agricultural Library**
**Document Delivery Services Branch**
**4th Floor, Photo Lab, 10301 Baltimore Avenue**
**Beltsville, MD 20705-2351**

**Phone: 1-301-504-5994**
**Fax: 1-301-504-5675**
**World Wide Web URL: http://www.nal.usda.gov/fnic**
**Email Address: lending@nal.usda.gov**

## Food Labels

This program is designed to help individuals read labels on food products and to develop healthy eating habits. Designed for school food preparation staff and students.

Availability: Staff at schools with NET, WIC, CSFP, FDPIR, CACFP, UMD or Child Nutrition Program food programs in the United States. Those not having such an affiliation should contact their library to place an interlibrary loan request.
Suggested Grade: 10-Adult
Order Number: NAL Video 2135
Production Date: 1994
Format: VHS videotape
Terms: Borrower pays return postage. RETURN the day after scheduled use. Book at least 4 weeks in advance. Requests must include your name, phone, mail address, eligibility program, title, NAL number, show date, and a statement, "I have read the warning on copyright restrictions and accept full responsibility for compliance." One title per request.

**Source: National Agricultural Library**
**Document Delivery Services Branch**
**4th Floor, Photo Lab**
**10301 Baltimore Avenue**
**Beltsville, MD 20705-2351**
**Phone: 1-301-504-5994**
**Fax: 1-301-504-5675**
**World Wide Web URL: http://www.nal.usda.gov/fnic**
**Email Address: lending@nal.usda.gov**

## Food Pyramid, The: High 5 for a Healthy You!

Teens and celebrities discuss healthy choices.

Availability: Staff at schools with NET, WIC, CSFP, FDPIR, CACFP, UMD or Child Nutrition Program food programs in the United States. Those not having such an affiliation should contact their library to place an interlibrary loan request.
Suggested Grade: 6-12
Order Number: NAL Video 2805
Production Date: 1997
Format: VHS videotape
Terms: Borrower pays return postage. RETURN the day after scheduled use. Book at least 4 weeks in advance. Requests must include your name, phone, mail address, eligibility program, title, NAL number, show date, and a statement, "I have read the warning on copyright restrictions and accept full responsibility for compliance." One title per request.

**Source: National Agricultural Library**
**Document Delivery Services Branch**
**4th Floor, Photo Lab**
**10301 Baltimore Avenue**
**Beltsville, MD 20705-2351**

Phone: 1-301-504-5994
Fax: 1-301-504-5675
World Wide Web URL: http://www.nal.usda.gov/fnic
Email Address: lending@nal.usda.gov

## Food Quality, Food Safety and You!

Information about food quality and food safety.

| | |
|---|---|
| Availability: | Schools, libraries, and nursing homes in the United States. |
| Suggested Grade: | 9-Adult |
| Order Number: | NAL Slide 307 |
| Production Date: | 1989 |
| Format: | Set of 80 slides |
| Special Notes: | Sound is provided on cassette. Includes a teacher's guide. |
| Terms: | Borrower pays return postage. RETURN the day after scheduled use. Book at least 4 weeks in advance. Requests must include your name, phone, mail address, eligibility program, title, NAL number, show date, and a statement, "I have read the warning on copyright restrictions and accept full responsibility for compliance." One title per request. |

Source: National Agricultural Library
Document Delivery Services Branch
4th Floor, Photo Lab
10301 Baltimore Avenue
Beltsville, MD   20705-2351
Phone: 1-301-504-5994
Fax: 1-301-504-5675
World Wide Web URL: http://www.nal.usda.gov/fnic
Email Address: lending@nal.usda.gov

## Food Safety at Home

Explains the four easy ways to keep food from spoiling.

| | |
|---|---|
| Availability: | All requesters |
| Suggested Grade: | 7-Adult |
| Order Number: | not applicable |
| Format: | Online Article; 2 pages |
| Special Notes: | Use the on-site search engine to easily find this title. You may request a printed copy mailed to you for a fee. |

Source: Federal Citizen Information Center
World Wide Web URL: http://www.pueblo.gsa.gov/

## Foods I Eat, the Foods You Eat, The

A multicultural nutrition program designed to encourage young children to explore and appreciate the foods of many cultures while learning such concepts as colors, shapes, and textures.

| | |
|---|---|
| Availability: | Librarians in the United States. |
| Suggested Grade: | preK |
| Order Number: | Kit No. 355 |
| Production Date: | 1996 |
| Format: | Audiotape |
| Special Notes: | Contains 2 wall charts, 1 poster, 3 books, and teacher's guide. |
| Terms: | Borrower pays return postage. RETURN the day after scheduled use. Book at least 4 weeks in advance. Requests must include your name, phone, mail address, |

eligibility program, title, NAL number, show date, and a statement, "I have read the warning on copyright restrictions and accept full responsibility for compliance." One title per request.

Source: National Agricultural Library
Document Delivery Services Branch
4th Floor, Photo Lab
10301 Baltimore Avenue
Beltsville, MD   20705-2351
Phone: 1-301-504-5994
Fax: 1-301-504-5675
World Wide Web URL: http://www.nal.usda.gov/fnic
Email Address: lending@nal.usda.gov

## Food Works:   An Integrated Approach to Teaching Nutrition

Teaches students how to choose a variety of foods; add more grains, vegetables and fruits to the foods they already eat; and construct a diet lower in fat.

| | |
|---|---|
| Availability: | Staff at schools with NET, WIC, CSFP, FDPIR, CACFP, UMD or Child Nutrition Program food programs in the United States. Those not having such an affiliation should contact their library to place an interlibrary loan request. |
| Suggested Grade: | 3-5 |
| Order Number: | NAL Kit 336 |
| Production Date: | 1995 |
| Format: | VHS videotape |
| Special Notes: | Includes a teacher's guide, student magazines, and more. |
| Terms: | Borrower pays return postage. RETURN the day after scheduled use. Book at least 4 weeks in advance. Requests must include your name, phone, mail address, eligibility program, title, NAL number, show date, and a statement, "I have read the warning on copyright restrictions and accept full responsibility for compliance." One title per request. |

Source: National Agricultural Library
Document Delivery Services Branch
4th Floor, Photo Lab
10301 Baltimore Avenue
Beltsville, MD   20705-2351
Phone: 1-301-504-5994
Fax: 1-301-504-5675
World Wide Web URL: http://www.nal.usda.gov/fnic
Email Address: lending@nal.usda.gov

## Fun with Food:   The Food Pyramid

Taught from an ESL perspective, this unit introduces students to the Food Guide Pyramid.

| | |
|---|---|
| Availability: | All requesters |
| Suggested Grade: | 3-4 |
| Order Number: | not applicable |
| Format: | Online Lesson Plan |

Source: Lisa Gassiott
World Wide Web URL: http://eduref.org/Virtual/Lessons/
Interdisciplinary/INT0100.html

*All materials listed in this 2018-2019 edition are* ***BRAND NEW!***

**"Get Fresh!" Nutrition Education Video Series: Apples, Potatoes, Broccoli, Squash**

Includes 5 minutes of each fruit and vegetable and shows how to select them. Also includes preparation of nutrition recipes.

Availability:     Staff at schools with NET, WIC, CSFP, FDPIR, CACFP, UMD or Child Nutrition Program food programs in the United States. Those not having such an affiliation should contact their library to place an interlibrary loan request.

Suggested Grade: 7-Adult
Languages:        English; Spanish
Order Number:     English NAL Video 3044; English/Spanish NAL Video 3045
Production Date:  2001
Format:           VHS videotape
Terms:            Borrower pays return postage. RETURN the day after scheduled use. Book at least 4 weeks in advance. Requests must include your name, phone, mail address, eligibility program, title, NAL number, show date, and a statement, "I have read the warning on copyright restrictions and accept full responsibility for compliance." One title per request.

  **Source: National Agricultural Library**
  **Document Delivery Services Branch**
  **4th Floor, Photo Lab**
  **10301 Baltimore Avenue**
  **Beltsville, MD 20705-2351**
  **Phone: 1-301-504-5994**
  **Fax: 1-301-504-5675**
**World Wide Web URL: http://www.nal.usda.gov/fnic**
  **Email Address: lending@nal.usda.gov**

**"Get Fresh!" Nutrition Education Video Series: Peaches, Kale, Carrots, Cabbage**

Includes 5 minutes of each fruit and vegetable and shows how to select them. Also includes preparation of nutrition recipes.

Availability:     Staff at schools with NET, WIC, CSFP, FDPIR, CACFP, UMD or Child Nutrition Program food programs in the United States. Those not having such an affiliation should contact their library to place an interlibrary loan request.

Suggested Grade: 7-Adult
Languages:        English; Spanish
Order Number:     English NAL Video 3044; English/Spanish NAL Video 3045
Production Date:  2001
Format:           VHS videotape
Terms:            Borrower pays return postage. RETURN the day after scheduled use. Book at least 4 weeks in advance. Requests must include your name, phone, mail address, eligibility program, title, NAL number, show date, and a statement, "I have read the warning on copyright restrictions and accept full responsibility for compliance." One title per request.

  **Source: National Agricultural Library**
  **Document Delivery Services Branch**
  **4th Floor, Photo Lab**
  **10301 Baltimore Avenue**
  **Beltsville, MD 20705-2351**
  **Phone: 1-301-504-5994**
  **Fax: 1-301-504-5675**
**World Wide Web URL: http://www.nal.usda.gov/fnic**
  **Email Address: lending@nal.usda.gov**

**Getting a Head Start with 5 a Day Fun Kit**

Designed to encourage young children and their families to eat more fruits and vegetables.

Availability:     Staff at schools with NET, WIC, CSFP, FDPIR, CACFP, UMD or Child Nutrition Program food programs in the United States. Those not having such an affiliation should contact their library to place an interlibrary loan request.

Suggested Grade: 2-Adult
Order Number:     NAL Kit 350
Production Date:  1995
Format:           VHS videotape
Terms:            Borrower pays return postage. RETURN the day after scheduled use. Book at least 4 weeks in advance. Requests must include your name, phone, mail address, eligibility program, title, NAL number, show date, and a statement, "I have read the warning on copyright restrictions and accept full responsibility for compliance." One title per request.

  **Source: National Agricultural Library**
  **Document Delivery Services Branch**
  **4th Floor, Photo Lab**
  **10301 Baltimore Avenue**
  **Beltsville, MD 20705-2351**
  **Phone: 1-301-504-5994**
  **Fax: 1-301-504-5675**
**World Wide Web URL: http://www.nal.usda.gov/fnic**
  **Email Address: lending@nal.usda.gov**

**Give Me 5! Colors that Jive! Trivia**

A fun way for students to learn more about nutrition.

Availability:     All requesters
Suggested Grade: K-6
Order Number:     not applicable
Format:           Web Site
  **Source: Penny McConnell**
  **World Wide Web URL:**
**http://www.fcps.edu/fs/food/food_facts/giveme5/index.htm**

**Give Yourself Five**

This humorous video highlights daily challenges teenagers face when making food selections.

Availability:     Staff at schools with NET, WIC, CSFP, FDPIR, CACFP, UMD or Child Nutrition Program food programs in the United States. Those not having such an affiliation should contact their library to place an interlibrary loan request.

# HEALTH--FOOD AND NUTRITION

Suggested Grade:   5-12
Order Number:      NAL Video 2211
Production Date:   1994
Format:            VHS videotape
Terms:   Borrower pays return postage.  RETURN the day after scheduled use.  Book at least 4 weeks in advance.  Requests must include your name, phone, mail address, eligibility program, title, NAL number, show date, and a statement, "I have read the warning on copyright restrictions and accept full responsibility for compliance."  One title per request.

**Source:  National Agricultural Library**
**Document Delivery Services Branch**
**4th Floor, Photo Lab**
**10301 Baltimore Avenue**
**Beltsville, MD   20705-2351**
**Phone:  1-301-504-5994**
**Fax:  1-301-504-5675**
**World Wide Web URL:  http://www.nal.usda.gov/fnic**
**Email Address:  lending@nal.usda.gov**

## Gold Peanut, The
Teaches students about the nutritional value of peanuts as well as the processing of them.
Availability:   One copy per student to schools, libraries, and homeschoolers in the United States.
Suggested Grade:   4-6
Order Number:      order by title
Format:            Comic Book
Special Notes:     A teacher's guide is also available for the asking.  May also be downloaded from the web site.

**Source:  Peanut Education Service**
**Marianne Copelan**
**P. O. Box 8**
**Nashville, NC   27856**
**Phone:  1-252-459-9977**
**Fax:  1-252-459-7396**
**World Wide Web URL:  http://www.aboutpeanuts.com**
**Email Address:  info@aboutpeanuts.com**

## Good Food Diner, The
This video teaches children how to choose healthy foods to make them feel better and give them energy.  It stresses the importance of breakfast.
Availability:   Staff at schools with NET, WIC, CSFP, FDPIR, CACFP, UMD or Child Nutrition Program food programs in the United States.  Those not having such an affiliation should contact their library to place an interlibrary loan request.
Suggested Grade:   preK-6
Order Number:      NAL Video 1630
Production Date:   1992
Format:            VHS videotape
Terms:   Borrower pays return postage.  RETURN the day after scheduled use.  Book at least 4 weeks in advance.  Requests must include your name, phone, mail address, eligibility program, title, NAL number, show date, and

a statement, "I have read the warning on copyright restrictions and accept full responsibility for compliance."  One title per request.

**Source:  National Agricultural Library**
**Document Delivery Services Branch**
**4th Floor, Photo Lab**
**10301 Baltimore Avenue**
**Beltsville, MD   20705-2351**
**Phone:  1-301-504-5994**
**Fax:  1-301-504-5675**
**World Wide Web URL:  http://www.nal.usda.gov/fnic**
**Email Address:  lending@nal.usda.gov**

## Goofy Over Health
This program introduces children to the issues of health and nutrition using live action and Disney animation.  The program explores issues such as the importance of exercise, nutrition, and sleep for maintaining good health.
Availability:   Staff at schools with NET, WIC, CSFP, FDPIR, CACFP, UMD or Child Nutrition Program food programs in the United States.  Those not having such an affiliation should contact their library to place an interlibrary loan request.
Suggested Grade:   preK-6
Order Number:      NAL Video 1630
Production Date:   1991
Format:            VHS videotape
Special Notes:     This Disney Educational Productions video includes 2 discussion guides.
Terms:   Borrower pays return postage.  RETURN the day after scheduled use.  Book at least 4 weeks in advance.  Requests must include your name, phone, mail address, eligibility program, title, NAL number, show date, and a statement, "I have read the warning on copyright restrictions and accept full responsibility for compliance."  One title per request.

**Source:  National Agricultural Library**
**Document Delivery Services Branch**
**4th Floor, Photo Lab**
**10301 Baltimore Avenue**
**Beltsville, MD   20705-2351**
**Phone:  1-301-504-5994**
**Fax:  1-301-504-5675**
**World Wide Web URL:  http://www.nal.usda.gov/fnic**
**Email Address:  lending@nal.usda.gov**

## Guide to Healthy Dining Out
Shows you how to make healthy choices in restaurants by understanding how to order, and by having a clearer idea of which foods represent the healthier choices.
Availability:   Limit of 1 copy to schools, libraries, and homeschoolers in the United States and Canada.
Suggested Grade:   5-Adult
Order Number:      order by title
Format:            Brochure
Special Notes:     May also be downloaded from the web site.

# HEALTH--FOOD AND NUTRITION

Source: American Institute for Cancer Research
Publication Orders
1759 R Street, N. W.
Washington, DC 20009
Phone: 1-800-843-8114
Fax: 1-202-328-7226
World Wide Web URL: http://www.aicr.org
Email Address: aicrweb@aicr.org

## Healthy Eating for the Whole Family

Discusses how the food parents eat, when they eat, and what they serve have an impact on children's health. It shows how to get children involved in menu planning and more.

Availability: Staff at schools with NET, WIC, CSFP, FDPIR, CACFP, UMD or Child Nutrition Program food programs in the United States. Those not having such an affiliation should contact their library to place an interlibrary loan request.
Suggested Grade: Adult
Order Number: NAL Video 2255
Production Date: 1995
Format: VHS videotape
Special Notes: A Mosby Great Performance production.
Terms: Borrower pays return postage. RETURN the day after scheduled use. Book at least 4 weeks in advance. Requests must include your name, phone, mail address, eligibility program, title, NAL number, show date, and a statement, "I have read the warning on copyright restrictions and accept full responsibility for compliance." One title per request.
Source: National Agricultural Library
Document Delivery Services Branch
4th Floor, Photo Lab
10301 Baltimore Avenue
Beltsville, MD 20705-2351
Phone: 1-301-504-5994
Fax: 1-301-504-5675
World Wide Web URL: http://www.nal.usda.gov/fnic
Email Address: lending@nal.usda.gov

## Healthy Eating: Nutrition for Infants and Children Under 5

Focuses on nutritional needs for three specific stages of development: birth to twelve months, 1 to 3 years, and 3 to 5 years.

Availability: Staff at schools with NET, WIC, CSFP, FDPIR, CACFP, UMD or Child Nutrition Program food programs in the United States. Those not having such an affiliation should contact their library to place an interlibrary loan request.
Suggested Grade: Adult
Order Number: NAL Video 2228
Production Date: 1994
Format: VHS videotape
Terms: Borrower pays return postage. RETURN the day after scheduled use. Book at least 4 weeks in advance.

Requests must include your name, phone, mail address, eligibility program, title, NAL number, show date, and a statement, "I have read the warning on copyright restrictions and accept full responsibility for compliance." One title per request.
Source: National Agricultural Library
Document Delivery Services Branch
4th Floor, Photo Lab
10301 Baltimore Avenue
Beltsville, MD 20705-2351
Phone: 1-301-504-5994
Fax: 1-301-504-5675
World Wide Web URL: http://www.nal.usda.gov/fnic
Email Address: lending@nal.usda.gov

## Healthy Kids: Germ Free

Contains materials designed to encourage safe food handling in a variety of settings and for a variety of audiences.

Availability: Staff at schools with NET, WIC, CSFP, FDPIR, CACFP, UMD or Child Nutrition Program food programs in the United States. Those not having such an affiliation should contact their library to place an interlibrary loan request.
Suggested Grade: 7-12
Order Number: NAL Kit 519
Production Date: 1998
Format: VHS videotape
Special Notes: Contains additional supplemental materials.
Terms: Borrower pays return postage. RETURN the day after scheduled use. Book at least 4 weeks in advance. Requests must include your name, phone, mail address, eligibility program, title, NAL number, show date, and a statement, "I have read the warning on copyright restrictions and accept full responsibility for compliance." One title per request.
Source: National Agricultural Library
Document Delivery Services Branch
4th Floor, Photo Lab
10301 Baltimore Avenue
Beltsville, MD 20705-2351
Phone: 1-301-504-5994
Fax: 1-301-504-5675
World Wide Web URL: http://www.nal.usda.gov/fnic
Email Address: lending@nal.usda.gov

## Heart and Soul: Foods and Facts for Your Heart

Shows African-Americans how to prepare typical soul food items with less fat, sodium, and calories, in order to provide better nutrition for the heart. Also discussed are how to shop and how to cook heart healthy foods and how it relates to heart disease and nutrition.

Availability: Staff at schools with NET, WIC, CSFP, FDPIR, CACFP, UMD or Child Nutrition Program food programs in the United States. Those not having such an affiliation should contact their library to place an interlibrary loan request.

# HEALTH--FOOD AND NUTRITION

Suggested Grade: 9-Adult
Order Number: NAL Video 1151
Production Date: 1989
Format: Set of 7 VHS videotapes
Terms: Borrower pays return postage. RETURN the day after scheduled use. Book at least 4 weeks in advance. Requests must include your name, phone, mail address, eligibility program, title, NAL number, show date, and a statement, "I have read the warning on copyright restrictions and accept full responsibility for compliance." One title per request.
Source: National Agricultural Library
Document Delivery Services Branch
4th Floor, Photo Lab
10301 Baltimore Avenue
Beltsville, MD 20705-2351
Phone: 1-301-504-5994
Fax: 1-301-504-5675
World Wide Web URL: http://www.nal.usda.gov/fnic
Email Address: lending@nal.usda.gov

## Heartcare Program, The: Dietary Management of Cholesterol

Describes how to revise your eating habits for a healthier life.
Availability: Staff at schools with NET, WIC, CSFP, FDPIR, CACFP, UMD or Child Nutrition Program food programs in the United States. Those not having such an affiliation should contact their library to place an interlibrary loan request.
Suggested Grade: 7-12
Order Number: NAL Video 2057
Production Date: 1994
Format: Set of 4 VHS videotapes
Terms: Borrower pays return postage. RETURN the day after scheduled use. Book at least 4 weeks in advance. Requests must include your name, phone, mail address, eligibility program, title, NAL number, show date, and a statement, "I have read the warning on copyright restrictions and accept full responsibility for compliance." One title per request.
Source: National Agricultural Library
Document Delivery Services Branch
4th Floor, Photo Lab
10301 Baltimore Avenue
Beltsville, MD 20705-2351
Phone: 1-301-504-5994
Fax: 1-301-504-5675
World Wide Web URL: http://www.nal.usda.gov/fnic
Email Address: lending@nal.usda.gov

## Heart Healthy Diet, A: Who Makes the Choices?

These materials are from a workshop that provides basic information about the relationship between diet and heart disease and the importance of limiting the amount of total fat, saturated fat, and cholesterol in the diet.

Availability: Staff at schools with NET, WIC, CSFP, FDPIR, CACFP, UMD or Child Nutrition Program food programs in the United States. Those not having such an affiliation should contact their library to place an interlibrary loan request.
Suggested Grade: 7-Adult
Order Number: NAL Kit 238
Production Date: 1994
Format: VHS videotape
Terms: Borrower pays return postage. RETURN the day after scheduled use. Book at least 4 weeks in advance. Requests must include your name, phone, mail address, eligibility program, title, NAL number, show date, and a statement, "I have read the warning on copyright restrictions and accept full responsibility for compliance." One title per request.
Source: National Agricultural Library
Document Delivery Services Branch
4th Floor, Photo Lab
10301 Baltimore Avenue
Beltsville, MD 20705-2351
Phone: 1-301-504-5994
Fax: 1-301-504-5675
World Wide Web URL: http://www.nal.usda.gov/fnic
Email Address: lending@nal.usda.gov

## Heart Healthy Eating Tips

Shows how to follow a vegetarian diet--which is ideal for your heart.
Availability: Classroom quantities to schools, libraries, and homeschoolers world-wide. Send a stamped, self-addressed envelope for reply.
Suggested Grade: 6-Adult
Languages: English; Spanish
Order Number: order by title
Format: Brochure
Source: Vegetarian Resource Group, The
P. O. Box 1463
Baltimore, MD 21203
Phone: 1-410-366-8343
Fax: 1-410-366-8804
World Wide Web URL: http://www.vrg.org
Email Address: vrg@vrg.org

## Herschel the Rabbit

Stresses the importance of including vegetables in one's daily diet to provide the body with energy and to help the body grow.
Availability: Staff at schools with NET, WIC, CSFP, FDPIR, CACFP, UMD or Child Nutrition Program food programs in the United States. Those not having such an affiliation should contact their library to place an interlibrary loan request.
Suggested Grade: preK-6
Order Number: NAL Video 1785
Production Date: 1992
Format: VHS videotape

Special Notes:    This is a Collie Craft production.
Terms:    Borrower pays return postage. RETURN the day after scheduled use. Book at least 4 weeks in advance. Requests must include your name, phone, mail address, eligibility program, title, NAL number, show date, and a statement, "I have read the warning on copyright restrictions and accept full responsibility for compliance." One title per request.
**Source:  National Agricultural Library**
**Document Delivery Services Branch**
**4th Floor, Photo Lab**
**10301 Baltimore Avenue**
**Beltsville, MD  20705-2351**
**Phone:  1-301-504-5994**
**Fax:  1-301-504-5675**
**World Wide Web URL:  http://www.nal.usda.gov/fnic**
**Email Address:  lending@nal.usda.gov**

## High Five:  Nutrition Program for High School Youth
Teens get together and discuss such topics as preparing quick, healthy snacks, eating disorders, and other topics.
Availability:    Staff at schools with NET, WIC, CSFP, FDPIR, CACFP, UMD or Child Nutrition Program food programs in the United States. Those not having such an affiliation should contact their library to place an interlibrary loan request.
Suggested Grade:    9-12
Order Number:    NAL Video 2230
Production Date:    1996
Format:    VHS videotape
Terms:    Borrower pays return postage. RETURN the day after scheduled use. Book at least 4 weeks in advance. Requests must include your name, phone, mail address, eligibility program, title, NAL number, show date, and a statement, "I have read the warning on copyright restrictions and accept full responsibility for compliance." One title per request.
**Source:  National Agricultural Library**
**Document Delivery Services Branch**
**4th Floor, Photo Lab**
**10301 Baltimore Avenue**
**Beltsville, MD  20705-2351**
**Phone:  1-301-504-5994**
**Fax:  1-301-504-5675**
**World Wide Web URL:  http://www.nal.usda.gov/fnic**
**Email Address:  lending@nal.usda.gov**

## Hip to Be Fit--A Production of California Raisins
Through music and fast-paced action, Kristi and her friends, the California Raisins, show kids that a healthy, well-balanced diet and plenty of exercise can make them champions in the classroom and on the playground.
Availability:    Staff at schools with NET, WIC, CSFP, FDPIR, CACFP, UMD or Child Nutrition Program food programs in the United States. Those not having such an affiliation should contact their library to place an interlibrary loan request.

Suggested Grade:    preK-6
Order Number:    NAL Video 1765
Production Date:    1993
Format:    VHS videotape
Special Notes:    This is a Wright Group production.
Terms:    Borrower pays return postage. RETURN the day after scheduled use. Book at least 4 weeks in advance. Requests must include your name, phone, mail address, eligibility program, title, NAL number, show date, and a statement, "I have read the warning on copyright restrictions and accept full responsibility for compliance." One title per request.
**Source:  National Agricultural Library**
**Document Delivery Services Branch**
**4th Floor, Photo Lab**
**10301 Baltimore Avenue**
**Beltsville, MD  20705-2351**
**Phone:  1-301-504-5994**
**Fax:  1-301-504-5675**
**World Wide Web URL:  http://www.nal.usda.gov/fnic**
**Email Address:  lending@nal.usda.gov**

## How Safe Is Your Food?
A CNN presentation on food safety, this program covers issues such as handling of chicken and beef from the slaughterhouse to the table.
Availability:    Staff at schools with NET, WIC, CSFP, FDPIR, CACFP, UMD or Child Nutrition Program food programs in the United States. Those not having such an affiliation should contact their library to place an interlibrary loan request.
Suggested Grade:    7-Adult
Order Number:    Video 2866
Production Date:    1997
Format:    VHS videotape
Terms:    Borrower pays return postage. RETURN the day after scheduled use. Book at least 4 weeks in advance. Requests must include your name, phone, mail address, eligibility program, title, NAL number, show date, and a statement, "I have read the warning on copyright restrictions and accept full responsibility for compliance." One title per request.
**Source:  National Agricultural Library**
**Document Delivery Services Branch**
**4th Floor, Photo Lab**
**10301 Baltimore Avenue**
**Beltsville, MD  20705-2351**
**Phone: 1-301-504-5994**
**Fax: 1-301-504-5675**
**World Wide Web URL:  http://www.nal.usda.gov/fnic**
**Email Address:  lending@nal.usda.gov**

## Incredible Adventures of the Amazing Food Detective, The
This online video games provides 20 minutes of lessons on healthy eating and exercise.
Availability:    All requesters
Suggested Grade:    4-5

Order Number: not applicable
Format: Online Video Game
**Source: Kaiser Permanente**
**World Wide Web URL:**
**http://members.kaiserpermanente.org/redirects/**
**landingpages/afd/**

**Invest in Yourself: A Sports Nutrition Manual for High School and Middle School Students, Trainers, and Teachers**
Discusses why athletes need fluid, how much and when an athlete needs fluid, what they should drink, and more.
Availability: Staff at schools with NET, WIC, CSFP, FDPIR, CACFP, UMD or Child Nutrition Program food programs in the United States. Those not having such an affiliation should contact their library to place an interlibrary loan request.
Suggested Grade: 7-Adult
Order Number: NAL Kit 364
Production Date: 1996
Format: VHS videotape
Special Notes: Includes a manual.
Terms: Borrower pays return postage. RETURN the day after scheduled use. Book at least 4 weeks in advance. Requests must include your name, phone, mail address, eligibility program, title, NAL number, show date, and a statement, "I have read the warning on copyright restrictions and accept full responsibility for compliance." One title per request.
**Source: National Agricultural Library**
**Document Delivery Services Branch**
**4th Floor, Photo Lab**
**10301 Baltimore Avenue**
**Beltsville, MD 20705-2351**
**Phone: 1-301-504-5994**
**Fax: 1-301-504-5675**
**World Wide Web URL: http://www.nal.usda.gov/fnic**
**Email Address: lending@nal.usda.gov**

**Kellogg's Fit to Be**
Tells the story of nine-year-old Michael who improved his physical fitness by eating more nutritionally and exercising daily. Instead of junk food, he began to eat a balanced diet including fruit. Michael also began to exercise with his friends.
Availability: Staff at schools with NET, WIC, CSFP, FDPIR, CACFP, UMD or Child Nutrition Program food programs in the United States. Those not having such an affiliation should contact their library to place an interlibrary loan request.
Suggested Grade: preK-6
Order Number: NAL Video 620
Production Date: 1989
Format: VHS videotape
Terms: Borrower pays return postage. RETURN the day after scheduled use. Book at least 4 weeks in advance. Requests must include your name, phone, mail address,

eligibility program, title, NAL number, show date, and a statement, "I have read the warning on copyright restrictions and accept full responsibility for compliance." One title per request.
**Source: National Agricultural Library**
**Document Delivery Services Branch**
**4th Floor, Photo Lab**
**10301 Baltimore Avenue**
**Beltsville, MD 20705-2351**
**Phone: 1-301-504-5994**
**Fax: 1-301-504-5675**
**World Wide Web URL: http://www.nal.usda.gov/fnic**
**Email Address: lending@nal.usda.gov**

**Ken McKan the Food Safety Man Evaluates Cans, Jars and Boxes**
Uses humor to demonstrate how to recognize dangerous food contamination in these containers.
Availability: Staff at schools with NET, WIC, CSFP, FDPIR, CACFP, UMD or Child Nutrition Program food programs in the United States. Those not having such an affiliation should contact their library to place an interlibrary loan request.
Suggested Grade: All ages
Order Number: Video 2869
Production Date: 1997
Format: VHS videotape
Terms: Borrower pays return postage. RETURN the day after scheduled use. Book at least 4 weeks in advance. Requests must include your name, phone, mail address, eligibility program, title, NAL number, show date, and a statement, "I have read the warning on copyright restrictions and accept full responsibility for compliance." One title per request.
**Source: National Agricultural Library**
**Document Delivery Services Branch**
**4th Floor, Photo Lab**
**10301 Baltimore Avenue**
**Beltsville, MD 20705-2351**
**Phone: 1-301-504-5994**
**Fax: 1-301-504-5675**
**World Wide Web URL: http://www.nal.usda.gov/fnic**
**Email Address: lending@nal.usda.gov**

**Ken McKan the Food Safety Man Examines the Effects of Time and Temperature on Food Safety**
Shows the right way to keep foods at safe temperatures to prevent harmful microorganisms from contaminating it.
Availability: Staff at schools with NET, WIC, CSFP, FDPIR, CACFP, UMD or Child Nutrition Program food programs in the United States. Those not having such an affiliation should contact their library to place an interlibrary loan request.
Suggested Grade: All ages
Order Number: Video 2870
Production Date: 1998
Format: VHS videotape

Terms: Borrower pays return postage. RETURN the day after scheduled use. Book at least 4 weeks in advance. Requests must include your name, phone, mail address, eligibility program, title, NAL number, show date, and a statement, "I have read the warning on copyright restrictions and accept full responsibility for compliance." One title per request.

**Source: National Agricultural Library**
**Document Delivery Services Branch**
**4th Floor, Photo Lab**
**10301 Baltimore Avenue**
**Beltsville, MD 20705-2351**
**Phone: 1-301-504-5994**
**Fax: 1-301-504-5675**
**World Wide Web URL: http://www.nal.usda.gov/fnic**
**Email Address: lending@nal.usda.gov**

## Kernel of Wheat
Graphically depicts the nutrient makeup of wheat.

Availability: Single copies to schools, libraries, and homeschoolers in the United States.
Suggested Grade: 3-12
Order Number: order by title
Format: Poster; 8 1/2 x 11 inches; full color

**Source: North Dakota Wheat Commission**
**2401 46th Avenue SE, Suite 104**
**Mandan, ND 58554-4829**
**Phone: 1-701-328-5111**
**Fax: 1-701-663-5787**
**World Wide Web URL: http://www.ndwheat.com**
**Email Address: ndwheat@ndwheat.com**

## Kidnetic.com
Designed to help kids tap into their own energy through good nutrition and regular physical activity, this fun site presents activities and ideas.

Availability: All requesters
Suggested Grade: All ages
Order Number: not applicable
Format: Web Site

**Source: International Food Information Council Foundation**
**World Wide Web URL: http://www.kidnetic.com/**

## Label-Ease: A Guide to Using the New Food Labels
Teaches a simple system to evaluate the nutrient density of a food using just the fingers on one hand and the new food labels.

Availability: Staff at schools with NET, WIC, CSFP, FDPIR, CACFP, UMD or Child Nutrition Program food programs in the United States. Those not having such an affiliation should contact their library to place an interlibrary loan request.
Suggested Grade: 6-Adult
Order Number: NAL Video 2210
Format: VHS videotape
Special Notes: Includes a teacher's guide.

Terms: Borrower pays return postage. RETURN the day after scheduled use. Book at least 4 weeks in advance. Requests must include your name, phone, mail address, eligibility program, title, NAL number, show date, and a statement, "I have read the warning on copyright restrictions and accept full responsibility for compliance." One title per request.

**Source: National Agricultural Library**
**Document Delivery Services Branch**
**4th Floor, Photo Lab, 10301 Baltimore Avenue**
**Beltsville, MD 20705-2351**
**Phone: 1-301-504-5994**
**Fax: 1-301-504-5675**
**World Wide Web URL: http://www.nal.usda.gov/fnic**
**Email Address: lending@nal.usda.gov**

## Lean Life Food Series, The
Compares typical breakfast/lunch/dinner menus to lower fat versions of the same meals.

Availability: Staff at schools with NET, WIC, CSFP, FDPIR, CACFP, UMD or Child Nutrition Program food programs in the United States. Those not having such an affiliation should contact their library to place an interlibrary loan request.
Suggested Grade: 6-12
Order Number: NAL Video 135
Format: VHS videotape
Special Notes: A slide script and low-fat recipes accompany the video kit.

Terms: Borrower pays return postage. RETURN the day after scheduled use. Book at least 4 weeks in advance. Requests must include your name, phone, mail address, eligibility program, title, NAL number, show date, and a statement, "I have read the warning on copyright restrictions and accept full responsibility for compliance." One title per request.

**Source: National Agricultural Library**
**Document Delivery Services Branch**
**4th Floor, Photo Lab, 10301 Baltimore Avenue**
**Beltsville, MD 20705-2351**
**Phone: 1-301-504-5994**
**Fax: 1-301-504-5675**
**World Wide Web URL: http://www.nal.usda.gov/fnic**
**Email Address: lending@nal.usda.gov**

## Lean 'n Easy: Preparing Meat with Less Fat and More Taste
This program teaches that a low-fat diet doesn't need to be costly, tasteless, or time consuming. It is not necessary to avoid favorite foods to lower fat intake. Included are tips for shopping, label reading, food preparation, cooking techniques, and safe storage and handling of foods.

Availability: Staff at schools with NET, WIC, CSFP, FDPIR, CACFP, UMD or Child Nutrition Program food programs in the United States. Those not having such an affiliation should contact their library to place an interlibrary loan request.

# HEALTH--FOOD AND NUTRITION

Suggested Grade:  6-12
Order Number:  NAL Video 2133
Production Date:  1994
Format:  VHS videotape
Special Notes:  This American Dietetic Association and National Live Stock and Meat Board production is accompanied by a leader's guide.
Terms:  Borrower pays return postage. RETURN the day after scheduled use. Book at least 4 weeks in advance. Requests must include your name, phone, mail address, eligibility program, title, NAL number, show date, and a statement, "I have read the warning on copyright restrictions and accept full responsibility for compliance." One title per request.

      **Source:  National Agricultural Library**
      **Document Delivery Services Branch**
      **4th Floor, Photo Lab**
      **10301 Baltimore Avenue**
      **Beltsville, MD  20705-2351**
      **Phone: 1-301-504-5994**
      **Fax: 1-301-504-5675**
**World Wide Web URL:  http://www.nal.usda.gov/fnic**
      **Email Address:  lending@nal.usda.gov**

## Learning the New Food Labels:  An Educator's Slide Kit

Intended to provide nutrition educators with an overview of the food label changes that were brought about by the Nutrition Education and Labeling Act of 1990.

Availability:  Librarians in the United States.
Suggested Grade:  preK-6
Order Number:  464
Format:  Set of 52 slides
Special Notes:  Accompanied by an educator's guide.
Terms:  Borrower pays return postage. RETURN the day after scheduled use. Book at least 4 weeks in advance. Requests must include your name, phone, mail address, eligibility program, title, NAL number, show date, and a statement, "I have read the warning on copyright restrictions and accept full responsibility for compliance." One title per request.

      **Source:  National Agricultural Library**
      **Document Delivery Services Branch**
    **4th Floor, Photo Lab, 10301 Baltimore Avenue**
      **Beltsville, MD  20705-2351**
      **Phone: 1-301-504-5994**
      **Fax: 1-301-504-5675**
**World Wide Web URL:  http://www.nal.usda.gov/fnic**
      **Email Address:  lending@nal.usda.gov**

## Lowdown on Cholesterol, The

Practical information concerning cholesterol in the average American diet. The role of fat in the diet and its part in the production of cholesterol is discussed. Topics included are total fat consumption, saturation and hydrogenation, and omega-3 fatty acids and soluble fiber. The program shows how to achieve a low cholesterol diet by avoiding fat in the preparation of meals.

Availability:  Staff at schools with NET, WIC, CSFP, FDPIR, CACFP, UMD or Child Nutrition Program food programs in the United States. Those not having such an affiliation should contact their library to place an interlibrary loan request.
Suggested Grade:  9-12
Order Number:  NAL Video 788
Production Date:  1989
Format:  VHS videotape
Special Notes:  A collection of recipes is included.
Terms:  Borrower pays return postage. RETURN the day after scheduled use. Book at least 4 weeks in advance. Requests must include your name, phone, mail address, eligibility program, title, NAL number, show date, and a statement, "I have read the warning on copyright restrictions and accept full responsibility for compliance." One title per request.

      **Source:  National Agricultural Library**
      **Document Delivery Services Branch**
      **4th Floor, Photo Lab**
      **10301 Baltimore Avenue**
      **Beltsville, MD  20705-2351**
      **Phone: 1-301-504-5994**
      **Fax: 1-301-504-5675**
**World Wide Web URL:  http://www.nal.usda.gov/fnic**
      **Email Address:  lending@nal.usda.gov**

## Managing Your Weight Without Dieting

Introduces students to some common misconceptions about dieting. Contains a report on the impact of fast-food restaurants on the modern teen's diet.

Availability:  Staff at schools with NET, WIC, CSFP, FDPIR, CACFP, UMD or Child Nutrition Program food programs in the United States. Those not having such an affiliation should contact their library to place an interlibrary loan request.
Suggested Grade:  5-12
Order Number:  NAL Video 2229
Production Date:  1993
Format:  VHS videotape
Special Notes:  Accompanied by a teacher's guide.
Terms:  Borrower pays return postage. RETURN the day after scheduled use. Book at least 4 weeks in advance. Requests must include your name, phone, mail address, eligibility program, title, NAL number, show date, and a statement, "I have read the warning on copyright restrictions and accept full responsibility for compliance." One title per request.

      **Source:  National Agricultural Library**
      **Document Delivery Services Branch**
      **4th Floor, Photo Lab**
      **10301 Baltimore Avenue**
      **Beltsville, MD  20705-2351**
      **Phone: 1-301-504-5994**
      **Fax: 1-301-504-5675**
**World Wide Web URL:  http://www.nal.usda.gov/fnic**
      **Email Address:  lending@nal.usda.gov**

**58**

## Maryland Seafood--Crabs
A variety of recipes using crabs.

Availability: Classroom quantities to schools, libraries, and homeschoolers in the United States and Canada.
Suggested Grade: 6-Adult
Order Number: order by title
Format: Leaflet
**Source: Maryland Department of Agriculture**
**Seafood Marketing Program**
**50 Harry S. Truman Parkway**
**Annapolis, MD 21401**
**Phone: 1-410-841-5820**
**Fax: 1-410-841-5970**
**World Wide Web URL:**
**Email Address: eberlynl@mda.state.md.us**

## Matter of Balance, A: Easy Steps for Good Nutrition
No food is intrinsically good or bad. Explains that wise selection of different foods throughout the day will let you reach the goal of consuming the recommended amount of fat.

Availability: Staff at schools with NET, WIC, CSFP, FDPIR, CACFP, UMD or Child Nutrition Program food programs in the United States. Those not having such an affiliation should contact their library to place an interlibrary loan request.
Suggested Grade: 4-12
Order Number: NAL Video 1295
Production Date: 1989
Format: VHS videotape
Terms: Borrower pays return postage. RETURN the day after scheduled use. Book at least 4 weeks in advance. Requests must include your name, phone, mail address, eligibility program, title, NAL number, show date, and a statement, "I have read the warning on copyright restrictions and accept full responsibility for compliance." One title per request.
**Source: National Agricultural Library**
**Document Delivery Services Branch**
**4th Floor, Photo Lab**
**10301 Baltimore Avenue**
**Beltsville, MD 20705-2351**
**Phone: 1-301-504-5994**
**Fax: 1-301-504-5675**
**World Wide Web URL: http://www.nal.usda.gov/fnic**
**Email Address: lending@nal.usda.gov**

## Meal Planning: The Food Pyramid in Action
Shows how to plan, shop for and prepare meals based on the food guide pyramid.

Availability: Staff at schools with NET, WIC, CSFP, FDPIR, CACFP, UMD or Child Nutrition Program food programs in the United States. Those not having such an affiliation should contact their library to place an interlibrary loan request.
Suggested Grade: 6-12

Order Number: NAL Video 2271
Production Date: 1996
Format: VHS videotape
Terms: Borrower pays return postage. RETURN the day after scheduled use. Book at least 4 weeks in advance. Requests must include your name, phone, mail address, eligibility program, title, NAL number, show date, and a statement, "I have read the warning on copyright restrictions and accept full responsibility for compliance." One title per request.
**Source: National Agricultural Library**
**Document Delivery Services Branch**
**4th Floor, Photo Lab**
**10301 Baltimore Avenue**
**Beltsville, MD 20705-2351**
**Phone: 1-301-504-5994**
**Fax: 1-301-504-5675**
**World Wide Web URL: http://www.nal.usda.gov/fnic**
**Email Address: lending@nal.usda.gov**

## Meaning of Food, The
Introduces students to diverse culture through food.

Availability: All requesters
Suggested Grade: 5-8
Order Number: not applicable
Format: Online Lesson Plan
**Source: Pie in the Sky Productions**
**World Wide Web URL:**
**http://www.pbs.org/opb/meaningoffood/classroom/**

## Mid-LINC: Middle Level Interdisciplinary Curriculum
Developed to help students make connections between nutrition and social studies, math, science, language arts, health, and home economics.

Availability: Staff at schools with NET, WIC, CSFP, FDPIR, CACFP, UMD or Child Nutrition Program food programs in the United States. Those not having such an affiliation should contact their library to place an interlibrary loan request.
Suggested Grade: 6-8
Order Number: NAL Kit 160
Production Date: 1993
Format: VHS videotape
Special Notes: This production from Penn State Nutrition Center includes a science video kit, 3 notebooks, and a meal ready-to-eat.
Terms: Borrower pays return postage. RETURN the day after scheduled use. Book at least 4 weeks in advance. Requests must include your name, phone, mail address, eligibility program, title, NAL number, show date, and a statement, "I have read the warning on copyright restrictions and accept full responsibility for compliance." One title per request.
**Source: National Agricultural Library**
**Document Delivery Services Branch**
**4th Floor, Photo Lab**
**10301 Baltimore Avenue**
**Beltsville, MD 20705-2351**
**Phone: 1-301-504-5994**

Fax: 1-301-504-5675
World Wide Web URL: http://www.nal.usda.gov/fnic
Email Address: lending@nal.usda.gov

## Mid-LINC: Middle Level Interdisciplinary Curriculum (Revised Edition)

Developed to help students make connections between nutrition and social studies, math, science, language arts, health, and home economics.

Availability: Staff at schools with NET, WIC, CSFP, FDPIR, CACFP, UMD or Child Nutrition Program food programs in the United States. Those not having such an affiliation should contact their library to place an interlibrary loan request.
Suggested Grade: 6-8
Order Number: NAL Kit 310
Production Date: 1995
Format: VHS videotape
Special Notes: This production from Penn State Nutrition Center includes a science video kit, 3 notebooks, and a meal ready-to-eat.
Terms: Borrower pays return postage. RETURN the day after scheduled use. Book at least 4 weeks in advance. Requests must include your name, phone, mail address, eligibility program, title, NAL number, show date, and a statement, "I have read the warning on copyright restrictions and accept full responsibility for compliance." One title per request.

Source: National Agricultural Library
Document Delivery Services Branch
4th Floor, Photo Lab, 10301 Baltimore Avenue
Beltsville, MD 20705-2351
Phone: 1-301-504-5994
Fax: 1-301-504-5675
World Wide Web URL: http://www.nal.usda.gov/fnic
Email Address: lending@nal.usda.gov

## MVE-TV: The Channel for Moderation, Variety and Exercise

This program is designed to help students develop good eating habits. It provides an overview of essentials for a low-fat, balanced diet.

Availability: Staff at schools with NET, WIC, CSFP, FDPIR, CACFP, UMD or Child Nutrition Program food programs in the United States. Those not having such an affiliation should contact their library to place an interlibrary loan request.
Suggested Grade: 7-12
Order Number: NAL Video 2156
Format: VHS videotape
Terms: Borrower pays return postage. RETURN the day after scheduled use. Book at least 4 weeks in advance. Requests must include your name, phone, mail address, eligibility program, title, NAL number, show date, and a statement, "I have read the warning on copyright restrictions and accept full responsibility for compliance." One title per request.

Source: National Agricultural Library
Document Delivery Services Branch
4th Floor, Photo Lab
10301 Baltimore Avenue
Beltsville, MD 20705-2351
Phone: 1-301-504-5994
Fax: 1-301-504-5675
World Wide Web URL: http://www.nal.usda.gov/fnic
Email Address: lending@nal.usda.gov

## New American Plate for Breakfast, The

Describes what a healthful breakfast should supply and why it is so important to have one. Includes recipes.

Availability: Limit of 1 copy to schools, libraries, and homeschoolers in the United States and Canada.
Suggested Grade: 10-Adult
Order Number: order by title
Format: Booklet
Special Notes: May also be downloaded from the web site.

Source: American Institute for Cancer Research
Publication Orders
1759 R Street, N. W.
Washington, DC 20009
Phone: 1-800-843-8114
Fax: 1-202-328-7226
World Wide Web URL: http://www.aicr.org
Email Address: aicrweb@aicr.org

## New American Plate, The--Comfort Foods

Shows how to add nutrition to your favorite foods without sacrificing their nostalgic flavors. Includes recipes and a list of healthy substitutions for baking and cooking.

Availability: Limit of 1 copy to schools, libraries, and homeschoolers in the United States and Canada.
Suggested Grade: 10-Adult
Order Number: order by title
Format: Booklet
Special Notes: May also be downloaded from the web site.

Source: American Institute for Cancer Research
Publication Orders
1759 R Street, N. W.
Washington, DC 20009
Phone: 1-800-843-8114
Fax: 1-202-328-7226
World Wide Web URL: http://www.aicr.org
Email Address: aicrweb@aicr.org

## New American Plate, The--One-Pot Meals

Explains how to reshape your diet to prevent cancer and maintain a healthy weight--with simple to prepare recipes that involve only one pot!

Availability: Limit of 1 copy to schools, libraries, and homeschoolers in the United States and Canada.
Suggested Grade: 10-Adult
Order Number: order by title
Format: Booklet

Special Notes: May also be downloaded from the web site.
**Source: American Institute for Cancer Research**
**Publication Orders**
**1759 R Street, N. W.**
**Washington, DC 20009**
**Phone: 1-800-843-8114**
**Fax: 1-202-328-7226**
**World Wide Web URL: http://www.aicr.org**
**Email Address: aicrweb@aicr.org**

## New American Plate, The--Veggies
Information about the health benefits of vegetables as well as tips on how to select, store, and prepare them. Includes recipes.

Availability: Limit of 1 copy to schools, libraries, and homeschoolers in the United States and Canada.
Suggested Grade: 10-Adult
Order Number: order by title
Format: Booklet
Special Notes: May also be downloaded from the web site.
**Source: American Institute for Cancer Research**
**Publication Orders**
**1759 R Street, N. W.**
**Washington, DC 20009**
**Phone: 1-800-843-8114**
**Fax: 1-202-328-7226**
**World Wide Web URL: http://www.aicr.org**
**Email Address: aicrweb@aicr.org**

## New Nutrition Facts Food Label, The
Explains the new federally-mandated food labels and shows how consumers can use them to make healthier food choices.

Availability: Staff at schools with NET, WIC, CSFP, FDPIR, CACFP, UMD or Child Nutrition Program food programs in the United States. Those not having such an affiliation should contact their library to place an interlibrary loan request.
Suggested Grade: 7-12
Order Number: NAL Video 2016
Production Date: 1995
Format: VHS videotape
Special Notes: An Educational Video Network production.
Terms: Borrower pays return postage. RETURN the day after scheduled use. Book at least 4 weeks in advance. Requests must include your name, phone, mail address, eligibility program, title, NAL number, show date, and a statement, "I have read the warning on copyright restrictions and accept full responsibility for compliance." One title per request.
**Source: National Agricultural Library**
**Document Delivery Services Branch**
**4th Floor, Photo Lab**
**10301 Baltimore Avenue**
**Beltsville, MD 20705-2351**
**Phone: 1-301-504-5994**
**Fax: 1-301-504-5675**

**World Wide Web URL: http://www.nal.usda.gov/fnic**
**Email Address: lending@nal.usda.gov**

## Nifty Nutrition with Skill Integration Activities
A developmentally appropriate curriculum with sequential nutrition and health concepts based on the U. S. Dietary Guidelines and Food Guide Pyramid. Basic language, math, social studies, science, art and health skills are integrated into the curriculum and coded to each lesson.

Availability: Staff at schools with NET, WIC, CSFP, FDPIR, CACFP, UMD or Child Nutrition Program food programs in the United States. Those not having such an affiliation should contact their library to place an interlibrary loan request.
Suggested Grade: preK-6
Order Number: NAL Kit 229
Production Date: 1995
Format: Set of 7 VHS videotapes
Special Notes: This Arkansas Department of Education kit includes 7 teacher guides.
Terms: Borrower pays return postage. RETURN the day after scheduled use. Book at least 4 weeks in advance. Requests must include your name, phone, mail address, eligibility program, title, NAL number, show date, and a statement, "I have read the warning on copyright restrictions and accept full responsibility for compliance." One title per request.
**Source: National Agricultural Library**
**Document Delivery Services Branch**
**4th Floor, Photo Lab**
**10301 Baltimore Avenue**
**Beltsville, MD 20705-2351**
**Phone: 1-301-504-5994**
**Fax: 1-301-504-5675**
**World Wide Web URL: http://www.nal.usda.gov/fnic**
**Email Address: lending@nal.usda.gov**

## Now We're Cooking
This campaign and curriculum has its origins in an ongoing national coalition project, "Resetting the American table: creating a new alliance of taste and health." The goals of this project are to facilitate elementary school students in experiencing the positive social, psychological, and nutritional value of eating together with family and friends. It is to help children share responsibility for family meals by teaching them some basic food preparation skills that encourage healthful eating.

Availability: Staff at schools with NET, WIC, CSFP, FDPIR, CACFP, UMD or Child Nutrition Program food programs in the United States. Those not having such an affiliation should contact their library to place an interlibrary loan request.
Suggested Grade: preK-6
Order Number: NAL Kit 252
Production Date: 1995
Format: VHS videotape

Special Notes: This campaign packet includes materials to support classroom and cafeteria activities.

Terms: Borrower pays return postage. RETURN the day after scheduled use. Book at least 4 weeks in advance. Requests must include your name, phone, mail address, eligibility program, title, NAL number, show date, and a statement, "I have read the warning on copyright restrictions and accept full responsibility for compliance." One title per request.

**Source: National Agricultural Library**
**Document Delivery Services Branch**
**4th Floor, Photo Lab, 10301 Baltimore Avenue**
**Beltsville, MD 20705-2351**
**Phone: 1-301-504-5994**
**Fax: 1-301-504-5675**
**World Wide Web URL: http://www.nal.usda.gov/fnic**
**Email Address: lending@nal.usda.gov**

## Nutricion a Traves de la Vida

Discusses food groups and recommended portions for healthy eating.

Availability: Staff at schools with NET, WIC, CSFP, FDPIR, CACFP, UMD or Child Nutrition Program food programs in the United States. Those not having such an affiliation should contact their library to place an interlibrary loan request.

Suggested Grade: 7-Adult
Language: Spanish
Order Number: NAL Video 2847
Production Date: 1997
Format: VHS videotape

Terms: Borrower pays return postage. RETURN the day after scheduled use. Book at least 4 weeks in advance. Requests must include your name, phone, mail address, eligibility program, title, NAL number, show date, and a statement, "I have read the warning on copyright restrictions and accept full responsibility for compliance." One title per request.

**Source: National Agricultural Library**
**Document Delivery Services Branch**
**4th Floor, Photo Lab, 10301 Baltimore Avenue**
**Beltsville, MD 20705-2351**
**Phone: 1-301-504-5994**
**Fax: 1-301-504-5675**
**World Wide Web URL: http://www.nal.usda.gov/fnic**
**Email Address: lending@nal.usda.gov**

## Nutrition: A Family Affair

This program discusses the importance of nutrition to children's health and growth. In this light, it suggests various possibilities for breakfast, lunch and snack foods and which types of food not to serve to children.

Availability: Staff at schools with NET, WIC, CSFP, FDPIR, CACFP, UMD or Child Nutrition Program food programs in the United States. Those not having such an affiliation should contact their library to place an interlibrary loan request.

Suggested Grade: Adult
Order Number: NAL Video 656
Production Date: 1987
Format: VHS videotape
Special Notes: This program includes an 8-page pre-test sheet and a post-test sheet.

Terms: Borrower pays return postage. RETURN the day after scheduled use. Book at least 4 weeks in advance. Requests must include your name, phone, mail address, eligibility program, title, NAL number, show date, and a statement, "I have read the warning on copyright restrictions and accept full responsibility for compliance." One title per request.

**Source: National Agricultural Library**
**Document Delivery Services Branch**
**4th Floor, Photo Lab, 10301 Baltimore Avenue**
**Beltsville, MD 20705-2351**
**Phone: 1-301-504-5994**
**Fax: 1-301-504-5675**
**World Wide Web URL: http://www.nal.usda.gov/fnic**
**Email Address: lending@nal.usda.gov**

## Nutrition After Fifty

Tips and recipes for staying fit and healthy after reaching this milestone.

Availability: Limit of 1 copy to schools, libraries, and homeschoolers in the United States and Canada.

Suggested Grade: Adult
Order Number: order by title
Format: Booklet
Special Notes: May also be downloaded from the web site.

**Source: American Institute for Cancer Research**
**Publication Orders**
**1759 R Street, N. W.**
**Washington, DC 20009**
**Phone: 1-800-843-8114**
**Fax: 1-202-328-7226**
**World Wide Web URL: http://www.aicr.org**
**Email Address: aicrweb@aicr.org**

## Nutritional Rap

Simulates a television program on the "N-TV" network.

Availability: Staff at schools with NET, WIC, CSFP, FDPIR, CACFP, UMD or Child Nutrition Program food programs in the United States. Those not having such an affiliation should contact their library to place an interlibrary loan request.

Suggested Grade: preK-6
Order Number: NAL Video 1492
Format: VHS videotape
Special Notes: Accompanied by a pamphlet.

Terms: Borrower pays return postage. RETURN the day after scheduled use. Book at least 4 weeks in advance. Requests must include your name, phone, mail address, eligibility program, title, NAL number, show date, and a statement, "I have read the warning on copyright restrictions and accept full responsibility for compliance." One title per request.

Source: National Agricultural Library
Document Delivery Services Branch
4th Floor, Photo Lab
10301 Baltimore Avenue
Beltsville, MD 20705-2351
Phone: 1-301-504-5994
Fax: 1-301-504-5675
World Wide Web URL: http://www.nal.usda.gov/fnic
Email Address: lending@nal.usda.gov

## Nutrition & Diet

In this video, a registered dietician and nutritionist work with teens to explain the principles of good nutrition and to demonstrate good eating habits, from reading product labels to selecting menu items and preparing food at home.

Availability: Staff at schools with NET, WIC, CSFP, FDPIR, CACFP, UMD or Child Nutrition Program food programs in the United States. Those not having such an affiliation should contact their library to place an interlibrary loan request.
Suggested Grade: 5-12
Order Number: NAL Video 2287
Production Date: 1994
Format: VHS videotape
Terms: Borrower pays return postage. RETURN the day after scheduled use. Book at least 4 weeks in advance. Requests must include your name, phone, mail address, eligibility program, title, NAL number, show date, and a statement, "I have read the warning on copyright restrictions and accept full responsibility for compliance." One title per request.

Source: National Agricultural Library
Document Delivery Services Branch
4th Floor, Photo Lab
10301 Baltimore Avenue
Beltsville, MD 20705-2351
Phone: 1-301-504-5994
Fax: 1-301-504-5675
World Wide Web URL: http://www.nal.usda.gov/fnic
Email Address: lending@nal.usda.gov

## Nutrition and Exercise for the 1990's

Designed to give students the latest facts about nutrition and exercise. It explains the components that make up a nutritionally adequate diet and demonstrates the effect of exercise on energy requirements.

Availability: Staff at schools with NET, WIC, CSFP, FDPIR, CACFP, UMD or Child Nutrition Program food programs in the United States. Those not having such an affiliation should contact their library to place an interlibrary loan request.
Suggested Grade: 4-12
Order Number: NAL Video 516
Production Date: 1989
Format: VHS videotape
Special Notes: The accompanying teacher's guide includes a food list.

Terms: Borrower pays return postage. RETURN the day after scheduled use. Book at least 4 weeks in advance. Requests must include your name, phone, mail address, eligibility program, title, NAL number, show date, and a statement, "I have read the warning on copyright restrictions and accept full responsibility for compliance." One title per request.
Source: National Agricultural Library
Document Delivery Services Branch
4th Floor, Photo Lab
10301 Baltimore Avenue
Beltsville, MD 20705-2351
Phone: 1-301-504-5994
Fax: 1-301-504-5675
World Wide Web URL: http://www.nal.usda.gov/fnic
Email Address: lending@nal.usda.gov

## Nutrition and Me

This is a curriculum-based health package for students. It focuses on three areas: categories of foods as organized in the Food Pyramid; digestion of food, with emphasis on the influence of food on growth; and the food industry. It is structured to involve student participation, as well as written follow-up activities.

Availability: Staff at schools with NET, WIC, CSFP, FDPIR, CACFP, UMD or Child Nutrition Program food programs in the United States. Those not having such an affiliation should contact their library to place an interlibrary loan request.
Suggested Grade: 4-6
Order Number: NAL Kit 217
Production Date: 1993
Format: Set of 3 VHS videotapes
Special Notes: This Churchill Media kit includes 10 transparencies, a wall chart, 2 books, 7 duplicating master sheets, and a classroom guide.
Terms: Borrower pays return postage. RETURN the day after scheduled use. Book at least 4 weeks in advance. Requests must include your name, phone, mail address, eligibility program, title, NAL number, show date, and a statement, "I have read the warning on copyright restrictions and accept full responsibility for compliance." One title per request.

Source: National Agricultural Library
Document Delivery Services Branch
4th Floor, Photo Lab
10301 Baltimore Avenue
Beltsville, MD 20705-2351
Phone: 1-301-504-5994
Fax: 1-301-504-5675
World Wide Web URL: http://www.nal.usda.gov/fnic
Email Address: lending@nal.usda.gov

## Nutrition and the Cancer Survivor

The right diet is essential for regaining and maintaining health. Tells what science knows about eating to prevent secondary tumors and recurrence.

*All materials listed in this 2018-2019 edition are BRAND NEW!*

Availability: Limit of 1 copy to schools, libraries, and homeschoolers in the United States and Canada.
Suggested Grade: 10-Adult
Order Number: order by title
Format: Brochure
Special Notes: May also be downloaded from the web site.

**Source: American Institute for Cancer Research**
**Publication Orders**
**1759 R Street, N. W.**
**Washington, DC 20009**
**Phone: 1-800-843-8114**
**Fax: 1-202-328-7226**
**World Wide Web URL: http://www.aicr.org**
**Email Address: aicrweb@aicr.org**

## Nutrition and Your Health: Dietary Guidelines for Americans

Reviews the seven nutrition and dietary recommendations of the USDA.
Availability: Librarians in the United States.
Suggested Grade: Adult
Order Number: NAL Slide 377
Production Date: 1990
Format: Set of 63 slides
Special Notes: Accompanied by a script.
Terms: Borrower pays return postage. RETURN the day after scheduled use. Book at least 4 weeks in advance. Requests must include your name, phone, mail address, eligibility program, title, NAL number, show date, and a statement, "I have read the warning on copyright restrictions and accept full responsibility for compliance." One title per request.

**Source: National Agricultural Library**
**Document Delivery Services Branch**
**4th Floor, Photo Lab**
**10301 Baltimore Avenue**
**Beltsville, MD 20705-2351**
**Phone: 1-301-504-5994**
**Fax: 1-301-504-5675**
**World Wide Web URL: http://www.nal.usda.gov/fnic**
**Email Address: lending@nal.usda.gov**

## Nutrition and Your Health: Dietary Guidelines for Americans

This program reviews the seven (7) nutrition and dietary recommendations of the USDA and the U. S. Department of Health and Human Services.
Availability: Staff at schools with NET, WIC, CSFP, FDPIR, CACFP, UMD or Child Nutrition Program food programs in the United States. Those not having such an affiliation should contact their library to place an interlibrary loan request.
Suggested Grade: 7-12
Order Number: NAL Video 1194
Production Date: 1991
Format: VHS videotape

Terms: Borrower pays return postage. RETURN the day after scheduled use. Book at least 4 weeks in advance. Requests must include your name, phone, mail address, eligibility program, title, NAL number, show date, and a statement, "I have read the warning on copyright restrictions and accept full responsibility for compliance." One title per request.

**Source: National Agricultural Library**
**Document Delivery Services Branch**
**4th Floor, Photo Lab**
**10301 Baltimore Avenue**
**Beltsville, MD 20705-2351**
**Phone: 1-301-504-5994**
**Fax: 1-301-504-5675**
**World Wide Web URL: http://www.nal.usda.gov/fnic**
**Email Address: lending@nal.usda.gov**

## Nutrition Cafe

Games and activities designed to teach important nutrition concepts.
Availability: All requesters
Suggested Grade: 3-5
Order Number: not applicable
Format: Web Site

**Source: Pacific Science Center and Washington State Dairy**
**Council**
**World Wide Web URL: http://exhibits.pacsci.org/nutrition/**

## Nutrition: Eating Well

This video teaches young children about the importance of healthful eating and good nutrition using humorous circus characters. It teaches the importance of proteins, fats, water, carbohydrates, fiber, vitamins and minerals.
Availability: Staff at schools with NET, WIC, CSFP, FDPIR, CACFP, UMD or Child Nutrition Program food programs in the United States. Those not having such an affiliation should contact their library to place an interlibrary loan request.
Suggested Grade: preK-6
Order Number: NAL Video 1280
Production Date: 1985
Format: VHS videotape
Special Notes: This video was created by the National Geographic Society, Mass Audiovisual Productions, and Photosynthesis Productions.
Terms: Borrower pays return postage. RETURN the day after scheduled use. Book at least 4 weeks in advance. Requests must include your name, phone, mail address, eligibility program, title, NAL number, show date, and a statement, "I have read the warning on copyright restrictions and accept full responsibility for compliance." One title per request.

**Source: National Agricultural Library**
**Document Delivery Services Branch**
**4th Floor, Photo Lab**
**10301 Baltimore Avenue**
**Beltsville, MD 20705-2351**
**Phone: 1-301-504-5994**

Fax: 1-301-504-5675
World Wide Web URL: http://www.nal.usda.gov/fnic
Email Address: lending@nal.usda.gov

## Nutrition Guide for Teenage Vegetarians, A
Addresses how nutrition needs of teenagers can be met with a vegetarian diet.

| | |
|---|---|
| Availability: | Classroom quantities to schools, libraries, and homeschoolers world-wide. Send a stamped, self-addressed envelope for reply. |
| Suggested Grade: | 6-12 |
| Languages: | English; Spanish |
| Order Number: | order by title |
| Format: | Brochure |

Source: **Vegetarian Resource Group, The**
P. O. Box 1463
Baltimore, MD 21203
Phone: 1-410-366-8343
Fax: 1-410-366-8804
World Wide Web URL: http://www.vrg.org
Email Address: vrg@vrg.org

## Nutrition Information and Misinformation
This video's purposes are to identify types of nutrition information which may influence children's food choices; analyze the information according to its content, source and motives; and review visual, audio and print media as ways in which nutrition information is exhibited. Classroom activities which help students identify reliable nutrition information are shown. Aspects to consider in analyzing nutrition information are: is the product a cure-all?, does someone profit from one using the product?, is the information biased? Advertising tactics utilized by the media to influence children's food selections are: emotional appeals, good looks, excitement, attention getters, incomplete truths are reviewed.

| | |
|---|---|
| Availability: | Staff at schools with NET, WIC, CSFP, FDPIR, CACFP, UMD or Child Nutrition Program food programs in the United States. Those not having such an affiliation should contact their library to place an interlibrary loan request. |
| Suggested Grade: | preK-6 |
| Order Number: | NAL Video 348 |
| Format: | VHS videotape |
| Special Notes: | This is ninth in the Nutrition in Action series designed by Penn State University. |
| Terms: | Borrower pays return postage. RETURN the day after scheduled use. Book at least 4 weeks in advance. Requests must include your name, phone, mail address, eligibility program, title, NAL number, show date, and a statement, "I have read the warning on copyright restrictions and accept full responsibility for compliance." One title per request. |

Source: **National Agricultural Library**
**Document Delivery Services Branch**
**4th Floor, Photo Lab, 10301 Baltimore Avenue**
**Beltsville, MD 20705-2351**

Phone: 1-301-504-5994
Fax: 1-301-504-5675
World Wide Web URL: http://www.nal.usda.gov/fnic
Email Address: lending@nal.usda.gov

## Nutrition Labeling
This program discusses the nature of nutrients, what has to be included on nutrition labels, what information can be found on nutrition labels, and the meaning of the term U. S. RDA.

| | |
|---|---|
| Availability: | Staff at schools with NET, WIC, CSFP, FDPIR, CACFP, UMD or Child Nutrition Program food programs in the United States. Those not having such an affiliation should contact their library to place an interlibrary loan request. |
| Suggested Grade: | preK-6 |
| Order Number: | NAL Video 1474 |
| Production Date: | 1989 |
| Format: | VHS videotape |
| Special Notes: | This is a WIC Program, Austin, Texas. |
| Terms: | Borrower pays return postage. RETURN the day after scheduled use. Book at least 4 weeks in advance. Requests must include your name, phone, mail address, eligibility program, title, NAL number, show date, and a statement, "I have read the warning on copyright restrictions and accept full responsibility for compliance." One title per request. |

Source: **National Agricultural Library**
**Document Delivery Services Branch**
**4th Floor, Photo Lab**
**10301 Baltimore Avenue**
**Beltsville, MD 20705-2351**
Phone: 1-301-504-5994
Fax: 1-301-504-5675
World Wide Web URL: http://www.nal.usda.gov/fnic
Email Address: lending@nal.usda.gov

## Nutrition Labels: Our Guides to Healthy Eating
Explains how to read the new food labels and how to interpret the nutrition facts on labels.

| | |
|---|---|
| Availability: | Staff at schools with NET, WIC, CSFP, FDPIR, CACFP, UMD or Child Nutrition Program food programs in the United States. Those not having such an affiliation should contact their library to place an interlibrary loan request. |
| Suggested Grade: | 6-12 |
| Order Number: | NAL Video 2135 |
| Format: | VHS videotape |
| Special Notes: | Includes a teacher's guide. |
| Terms: | Borrower pays return postage. RETURN the day after scheduled use. Book at least 4 weeks in advance. Requests must include your name, phone, mail address, eligibility program, title, NAL number, show date, and a statement, "I have read the warning on copyright restrictions and accept full responsibility for compliance." One title per request. |

Source: National Agricultural Library
Document Delivery Services Branch
4th Floor, Photo Lab
10301 Baltimore Avenue
Beltsville, MD  20705-2351
Phone: 1-301-504-5994
Fax: 1-301-504-5675
World Wide Web URL: http://www.nal.usda.gov/fnic
Email Address: lending@nal.usda.gov

## Nutritionland Mall with Sammy Chef

Designed to complement the basic nutrition curriculum used in schools.

Availability: Staff at schools with NET, WIC, CSFP, FDPIR, CACFP, UMD or Child Nutrition Program food programs in the United States. Those not having such an affiliation should contact their library to place an interlibrary loan request.
Suggested Grade: 3-4
Order Number: NAL Kit 513
Production Date: 1996
Format: VHS videotape
Special Notes: Includes camera-ready handouts.
Terms: Borrower pays return postage. RETURN the day after scheduled use. Book at least 4 weeks in advance. Requests must include your name, phone, mail address, eligibility program, title, NAL number, show date, and a statement, "I have read the warning on copyright restrictions and accept full responsibility for compliance." One title per request.
Source: National Agricultural Library
Document Delivery Services Branch
4th Floor, Photo Lab, 10301 Baltimore Avenue
Beltsville, MD  20705-2351
Phone: 1-301-504-5994
Fax: 1-301-504-5675
World Wide Web URL: http://www.nal.usda.gov/fnic
Email Address: lending@nal.usda.gov

## Nutrition Programs for Children

Explores this issue in a concise report.
Availability: All requesters
Suggested Grade: Teacher Reference
Order Number: not applicable
Production Date: 1994
Format: Online Article
Source: National Health/Education Consortium
World Wide Web URL:
http://ceep.crc.uiuc.edu/eecearchive/digests/1994/nhec294.html

## Nutrition to Grow on Human Relations Media

Designed to acquaint students with the fundamentals of nutrition, and to show that good nutrition, coupled with regular exercise, is the key to looking and feeling your best. Combines live-action video, animated graphics, and animated cartoons to deliver the basic on nutrition in a format that is engaging and informative.

Availability: Staff at schools with NET, WIC, CSFP, FDPIR, CACFP, UMD or Child Nutrition Program food programs in the United States. Those not having such an affiliation should contact their library to place an interlibrary loan request.
Suggested Grade: 5-8
Order Number: NAL Video 546
Production Date: 1989
Format: VHS videotape
Terms: Borrower pays return postage. RETURN the day after scheduled use. Book at least 4 weeks in advance. Requests must include your name, phone, mail address, eligibility program, title, NAL number, show date, and a statement, "I have read the warning on copyright restrictions and accept full responsibility for compliance." One title per request.
Source: National Agricultural Library
Document Delivery Services Branch
4th Floor, Photo Lab
10301 Baltimore Avenue
Beltsville, MD  20705-2351
Phone: 1-301-504-5994
Fax: 1-301-504-5675
World Wide Web URL: http://www.nal.usda.gov/fnic
Email Address: lending@nal.usda.gov

## Oatmeal in My Hair:  The Challenge of Feeding Kids

Several parents discuss their problems with feeding their preschool children. Topics discussed include: ideas for snacks, ways to make mealtime more pleasant, shopping tips, typical characteristics of preschooler parents as role models. A variety of ethnic groups and family types are represented, including a divorced father and a single mother.

Availability: Staff at schools with NET, WIC, CSFP, FDPIR, CACFP, UMD or Child Nutrition Program food programs in the United States. Those not having such an affiliation should contact their library to place an interlibrary loan request.
Suggested Grade: Adult
Order Number: NAL Video 1301
Production Date: 1992
Format: VHS videotape
Special Notes: This production is from The Services, Minneapolis, MN.
Terms: Borrower pays return postage. RETURN the day after scheduled use. Book at least 4 weeks in advance. Requests must include your name, phone, mail address, eligibility program, title, NAL number, show date, and a statement, "I have read the warning on copyright restrictions and accept full responsibility for compliance." One title per request.
Source: National Agricultural Library
Document Delivery Services Branch
4th Floor, Photo Lab
10301 Baltimore Avenue
Beltsville, MD  20705-2351

Phone: 1-301-504-5994
Fax: 1-301-504-5675
World Wide Web URL: http://www.nal.usda.gov/fnic
Email Address: lending@nal.usda.gov

## Our Wonderful Body. How It Uses Food

Space explorer Zork comes from a planet where the inhabitants do not eat. He discovers why humans eat and learns about the digestive process.

| | |
|---|---|
| Availability: | Staff at schools with NET, WIC, CSFP, FDPIR, CACFP, UMD or Child Nutrition Program food programs in the United States. Those not having such an affiliation should contact their library to place an interlibrary loan request. |
| Suggested Grade: | preK-6 |
| Order Number: | NAL Video 1574 |
| Production Date: | 1992 |
| Format: | VHS videotape |
| Special Notes: | This Coronet/MIT Film and Video production includes 2 discussion guides. |

Terms: Borrower pays return postage. RETURN the day after scheduled use. Book at least 4 weeks in advance. Requests must include your name, phone, mail address, eligibility program, title, NAL number, show date, and a statement, "I have read the warning on copyright restrictions and accept full responsibility for compliance." One title per request.

Source: National Agricultural Library
Document Delivery Services Branch
4th Floor, Photo Lab
10301 Baltimore Avenue
Beltsville, MD 20705-2351
Phone: 1-301-504-5994
Fax: 1-301-504-5675
World Wide Web URL: http://www.nal.usda.gov/fnic
Email Address: lending@nal.usda.gov

## Para Vivir Bien

Explains how eating a variety of foods daily can promote good health.

| | |
|---|---|
| Availability: | Staff at schools with NET, WIC, CSFP, FDPIR, CACFP, UMD or Child Nutrition Program food programs in the United States. Those not having such an affiliation should contact their library to place an interlibrary loan request. |
| Suggested Grade: | 4-12 |
| Language: | Spanish |
| Order Number: | NAL Video 2121 |
| Production Date: | 1994 |
| Format: | VHS videotape |

Terms: Borrower pays return postage. RETURN the day after scheduled use. Book at least 4 weeks in advance. Requests must include your name, phone, mail address, eligibility program, title, NAL number, show date, and a statement, "I have read the warning on copyright restrictions and accept full responsibility for compliance." One title per request.

Source: National Agricultural Library
Document Delivery Services Branch
4th Floor, Photo Lab
10301 Baltimore Avenue
Beltsville, MD 20705-2351
Phone: 1-301-504-5994
Fax: 1-301-504-5675
World Wide Web URL: http://www.nal.usda.gov/fnic
Email Address: lending@nal.usda.gov

## Personal Nutrition Planner

A quick assessment of your personal nutrition habits and recommendations for optimizing your health according to your individual lifestyle and risk factors.

| | |
|---|---|
| Availability: | All requesters |
| Suggested Grade: | Adult |
| Order Number: | not applicable |
| Format: | Online Evaluation Tool |

Source: Dairy Council of California
World Wide Web URL:
http://www.dairycouncilofca.org/activities/pnp/
pnp_main.htm

## Pesticides and Food: What You and Your Family Need to Know

Information about the levels of exposure to pesticides in food which can cause health problems.

| | |
|---|---|
| Availability: | All requesters |
| Suggested Grade: | 4-Adult |
| Order Number: | not applicable |
| Format: | Online Article; 4 pages |
| Special Notes: | Use the on-site search engine to easily find this title. You may request a printed copy mailed to you for a fee. |

Source: Federal Citizen Information Center
World Wide Web URL: http://www.pueblo.gsa.gov/

## Picky Pedro's Adventures in Eating

Contains material to be used in the cafeteria or classroom and is intended to increase students' awareness of the benefits of eating right.

| | |
|---|---|
| Availability: | Librarians in the United States. |
| Suggested Grade: | preK-6 |
| Order Number: | Kit 306 |
| Production Date: | 1994 |
| Format: | Audiotape |
| Special Notes: | The kit includes 2 cassettes, 1 wall chart, 1 booklet, 2 fliers, and 1 duplicating master. |

Terms: Borrower pays return postage. RETURN the day after scheduled use. Book at least 4 weeks in advance. Requests must include your name, phone, mail address, eligibility program, title, NAL number, show date, and a statement, "I have read the warning on copyright restrictions and accept full responsibility for compliance." One title per request.

Source: National Agricultural Library
Document Delivery Services Branch
4th Floor, Photo Lab, 10301 Baltimore Avenue
Beltsville, MD 20705-2351

Phone: 1-301-504-5994
Fax: 1-301-504-5675
World Wide Web URL: http://www.nal.usda.gov/fnic
Email Address: lending@nal.usda.gov

## Pig Talk

A newsletter with nutrition information and puzzles about pork.

| | |
|---|---|
| Availability: | Single copies to schools, libraries, and homeschoolers in the United States. |
| Suggested Grade: | 3-6 |
| Order Number: | order by title |
| Format: | Newsletter |

Source: Minnesota Pork Board
151 St. Andrews Court, Suite 810
Mankato, MN 56001
Phone: 1-507-345-8814
Fax: 1-507-345-8681
World Wide Web URL: http://www.mnpork.com
Email Address: mnpork@mnpork.com

## Piramide del Dia con el Sabor Popular Mexicano: A Food Pyramid for Today's Mexican-American Family

Discusses the food pyramid with emphasis on foods of special interest to the Mexican culture.

| | |
|---|---|
| Availability: | Staff at schools with NET, WIC, CSFP, FDPIR, CACFP, UMD or Child Nutrition Program food programs in the United States. Those not having such an affiliation should contact their library to place an interlibrary loan request. |
| Suggested Grade: | 7-12 |
| Languages: | English and Spanish together |
| Order Number: | NAL Video 2888 |
| Production Date: | 1996 |
| Format: | VHS videotape |
| Terms: | Borrower pays return postage. RETURN the day after scheduled use. Book at least 4 weeks in advance. Requests must include your name, phone, mail address, eligibility program, title, NAL number, show date, and a statement, "I have read the warning on copyright restrictions and accept full responsibility for compliance." One title per request. |

Source: National Agricultural Library
Document Delivery Services Branch
4th Floor, Photo Lab
10301 Baltimore Avenue
Beltsville, MD 20705-2351
Phone: 1-301-504-5994
Fax: 1-301-504-5675
World Wide Web URL: http://www.nal.usda.gov/fnic
Email Address: lending@nal.usda.gov

## Plastic Fork Diaries

Follows six middle school students as they experience first-hand the relationship between food and their changing bodies, cultural differences, the vanishing family meal, nutrition, and athletic performance.

| | |
|---|---|
| Availability: | All requesters |
| Suggested Grade: | 6-8 |
| Order Number: | not applicable |
| Format: | Web Site |

Source: Maryland Public Television and Corporation for Public Broadcasting
World Wide Web URL:
http://www.plasticforkdiaries.org/index_flash.cfm

## Preschool Nutrition Education Curriculum, A, 2nd Edition

These instructional resources are designed for preschool educators. Its objective is to help 3 to 5 year-old children develop sound attitudes and knowledge about food, nutrition, health, socially acceptable behavior, and their own growth and development. It emphasizes teaching concepts relating to food and nutrition through the use of developmentally appropriate activities.

| | |
|---|---|
| Availability: | Staff at schools with NET, WIC, CSFP, FDPIR, CACFP, UMD or Child Nutrition Program food programs in the United States. Those not having such an affiliation should contact their library to place an interlibrary loan request. |
| Suggested Grade: | preK |
| Order Number: | NAL Kit 182 |
| Production Date: | 1993 |
| Format: | VHS videotape |
| Special Notes: | This Florida Department of Education kit includes a curriculum guide and a training manual. |
| Terms: | Borrower pays return postage. RETURN the day after scheduled use. Book at least 4 weeks in advance. Requests must include your name, phone, mail address, eligibility program, title, NAL number, show date, and a statement, "I have read the warning on copyright restrictions and accept full responsibility for compliance." One title per request. |

Source: National Agricultural Library
Document Delivery Services Branch
4th Floor, Photo Lab
10301 Baltimore Avenue
Beltsville, MD 20705-2351
Phone: 1-301-504-5994
Fax: 1-301-504-5675
World Wide Web URL: http://www.nal.usda.gov/fnic
Email Address: lending@nal.usda.gov

## Produce Oasis

Just click on a letter of the alphabet and find out about nutrition information for the produce that begins with that letter.

| | |
|---|---|
| Availability: | All requesters |
| Suggested Grade: | 4-12 |
| Order Number: | not applicable |
| Format: | Web Site |

Source: Produce Oasis
World Wide Web URL:
http://www.produceoasis.com/Alpha_Folder/Alpha.html

## Project 2001:  Nutrition for a New Century

Project 2001 is an invitation to schools to shape their food service around the concept of the Food Guide Pyramid.

| | |
|---|---|
| Availability: | Staff at schools with NET, WIC, CSFP, FDPIR, CACFP, UMD or Child Nutrition Program food programs in the United States. Those not having such an affiliation should contact their library to place an interlibrary loan request. |
| Suggested Grade: | Teacher Reference |
| Order Number: | NAL Video 2549 |
| Production Date: | 1997 |
| Format: | VHS videotape |
| Terms: | Borrower pays return postage.  RETURN the day after scheduled use.  Book at least 4 weeks in advance.  Requests must include your name, phone, mail address, eligibility program, title, NAL number, show date, and a statement, "I have read the warning on copyright restrictions and accept full responsibility for compliance."  One title per request. |

> **Source:  National Agricultural Library**
> **Document Delivery Services Branch**
> **4th Floor, Photo Lab**
> **10301 Baltimore Avenue**
> **Beltsville, MD  20705-2351**
> **Phone:  1-301-504-5994**
> **Fax:  1-301-504-5675**
> **World Wide Web URL:  http://www.nal.usda.gov/fnic**
> **Email Address:  lending@nal.usda.gov**

## Putting the Pyramid into Practice

Explains what the Food Guide Pyramid is and discusses how to use it.

| | |
|---|---|
| Availability: | Librarians in the United States. |
| Suggested Grade: | 7-Adult |
| Order Number: | NAL Kit 192 |
| Production Date: | 1993 |
| Format: | Set of 40 slides |
| Special Notes: | Includes a script, booklet, and lesson plans. |
| Terms: | Borrower pays return postage.  RETURN the day after scheduled use.  Book at least 4 weeks in advance.  Requests must include your name, phone, mail address, eligibility program, title, NAL number, show date, and a statement, "I have read the warning on copyright restrictions and accept full responsibility for compliance."  One title per request. |

> **Source:  National Agricultural Library**
> **Document Delivery Services Branch**
> **4th Floor, Photo Lab, 10301 Baltimore Avenue**
> **Beltsville, MD  20705-2351**
> **Phone:  1-301-504-5994**
> **Fax:  1-301-504-5675**
> **World Wide Web URL:  http://www.nal.usda.gov/fnic**
> **Email Address:  lending@nal.usda.gov**

## Que Deben Hacer Los Padres De Los Ninos Que Pesan Mucho

Offers advice to parents on their child's weight, body size and nutrition.

| | |
|---|---|
| Availability: | Staff at schools with NET, WIC, CSFP, FDPIR, CACFP, UMD or Child Nutrition Program food programs in the United States. Those not having such an affiliation should contact their library to place an interlibrary loan request. |
| Suggested Grade: | Adult |
| Language: | Spanish |
| Order Number: | NAL Video 2077 |
| Production Date: | 1991 |
| Format: | VHS videotape |
| Terms: | Borrower pays return postage.  RETURN the day after scheduled use.  Book at least 4 weeks in advance.  Requests must include your name, phone, mail address, eligibility program, title, NAL number, show date, and a statement, "I have read the warning on copyright restrictions and accept full responsibility for compliance."  One title per request. |

> **Source:  National Agricultural Library**
> **Document Delivery Services Branch**
> **4th Floor, Photo Lab**
> **10301 Baltimore Avenue**
> **Beltsville, MD  20705-2351**
> **Phone:  1-301-504-5994**
> **Fax:  1-301-504-5675**
> **World Wide Web URL:  http://www.nal.usda.gov/fnic**
> **Email Address:  lending@nal.usda.gov**

## Ralphie's Class Presents:  Keep Your Balance

This program focuses on proper eating habits and the role that food plays as fuel for the human body.  It discusses diets, fast food, fats, and processed foods in the balance process.

| | |
|---|---|
| Availability: | Staff at schools with NET, WIC, CSFP, FDPIR, CACFP, UMD or Child Nutrition Program food programs in the United States. Those not having such an affiliation should contact their library to place an interlibrary loan request. |
| Suggested Grade: | preK-6 |
| Order Number: | NAL Video 1763 |
| Production Date: | 1993 |
| Format: | VHS videotape |
| Terms: | Borrower pays return postage.  RETURN the day after scheduled use.  Book at least 4 weeks in advance.  Requests must include your name, phone, mail address, eligibility program, title, NAL number, show date, and a statement, "I have read the warning on copyright restrictions and accept full responsibility for compliance."  One title per request. |

> **Source:  National Agricultural Library**
> **Document Delivery Services Branch**
> **4th Floor, Photo Lab**
> **10301 Baltimore Avenue**
> **Beltsville, MD  20705-2351**
> **Phone:  1-301-504-5994**
> **Fax:  1-301-504-5675**
> **World Wide Web URL:  http://www.nal.usda.gov/fnic**
> **Email Address:  lending@nal.usda.gov**

## Recipes for Success

The video and cookbook in this program illustrate healthy eating styles for individuals, weight loss diets, rehabilitation programs and nutrition classes. The recipes emphasize foods with California summer fruits, and the recipes highlight dietary fiber, low sodium, low cholesterol and diabetic exchanges.

Availability: Staff at schools with NET, WIC, CSFP, FDPIR, CACFP, UMD or Child Nutrition Program food programs in the United States. Those not having such an affiliation should contact their library to place an interlibrary loan request.

Suggested Grade: 7-12
Order Number: NAL Video 847
Production Date: 1989
Format: VHS videotape
Terms: Borrower pays return postage. RETURN the day after scheduled use. Book at least 4 weeks in advance. Requests must include your name, phone, mail address, eligibility program, title, NAL number, show date, and a statement, "I have read the warning on copyright restrictions and accept full responsibility for compliance." One title per request.

Source: National Agricultural Library
Document Delivery Services Branch
4th Floor, Photo Lab
10301 Baltimore Avenue
Beltsville, MD 20705-2351
Phone: 1-301-504-5994
Fax: 1-301-504-5675
World Wide Web URL: http://www.nal.usda.gov/fnic
Email Address: lending@nal.usda.gov

## Red Riding Hood and the Well-Fed Wolf

Presents the traditional Little Red Riding Hood story with a twist. Here's the ugly wolf, all dressed up in Grandma's clothes and looking forward to a dinner of succulent Red Riding Hood; however, she and her walking talking foods have a different idea of what constitutes a good meal.

Availability: Staff at schools with NET, WIC, CSFP, FDPIR, CACFP, UMD or Child Nutrition Program food programs in the United States. Those not having such an affiliation should contact their library to place an interlibrary loan request.

Suggested Grade: 4-6
Order Number: NAL Video 2136
Production Date: 1993
Format: VHS videotape
Special Notes: A Churchill Media production.
Terms: Borrower pays return postage. RETURN the day after scheduled use. Book at least 4 weeks in advance. Requests must include your name, phone, mail address, eligibility program, title, NAL number, show date, and a statement, "I have read the warning on copyright restrictions and accept full responsibility for compliance." One title per request.

Source: National Agricultural Library
Document Delivery Services Branch
4th Floor, Photo Lab
10301 Baltimore Avenue
Beltsville, MD 20705-2351
Phone: 1-301-504-5994
Fax: 1-301-504-5675
World Wide Web URL: http://www.nal.usda.gov/fnic
Email Address: lending@nal.usda.gov

## Reflections and Recipes: A Workshop Model for School Food Service Personnel

Focuses on methods of preparation, meal service and promotion that provide consistent high quality foods that appeal to students.

Availability: Librarians in the United States.
Suggested Grade: Teacher Reference
Order Number: 338
Production Date: 1996
Format: Set of 47 slides
Terms: Borrower pays return postage. RETURN the day after scheduled use. Book at least 4 weeks in advance. Requests must include your name, phone, mail address, eligibility program, title, NAL number, show date, and a statement, "I have read the warning on copyright restrictions and accept full responsibility for compliance." One title per request.

Source: National Agricultural Library
Document Delivery Services Branch
4th Floor, Photo Lab
10301 Baltimore Avenue
Beltsville, MD 20705-2351
Phone: 1-301-504-5994
Fax: 1-301-504-5675
World Wide Web URL: http://www.nal.usda.gov/fnic
Email Address: lending@nal.usda.gov

## Road to Change, The

This self-instructional nutrition video and guidebook assist child nutrition staff in improving nutritional status through implementing the Dietary Guidelines. Both show realistic ways to change food gradually in school settings.

Availability: Staff at schools with NET, WIC, CSFP, FDPIR, CACFP, UMD or Child Nutrition Program food programs in the United States. Those not having such an affiliation should contact their library to place an interlibrary loan request.

Suggested Grade: Adult
Order Number: NAL Video 1112
Production Date: 1991
Format: VHS videotape
Terms: Borrower pays return postage. RETURN the day after scheduled use. Book at least 4 weeks in advance. Requests must include your name, phone, mail address, eligibility program, title, NAL number, show date, and a statement, "I have read the warning on copyright restrictions and accept full responsibility for compliance." One title per request.

## Room at the Table: Meeting Children's Special Needs at Mealtime
Offers child care providers mealtime strategies.

Availability: Staff at schools with NET, WIC, CSFP, FDPIR, CACFP, UMD or Child Nutrition Program food programs in the United States. Those not having such an affiliation should contact their library to place an interlibrary loan request.
Suggested Grade: Adult
Order Number: NAL Video 2807
Production Date: 1996
Format: VHS videotape
Terms: Borrower pays return postage. RETURN the day after scheduled use. Book at least 4 weeks in advance. Requests must include your name, phone, mail address, eligibility program, title, NAL number, show date, and a statement, "I have read the warning on copyright restrictions and accept full responsibility for compliance." One title per request.

## Safety First
A panel of food safety experts provides information and answers to questions about irradiated beef.

Availability: Staff at schools with NET, WIC, CSFP, FDPIR, CACFP, UMD or Child Nutrition Program food programs in the United States. Those not having such an affiliation should contact their library to place an interlibrary loan request.
Suggested Grade: Teacher Reference
Order Number: NAL DVD No. 14
Production Date: 2003
Format: DVD
Terms: Borrower pays return postage. RETURN the day after scheduled use. Book at least 4 weeks in advance. Requests must include your name, phone, mail address, eligibility program, title, NAL number, show date, and a statement, "I have read the warning on copyright restrictions and accept full responsibility for compliance." One title per request.

## Safety First
A panel of food safety experts provides information and answers to questions about irradiated beef.

Availability: Staff at schools with NET, WIC, CSFP, FDPIR, CACFP, UMD or Child Nutrition Program food programs in the United States. Those not having such an affiliation should contact their library to place an interlibrary loan request.
Suggested Grade: Teacher Reference
Order Number: NAL Video 3321
Production Date: 2003
Format: VHS videotape
Terms: Borrower pays return postage. RETURN the day after scheduled use. Book at least 4 weeks in advance. Requests must include your name, phone, mail address, eligibility program, title, NAL number, show date, and a statement, "I have read the warning on copyright restrictions and accept full responsibility for compliance." One title per request.

## Sanitary and Unsanitary Food Habits
Students will learn the difference between sanitary and unsanitary food habits.

Availability: All requesters
Suggested Grade: 4-5
Order Number: not applicable
Format: Online Lesson Plan
Source: Anne Gostonczik
World Wide Web URL: http://www.eduref.org/Virtual/Lessons/Health/Safety/SFY0010.html

## Sante7000
This online program looks up a table of 7,248 foods selected from the USDA survey database and identifies 29 nutrients.

Availability: All requesters
Suggested Grade: All ages
Order Number: not applicable

*All materials listed in this 2018-2019 edition are BRAND NEW!*

# HEALTH--FOOD AND NUTRITION

Format:        Online Program
**Source: Hopkins Technology, LLC
World Wide Web URL:
http://www.hoptechno.com/nightcrew/sante7000/
sante7000_search.cfm**

## Science Goes on a Diet
Shows a translucency test to detect fat in foods, calorie calculation of a peanut using a calorimeter, color expenditure, and more.

Availability:        Staff at schools with NET, WIC, CSFP, FDPIR, CACFP, UMD or Child Nutrition Program food programs in the United States. Those not having such an affiliation should contact their library to place an interlibrary loan request.
Suggested Grade:    7-12
Order Number:       NAL Video 1889
Production Date:    1994
Format:             VHS videotape
Terms:    Borrower pays return postage. RETURN the day after scheduled use. Book at least 4 weeks in advance. Requests must include your name, phone, mail address, eligibility program, title, NAL number, show date, and a statement, "I have read the warning on copyright restrictions and accept full responsibility for compliance." One title per request.

**Source: National Agricultural Library
Document Delivery Services Branch
4th Floor, Photo Lab, 10301 Baltimore Avenue
Beltsville, MD  20705-2351
Phone: 1-301-504-5994
Fax: 1-301-504-5675
World Wide Web URL: http://www.nal.usda.gov/fnic
Email Address: lending@nal.usda.gov**

## Shopping for Heart Health:  Lower Your Blood Cholesterol and Reduce Your Risk of Coronary Artery Disease
Features five guidelines for making smart choices at the supermarket and tips for moving toward a healthier, plant-based eating style.

Availability:        Staff at schools with NET, WIC, CSFP, FDPIR, CACFP, UMD or Child Nutrition Program food programs in the United States. Those not having such an affiliation should contact their library to place an interlibrary loan request.
Suggested Grade:    7-12
Order Number:       NAL Video 2621
Production Date:    1997
Format:             VHS videotape
Terms:    Borrower pays return postage. RETURN the day after scheduled use. Book at least 4 weeks in advance. Requests must include your name, phone, mail address, eligibility program, title, NAL number, show date, and a statement, "I have read the warning on copyright restrictions and accept full responsibility for compliance." One title per request.

**Source: National Agricultural Library
Document Delivery Services Branch
4th Floor, Photo Lab
10301 Baltimore Avenue
Beltsville, MD  20705-2351
Phone: 1-301-504-5994
Fax: 1-301-504-5675
World Wide Web URL: http://www.nal.usda.gov/fnic
Email Address: lending@nal.usda.gov**

## Smart Selections for Healthy Eating
Explains how the new food label offers more complete nutrition and health information than previous labels. Comedienne Carol Leifer walks through the aisles of a grocery store examining labels of various items.

Availability:        Staff at schools with NET, WIC, CSFP, FDPIR, CACFP, UMD or Child Nutrition Program food programs in the United States. Those not having such an affiliation should contact their library to place an interlibrary loan request.
Suggested Grade:    7-Adult
Order Number:       NAL Video 1600
Production Date:    1993
Format:             VHS videotape
Special Notes:      This Public Voice for Food and Health Policy production includes a booklet.
Terms:    Borrower pays return postage. RETURN the day after scheduled use. Book at least 4 weeks in advance. Requests must include your name, phone, mail address, eligibility program, title, NAL number, show date, and a statement, "I have read the warning on copyright restrictions and accept full responsibility for compliance." One title per request.

**Source: National Agricultural Library
Document Delivery Services Branch
4th Floor, Photo Lab
10301 Baltimore Avenue
Beltsville, MD  20705-2351
Phone: 1-301-504-5994
Fax: 1-301-504-5675
World Wide Web URL: http://www.nal.usda.gov/fnic
Email Address: lending@nal.usda.gov**

## Smart Snacking for Children
Demonstrates that snacking can be an opportunity to give children important nutrients, rather than junk food.  It stresses the importance of being prepared, sticking to a schedule when possible, and having children help in snack preparation.

Availability:        Staff at schools with NET, WIC, CSFP, FDPIR, CACFP, UMD or Child Nutrition Program food programs in the United States. Those not having such an affiliation should contact their library to place an interlibrary loan request.
Suggested Grade:    preK-6
Order Number:       NAL Video 2074
Production Date:    1994

*All materials listed in this 2018-2019 edition are **BRAND NEW!***

Format: VHS videotape

Terms: Borrower pays return postage. RETURN the day after scheduled use. Book at least 4 weeks in advance. Requests must include your name, phone, mail address, eligibility program, title, NAL number, show date, and a statement, "I have read the warning on copyright restrictions and accept full responsibility for compliance." One title per request.

**Source: National Agricultural Library**
**Document Delivery Services Branch**
**4th Floor, Photo Lab**
**10301 Baltimore Avenue**
**Beltsville, MD 20705-2351**
**Phone: 1-301-504-5994**
**Fax: 1-301-504-5675**
**World Wide Web URL: http://www.nal.usda.gov/fnic**
**Email Address: lending@nal.usda.gov**

## Snack Attack

On their way to grab a snack in a supermarket, siblings Fred and Virginia encounter some talkative produce that persuades them to choose fresh, healthy alternatives to chips and cookies.

Availability: All requesters
Suggested Grade: 3-6
Order Number: not applicable
Format: Downloadable Theater Script

**Source: Cara Bafile**
**World Wide Web URL:**
**http://www.educationworld.com/a_curr/**
**reading/ReadersTheater/ReadersTheater026.shtml**

## Snacking Mouse

This is the saga of the cartoon character, Snacking Mouse, whose appetite for sweet and salty snacks makes him too fat for the mouse hole. It is designed to discourage children from excessive snacking, and introduces them to nutritious snack foods.

Availability: Staff at schools with NET, WIC, CSFP, FDPIR, CACFP, UMD or Child Nutrition Program food programs in the United States. Those not having such an affiliation should contact their library to place an interlibrary loan request.

Suggested Grade: preK-6
Order Number: NAL Video 2212
Production Date: 1977
Format: VHS videotape

Terms: Borrower pays return postage. RETURN the day after scheduled use. Book at least 4 weeks in advance. Requests must include your name, phone, mail address, eligibility program, title, NAL number, show date, and a statement, "I have read the warning on copyright restrictions and accept full responsibility for compliance." One title per request.

**Source: National Agricultural Library**
**Document Delivery Services Branch**
**4th Floor, Photo Lab, 10301 Baltimore Avenue**
**Beltsville, MD 20705-2351**

Phone: 1-301-504-5994
Fax: 1-301-504-5675
World Wide Web URL: http://www.nal.usda.gov/fnic
Email Address: lending@nal.usda.gov

## Sports and Nutrition: The Winning Connection

Explores the relationship between sports and exercise and the food you need to supply the energy needed.

Availability: All requesters
Suggested Grade: 6-Adult
Order Number: not applicable
Format: Web Site

**Source: University of Illinois Extension Urban Programs**
**Resource Network**
**World Wide Web URL:**
**http://www.urbanext.uiuc.edu/hsnut/index.html**

## Starting Smarter

Surveys school breakfast programs in Illinois. The video discusses how a program is established, the importance of coordinating the arrival of children to school with the eating of their breakfast, supervision of the food preparation staff, and menu selection.

Availability: Staff at schools with NET, WIC, CSFP, FDPIR, CACFP, UMD or Child Nutrition Program food programs in the United States. Those not having such an affiliation should contact their library to place an interlibrary loan request.

Suggested Grade: Teacher Reference
Order Number: NAL Video 1588
Production Date: 1992
Format: VHS videotape

Terms: Borrower pays return postage. RETURN the day after scheduled use. Book at least 4 weeks in advance. Requests must include your name, phone, mail address, eligibility program, title, NAL number, show date, and a statement, "I have read the warning on copyright restrictions and accept full responsibility for compliance." One title per request.

**Source: National Agricultural Library**
**Document Delivery Services Branch**
**4th Floor, Photo Lab**
**10301 Baltimore Avenue**
**Beltsville, MD 20705-2351**
**Phone: 1-301-504-5994**
**Fax: 1-301-504-5675**
**World Wide Web URL: http://www.nal.usda.gov/fnic**
**Email Address: lending@nal.usda.gov**

## Stay Young at Heart Recipes

A multitude of recipes for preparing delicious foods low in cholesterol.

Availability: One copy is free to schools, libraries, and homeschoolers world-wide. Shipping charges will apply if more than one publication is requested.

Suggested Grade: 4-12
Order Number: 55-648

Format:          Booklet
Special Notes:   May also be downloaded from the web site.
**Source: National Heart, Lung, and Blood Institute**
**Information Center**
**P. O. Box 30105**
**Bethesda, MD   20824-0105**
**Phone:  1-301-592-8573**
**Fax:  1-240-629-3246**
**World Wide Web URL:  http://www.nhlbi.nih.gov/**
**Email Address:  nhlbiinfo@nhlbi.nih.gov**

## Story of Wheat, The
Explains the production, marketing, and nutritional value of hard red spring wheat and durum wheat.  Includes activities.
Availability:      Single copies to schools, libraries, and homeschoolers in the United States.
Suggested Grade:  4-6
Order Number:    order by title
Format:          Booklet; 20 pages
**Source: North Dakota Wheat Commission**
**2401  46th Avenue SE, Suite 104**
**Mandan, ND   58554-4829**
**Phone:  1-701-328-5111**
**Fax:  1-701-663-5787**
**World Wide Web URL:  http://www.ndwheat.com**
**Email Address:  ndwheat@ndwheat.com**

## Summer Vacation with Sammy Spaghetti and Becky Bread
Explains the production and nutritional value of wheat raised in North Dakota.  Activities included.
Availability:      Single copies to schools, libraries, and homeschoolers in the United States.
Suggested Grade:  K-2
Order Number:    order by title
Format:          Activity and Story Book
**Source: North Dakota Wheat Commission**
**2401  46th Avenue SE, Suite 104**
**Mandan, ND   58554-4829**
**Phone:  1-701-328-5111**
**Fax:  1-701-663-5787**
**World Wide Web URL:  http://www.ndwheat.com**
**Email Address:  ndwheat@ndwheat.com**

## Teaching for a Lifetime:  Nutrition Education for Young Children
This program is designed to provide training in doing nutrition education with young children.
Availability:      Staff at schools with NET, WIC, CSFP, FDPIR, CACFP, UMD or Child Nutrition Program food programs in the United States.  Those not having such an affiliation should contact their library to place an interlibrary loan request.
Suggested Grade:  Adult
Order Number:    NAL Video 2145
Production Date:  1994
Format:          VHS videotape

Special Notes:   This Walters & Steinberg Productions video includes a resource manual.
Terms:   Borrower pays return postage.  RETURN the day after scheduled use.  Book at least 4 weeks in advance.  Requests must include your name, phone, mail address, eligibility program, title, NAL number, show date, and a statement, "I have read the warning on copyright restrictions and accept full responsibility for compliance."  One title per request.
**Source: National Agricultural Library**
**Document Delivery Services Branch**
**4th Floor, Photo Lab**
**10301 Baltimore Avenue**
**Beltsville, MD   20705-2351**
**Phone:  1-301-504-5994**
**Fax:  1-301-504-5675**
**World Wide Web URL:  http://www.nal.usda.gov/fnic**
**Email Address:  lending@nal.usda.gov**

## TerminEater
The TerminEater, a cyborg sent back from the future, teaches 11-year-old John Conner five simple ways to reduce fat in his diet without giving up his favorite foods, friends, or flavor.
Availability:      Staff at schools with NET, WIC, CSFP, FDPIR, CACFP, UMD or Child Nutrition Program food programs in the United States.  Those not having such an affiliation should contact their library to place an interlibrary loan request.
Suggested Grade:  preK-6
Order Number:    NAL Video 1583
Production Date:  1993
Format:          VHS videotape
Special Notes:   This Dream Street Films production includes an instructor's guide.
Terms:   Borrower pays return postage.  RETURN the day after scheduled use.  Book at least 4 weeks in advance.  Requests must include your name, phone, mail address, eligibility program, title, NAL number, show date, and a statement, "I have read the warning on copyright restrictions and accept full responsibility for compliance."  One title per request.
**Source: National Agricultural Library**
**Document Delivery Services Branch**
**4th Floor, Photo Lab, 10301 Baltimore Avenue**
**Beltsville, MD   20705-2351**
**Phone:  1-301-504-5994**
**Fax:  1-301-504-5675**
**World Wide Web URL:  http://www.nal.usda.gov/fnic**
**Email Address:  lending@nal.usda.gov**

## USDA's Great Nutrition Adventure
This project involves the forming of a partnership between chefs in America's finest restaurants with those in the food service community.  The goal of this partnership is to assist food service staff in the preparation of nutritious, tasty food and to excite and motivate children to make healthy food choices.

Availability: Staff at schools with NET, WIC, CSFP, FDPIR, CACFP, UMD or Child Nutrition Program food programs in the United States. Those not having such an affiliation should contact their library to place an interlibrary loan request.
Suggested Grade: Adult
Order Number: NAL Video 2189
Format: VHS videotape
Terms: Borrower pays return postage. RETURN the day after scheduled use. Book at least 4 weeks in advance. Requests must include your name, phone, mail address, eligibility program, title, NAL number, show date, and a statement, "I have read the warning on copyright restrictions and accept full responsibility for compliance." One title per request.
**Source: National Agricultural Library**
**Document Delivery Services Branch**
**4th Floor, Photo Lab**
**10301 Baltimore Avenue**
**Beltsville, MD 20705-2351**
**Phone: 1-301-504-5994**
**Fax: 1-301-504-5675**
**World Wide Web URL: http://www.nal.usda.gov/fnic**
**Email Address: lending@nal.usda.gov**

## Using the Dietary Guidelines for Americans
How to choose a diet that tastes good, is nutritious, and will reduce chronic disease risks.
Availability: All requesters
Suggested Grade: 6-Adult
Order Number: not applicable
Format: Online Article; 2 pages
Special Notes: Use the on-site search engine to easily find this title. You may request a printed copy mailed to you for a fee.
**Source: Federal Citizen Information Center**
**World Wide Web URL: http://www.pueblo.gsa.gov/**

## Vegan Diets in a Nutshell
Addresses the nutrition basics of vegan diets.
Availability: Classroom quantities to schools, libraries, and homeschoolers world-wide. Send a stamped, self-addressed envelope for reply.
Suggested Grade: 4-Adult
Order Number: order by title
Format: Brochure
**Source: Vegetarian Resource Group, The**
**P. O. Box 1463**
**Baltimore, MD 21203**
**Phone: 1-410-366-8343**
**Fax: 1-410-366-8804**
**World Wide Web URL: http://www.vrg.org**
**Email Address: vrg@vrg.org**

## What's on Your Plate
This program features claymation figure Willie Munchright presenting nutrition education to children.

Availability: Staff at schools with NET, WIC, CSFP, FDPIR, CACFP, UMD or Child Nutrition Program food programs in the United States. Those not having such an affiliation should contact their library to place an interlibrary loan request.
Suggested Grade: preK-6
Order Number: NAL Video 2268
Format: VHS videotape
Terms: Borrower pays return postage. RETURN the day after scheduled use. Book at least 4 weeks in advance. Requests must include your name, phone, mail address, eligibility program, title, NAL number, show date, and a statement, "I have read the warning on copyright restrictions and accept full responsibility for compliance." One title per request.
**Source: National Agricultural Library**
**Document Delivery Services Branch**
**4th Floor, Photo Lab**
**10301 Baltimore Avenue**
**Beltsville, MD 20705-2351**
**Phone: 1-301-504-5994**
**Fax: 1-301-504-5675**
**World Wide Web URL: http://www.nal.usda.gov/fnic**
**Email Address: lending@nal.usda.gov**

## When I Grow Up
Teaches young children what they need to do to "grow up and be what you want to be," and then focuses on nutrition by studying the Food Guide Pyramid. Includes intermissions for class discussion.
Availability: Staff at schools with NET, WIC, CSFP, FDPIR, CACFP, UMD or Child Nutrition Program food programs in the United States. Those not having such an affiliation should contact their library to place an interlibrary loan request.
Suggested Grade: preK-6
Order Number: NAL Video 2023
Production Date: 1994
Format: VHS videotape
Special Notes: Includes a teacher's guide and duplication masters.
Terms: Borrower pays return postage. RETURN the day after scheduled use. Book at least 4 weeks in advance. Requests must include your name, phone, mail address, eligibility program, title, NAL number, show date, and a statement, "I have read the warning on copyright restrictions and accept full responsibility for compliance." One title per request.
**Source: National Agricultural Library**
**Document Delivery Services Branch**
**4th Floor, Photo Lab**
**10301 Baltimore Avenue**
**Beltsville, MD 20705-2351**
**Phone: 1-301-504-5994**
**Fax: 1-301-504-5675**
**World Wide Web URL: http://www.nal.usda.gov/fnic**
**Email Address: lending@nal.usda.gov**

# HEALTH--FOOD AND NUTRITION

**You Are What You Eat: A Guide to Good Nutrition**
How does your diet measure up? Why is nutrition so important?

| | |
|---|---|
| Availability: | All requesters |
| Suggested Grade: | 6-12 |
| Order Number: | not applicable |
| Format: | Web Site |
| Special Notes: | This URL will lead you to a subject page. Then click on the appropriate subject heading. |

Source: ThinkQuest
World Wide Web URL:
http://www.thinkquest.org/pls/html/think.library

**Your Active Body: Digestion and Absorption**
Designed to introduce young people to the processes of digesting food and absorbing the nutrients from that food. Presented in a zoo-type setting for easy comparison.

| | |
|---|---|
| Availability: | Staff at schools with NET, WIC, CSFP, FDPIR, CACFP, UMD or Child Nutrition Program food programs in the United States. Those not having such an affiliation should contact their library to place an interlibrary loan request. |
| Suggested Grade: | preK-6 |
| Order Number: | NAL Video 752 |
| Production Date: | 1987 |
| Format: | VHS videotape |
| Terms: | Borrower pays return postage. RETURN the day after scheduled use. Book at least 4 weeks in advance. Requests must include your name, phone, mail address, eligibility program, title, NAL number, show date, and a statement, "I have read the warning on copyright restrictions and accept full responsibility for compliance." One title per request. |

Source: National Agricultural Library
Document Delivery Services Branch
4th Floor, Photo Lab
10301 Baltimore Avenue
Beltsville, MD 20705-2351
Phone: 1-301-504-5994
Fax: 1-301-504-5675
World Wide Web URL: http://www.nal.usda.gov/fnic
Email Address: lending@nal.usda.gov

**Your Body, Your Diet, and Cholesterol**
This program on cardiovascular disease discusses the risk factors associated with the disease, the role of diet (particularly fats and cholesterol), and stresses the importance of having your blood cholesterol and blood pressure checked regularly.

| | |
|---|---|
| Availability: | Staff at schools with NET, WIC, CSFP, FDPIR, CACFP, UMD or Child Nutrition Program food programs in the United States. Those not having such an affiliation should contact their library to place an interlibrary loan request. |
| Suggested Grade: | 7-12 |
| Order Number: | NAL Video 441 |
| Production Date: | 1989 |

| | |
|---|---|
| Format: | VHS videotape |
| Terms: | Borrower pays return postage. RETURN the day after scheduled use. Book at least 4 weeks in advance. Requests must include your name, phone, mail address, eligibility program, title, NAL number, show date, and a statement, "I have read the warning on copyright restrictions and accept full responsibility for compliance." One title per request. |

Source: National Agricultural Library
Document Delivery Services Branch
4th Floor, Photo Lab
10301 Baltimore Avenue
Beltsville, MD 20705-2351
Phone: 1-301-504-5994
Fax: 1-301-504-5675
World Wide Web URL: http://www.nal.usda.gov/fnic
Email Address: lending@nal.usda.gov

**YourSELF: Middle School Nutrition Education Kit**
Developed to help middle school students understand how their decisions about eating patterns and physical activity can affect the way they grow and their future health.

| | |
|---|---|
| Availability: | Staff at schools with NET, WIC, CSFP, FDPIR, CACFP, UMD or Child Nutrition Program food programs in the United States. Those not having such an affiliation should contact their library to place an interlibrary loan request. |
| Suggested Grade: | 5-8 |
| Order Number: | NAL Kit 512 |
| Production Date: | 1998 |
| Format: | VHS videotape |
| Special Notes: | Includes a teacher's guide and student activity guides. |
| Terms: | Borrower pays return postage. RETURN the day after scheduled use. Book at least 4 weeks in advance. Requests must include your name, phone, mail address, eligibility program, title, NAL number, show date, and a statement, "I have read the warning on copyright restrictions and accept full responsibility for compliance." One title per request. |

Source: National Agricultural Library
Document Delivery Services Branch
4th Floor, Photo Lab
10301 Baltimore Avenue
Beltsville, MD 20705-2351
Phone: 1-301-504-5994
Fax: 1-301-504-5675
World Wide Web URL: http://www.nal.usda.gov/fnic
Email Address: lending@nal.usda.gov

## Anxiety Disorders

Discusses treatments available and resources to contact for more information on panic phobias, stress, obsessive compulsive, and other disorders.

Availability:        All requesters
Suggested Grade:  4-Adult
Order Number:     not applicable
Format:            Online Article; 24 pages
Special Notes:     Use the on-site search engine to easily find this title.  You may request a printed copy mailed to you for a fee.

**Source:  Federal Citizen Information Center**
**World Wide Web URL:  http://www.pueblo.gsa.gov/**

## Anxiety--Fact Sheet

Describes different types of anxiety disorders and what you can do if you recognize these symptoms in yourself or a loved one.

Availability:        All requesters
Suggested Grade:  4-Adult
Order Number:     not applicable
Production Date:  2001
Format:            Online Article; 4 pages
Special Notes:     Use the on-site search engine to easily find this title.  You may request a printed copy mailed to you for a fee.

**Source:  Federal Citizen Information Center**
**World Wide Web URL:  http://www.pueblo.gsa.gov/**

## Backstroke

Danny, a high school student, fears he has AIDS and exhibits erratic mood swings. His friends can't figure him out, but Mr. Gray, a teacher, believes Danny may be suicidal, and decides to intervene. Explores some of the danger signals of a potentially suicidal person and suggests ways to deal with the individual.

Availability:        Schools, libraries, and homeschoolers in the United States who serve the hearing impaired.
Suggested Grade:  9-12
Order Number:     12377
Production Date:  1997
Format:            DVD
Special Notes:     Produced by Aims Multimedia.
Terms:            Sponsor pays all transportation costs.  Return one week after receipt.  Participation is limited to deaf or hard of hearing Americans, their parents, families, teachers, counselors, or others whose use would benefit a deaf or hard of hearing person.  Only one person in the audience needs to be hearing impaired.  You must register--which is free.  These videos are all open-captioned--no special equipment is required for viewing.

**Source:  Described and Captioned Media Program**
**National Association of the Deaf**
**4211 Church Street Ext.**
**Roebuck, SC  29376**
**Phone:  1-800-237-6213**
**Fax:  1-800-538-5636**
**World Wide Web URL:  http://www.dcmp.org**

## Bodies in Motion Minds at Rest

Sensible recommendations for diet and exercise, self esteem, parental divorce, and school stress.

Availability:        All requesters
Suggested Grade:  6-12
Order Number:     not applicable
Format:            Web Site
Special Notes:     This URL will lead you to a subject page.  Then click on the appropriate subject heading.

**Source:  ThinkQuest**
**World Wide Web URL:**
**http://www.thinkquest.org/pls/html/think.library**

## Depression and Disability in Children and Adolescents

Focuses on major depressive disorder, dysthymic disorder, and bipolar disorder as they are exhibited in childhood and adolescence.  Discusses their symptoms, casual factors, and treatment.

Availability:        All requesters
Suggested Grade:  Teacher Reference
Order Number:     not applicable
Production Date:  2003
Format:            Online Article

**Source:  Eleanor Guetzloe**
**World Wide Web URL:**
**http://www.ericdigests.org/2005-1/depression.htm**

## Dying to Be Thin

Life-threatening eating disorders such as anorexia and bulimia are on the rise among America's youth.

Availability:        All requesters
Suggested Grade:  7-Adult
Order Number:     not applicable
Production Date:  2000
Format:            Streaming Video

**Source:  NOVA**
**World Wide Web URL:**
**http://www.pbs.org/wgbh/nova/programs/index.html**

## Eating Disorder Awareness Website

Develop insight and power against diseases of Anorexia, Binge eating and Bulimia.

Availability:        All requesters
Suggested Grade:  6-12
Order Number:     not applicable
Format:            Web Site
Special Notes:     This URL will lead you to a subject page.  Then click on the appropriate subject heading.

**Source:  ThinkQuest**
**World Wide Web URL:**
**http://www.thinkquest.org/pls/html/think.library**

## Eating Disorders

Recognize the symptoms of different eating disorders, who is most likely to be affected, and various treatment options.

Availability:        All requesters
Suggested Grade:  4-Adult
Order Number:     not applicable

Production Date: 2001
Format: Online Article; 8 pages
Special Notes: Use the on-site search engine to easily find this title. You may request a printed copy mailed to you for a fee.
**Source: Federal Citizen Information Center**
**World Wide Web URL: http://www.pueblo.gsa.gov/**

## Eating Disorders
Compelling interviews with several young people who suffered from anorexia nervosa, bulimia, and compulsive overeating, provide a living portrait of these devastating diseases. Experts in the field discuss treatments available, the causes and symptoms o the diseases, and techniques of prevention and detection.
Availability: Staff at schools with NET, WIC, CSFP, FDPIR, CACFP, UMD or Child Nutrition Program food programs in the United States. Those not having such an affiliation should contact their library to place an interlibrary loan request.
Suggested Grade: 7-12
Order Number: NAL Video 2273
Production Date: 1994
Format: VHS videotape
Terms: Borrower pays return postage. RETURN the day after scheduled use. Book at least 4 weeks in advance. Requests must include your name, phone, mail address, eligibility program, title, NAL number, show date, and a statement, "I have read the warning on copyright restrictions and accept full responsibility for compliance." One title per request.
**Source: National Agricultural Library**
**Document Delivery Services Branch**
**4th Floor, Photo Lab**
**10301 Baltimore Avenue**
**Beltsville, MD 20705-2351**
**Phone: 1-301-504-5994**
**Fax: 1-301-504-5675**
**World Wide Web URL: http://www.nal.usda.gov/fnic**
**Email Address: lending@nal.usda.gov**

## Eating Disorders Awareness and Prevention Materials
Presents a number of articles on what eating disorders are and how you can help yourself--and others--who suffer from this problem.
Availability: All requesters
Suggested Grade: 4-Adult
Order Number: not applicable
Format: Web Site
**Source: Eating Disorders Awareness and Prevention, Inc.**
**World Wide Web URL: http://nationaleatingdisorders.org/**

## Eating Disorders for Teens
Explains eating disorders and presents information designed to help prevent them.
Availability: All requesters
Suggested Grade: 6-12

Order Number: not applicable
Format: Web Site
Special Notes: This URL will lead you to a subject page. Then click on the appropriate subject heading.
**Source: ThinkQuest**
**World Wide Web URL:**
**http://www.thinkquest.org/pls/html/think.library**

## Eating Disorders You Are Not Alone
This video defines anorexia nervosa, bulimia, and compulsive overeating. By including case studies of recovering patients and showing how they started and what the treatment is, the video helps teenagers understand such eating disorders and offers hope to those in their grip.
Availability: Staff at schools with NET, WIC, CSFP, FDPIR, CACFP, UMD or Child Nutrition Program food programs in the United States. Those not having such an affiliation should contact their library to place an interlibrary loan request.
Suggested Grade: 6-12
Order Number: NAL Video 988
Production Date: 1995
Format: VHS videotape
Terms: Borrower pays return postage. RETURN the day after scheduled use. Book at least 4 weeks in advance. Requests must include your name, phone, mail address, eligibility program, title, NAL number, show date, and a statement, "I have read the warning on copyright restrictions and accept full responsibility for compliance." One title per request.
**Source: National Agricultural Library**
**Document Delivery Services Branch**
**4th Floor, Photo Lab**
**10301 Baltimore Avenue**
**Beltsville, MD 20705-2351**
**Phone: 1-301-504-5994**
**Fax: 1-301-504-5675**
**World Wide Web URL: http://www.nal.usda.gov/fnic**
**Email Address: lending@nal.usda.gov**

## Food for Thought
Features science writer Roger Bingham in a fascinating update of information first presented in the film "Diet for a Small Planet" about the environmental consequences of a meat-centered diet. Using the example of an automobile, Bingham explains the inefficiency of using meat as fuel for the human body.
Availability: Schools, libraries, homeschoolers, and nursing homes in the United States.
Suggested Grade: 6-Adult
Order Number: order by title
Production Date: 1990
Format: VHS videotape
Terms: Borrower pays return postage. Return the day after scheduled showing, via UPS or Priority Mail, insured for $100.00. Book 4 weeks in advance and include an alternate date. Order should include name of person responsible for handling the video, and complete

mailing address. Please mention this Guide when ordering. Tapes may not be duplicated, edited or exhibited for a fee.

**Source: Church World Service**
**Film & Video Library**
**28606 Phillips Street, P. O. Box 968**
**Elkhart, IN 46515**
**Phone: 1-800-297-1516, ext. 338**
**Fax: 1-574-262-0966**
**World Wide Web URL: http://www.churchworldservice.org**
**Email Address: videos@churchworldservice.org**

## Food for Thought

Kathleen strives to win first place in the science fair while denying her symptoms of anorexia nervosa.

Availability: Staff at schools with NET, WIC, CSFP, FDPIR, CACFP, UMD or Child Nutrition Program food programs in the United States. Those not having such an affiliation should contact their library to place an interlibrary loan request.
Suggested Grade: 6-12
Order Number: NAL Video 1030
Format: VHS videotape
Terms: Borrower pays return postage. RETURN the day after scheduled use. Book at least 4 weeks in advance. Requests must include your name, phone, mail address, eligibility program, title, NAL number, show date, and a statement, "I have read the warning on copyright restrictions and accept full responsibility for compliance." One title per request.

**Source: National Agricultural Library**
**Document Delivery Services Branch**
**4th Floor, Photo Lab**
**10301 Baltimore Avenue**
**Beltsville, MD 20705-2351**
**Phone: 1-301-504-5994**
**Fax: 1-301-504-5675**
**World Wide Web URL: http://www.nal.usda.gov/fnic**
**Email Address: lending@nal.usda.gov**

## I Can't Stand It! - Phobias

Explores and explains phobias.

Availability: All requesters
Suggested Grade: All ages
Order Number: not applicable
Format: Web Site
Special Notes: This URL will lead you to a subject page. Then click on the appropriate subject heading.

**Source: ThinkQuest**
**World Wide Web URL:**
**http://www.thinkquest.org/pls/html/think.library**

## Real People Coping with Eating Disorders

This program documents the stories of three young people recovering from the eating disorders bulimia and anorexia nervosa.

---

Availability: Staff at schools with NET, WIC, CSFP, FDPIR, CACFP, UMD or Child Nutrition Program food programs in the United States. Those not having such an affiliation should contact their library to place an interlibrary loan request.
Suggested Grade: 7-12
Order Number: NAL Video 778
Production Date: 1989
Format: VHS videotape
Terms: Borrower pays return postage. RETURN the day after scheduled use. Book at least 4 weeks in advance. Requests must include your name, phone, mail address, eligibility program, title, NAL number, show date, and a statement, "I have read the warning on copyright restrictions and accept full responsibility for compliance." One title per request.

**Source: National Agricultural Library**
**Document Delivery Services Branch**
**4th Floor, Photo Lab**
**10301 Baltimore Avenue**
**Beltsville, MD 20705-2351**
**Phone: 1-301-504-5994**
**Fax: 1-301-504-5675**
**World Wide Web URL: http://www.nal.usda.gov/fnic**
**Email Address: lending@nal.usda.gov**

## Something Fishy Website on Eating Disorders, The

This website provides lots of information on eating disorders--what they are, who suffers from them, how to help others as well as yourself, and more.

Availability: All requesters
Suggested Grade: 6-12
Order Number: not applicable
Format: Web Site

**Source: Something Fishy Music & Publishing**
**World Wide Web URL: http://www.something-fishy.org/**

## Stress Double Dealer

Learn tips to cope with stress, as well as illnesses caused or made worse by stress.

Availability: All requesters
Suggested Grade: 4-12
IANGUAGES: English; Japanese
Order Number: not applicable
Format: Web Site
Special Notes: This URL will lead you to a subject page. Then click on the appropriate subject heading.

**Source: ThinkQuest**
**World Wide Web URL:**
**http://www.thinkquest.org/pls/html/think.library**

## Teens and Stress

Learn about the causes and results of stress and ways to prevent it.

Availability: All requesters
Suggested Grade: 6-12
IANGUAGES: English; Dutch; French; Spanish
Order Number: not applicable

Format: Web Site
Special Notes: This URL will lead you to a subject page.
Then click on the appropriate subject heading.
**Source: ThinkQuest**
**World Wide Web URL:**
**http://www.thinkquest.org/pls/html/think.library**

## Understanding Eating Disorders

Covers topics through professional information and real-life experiences with anorexia nervosa, bulimia and binge eating.

Availability: Staff at schools with NET, WIC, CSFP, FDPIR, CACFP, UMD or Child Nutrition Program food programs in the United States. Those not having such an affiliation should contact their library to place an interlibrary loan request.

Suggested Grade: 7-12
Order Number: NAL Video 3283
Production Date: 2003
Format: VHS videotape
Special Notes: Includes a teacher's guide.
Terms: Borrower pays return postage. RETURN the day after scheduled use. Book at least 4 weeks in advance. Requests must include your name, phone, mail address, eligibility program, title, NAL number, show date, and a statement, "I have read the warning on copyright restrictions and accept full responsibility for compliance." One title per request.

**Source: National Agricultural Library**
**Document Delivery Services Branch**
**4th Floor, Photo Lab**
**10301 Baltimore Avenue**
**Beltsville, MD 20705-2351**
**Phone: 1-301-504-5994**
**Fax: 1-301-504-5675**
**World Wide Web URL: http://www.nal.usda.gov/fnic**
**Email Address: lending@nal.usda.gov**

*All materials listed in this 2018-2019 edition are **BRAND NEW!***

## Adverse Reactions to Medications

Tells which medications most commonly cause problems, and how to identify an allergic reaction.

| | |
|---|---|
| Availability: | Limit of one copy to non-profit schools, libraries, and homeschoolers world-wide. |
| Suggested Grade: | 7-Adult |
| Languages: | English; Spanish |
| Order Number: | order by title |
| Format: | Brochure |
| Special Notes: | Requests must be made via web site or email ONLY. |

**Source: American Academy of Allergy, Asthma & Immunology**
**Attn: Membership Assistant**
**555 East Wells Street, Suite 1100**
**Milwaukee, WI 53202**
**World Wide Web URL: http://www.aaaai.org**
**Email Address: info@aaaai.org**

## All About Me: My Senses

Discusses the senses, and introduces the parts of the body that are sense organs and develops the concept that using the senses helps people learn about the world around them.

| | |
|---|---|
| Availability: | All requesters |
| Suggested Grade: | K |
| Order Number: | not applicable |
| Format: | Online Lesson Plan |

**Source: Mary L. Nisewander**
**World Wide Web URL:**
**http://www.eduref.org/Virtual/Lessons/Health/**
**Body_Systems_and_Senses/BSS0001.html**

## Allergic Skin Conditions

Teaches how plants, metals, and other substances can cause an allergic reaction.

| | |
|---|---|
| Availability: | Limit of one copy to non-profit schools, libraries, and homeschoolers world-wide. |
| Suggested Grade: | 7-Adult |
| Languages: | English; Spanish |
| Order Number: | order by title |
| Format: | Brochure |
| Special Notes: | Requests must be made via web site or email ONLY. |

**Source: American Academy of Allergy, Asthma & Immunology**
**Attn: Membership Assistant**
**555 East Wells Street, Suite 1100**
**Milwaukee, WI 53202**
**World Wide Web URL: http://www.aaaai.org**
**Email Address: info@aaaai.org**

## BAM! Body and Mind

Written to given children the information they need to make wise and healthy lifestyle choices.

| | |
|---|---|
| Availability: | All requesters |
| Suggested Grade: | 4-8 |
| Order Number: | not applicable |
| Format: | Web Site |
| Special Notes: | Includes a teacher's corner. |

**Source: Centers for Disease Control and Prevention (bam)**
**World Wide Web URL:**
**http://www.bam.gov/http://www.bam.gov/**

## Basic Lasik: Tips on Lasik Eye Surgery

Provides information on this very popular eye surgery.

| | |
|---|---|
| Availability: | Limit of 49 copies to schools, libraries, and homeschoolers world-wide. |
| Suggested Grade: | 10-Adult |
| Order Number: | order by title |
| Format: | Brochure |
| Special Notes: | May also be downloaded from the Web site. Quantities in excess of 50 are available from Federal Trade Commission, Distribution Office, 600 Pennsylvania Avenue, NW, Washington, D. C. 20580-0001 or fax to: 1-703-739-0991. |

**Source: Federal Trade Commission**
**Consumer Response Center**
**600 Pennsylvania, N. W., Room H-130**
**Washington, DC 20580**
**World Wide Web URL:**
**http://www.ftc.gov/bcp/consumer.shtm**

## Basik Lasik

Learn the details about this new eye surgery which eliminates the need for glasses.

| | |
|---|---|
| Availability: | All requesters |
| Suggested Grade: | 8-Adult |
| Order Number: | not applicable |
| Format: | Online Article; 5 pages |
| Special Notes: | Use the on-site search engine to easily find this title. You may request a printed copy mailed to you for a fee. |

**Source: Federal Citizen Information Center**
**World Wide Web URL: http://www.pueblo.gsa.gov/**

## Brushing Chart

Use this "Brushing Chart" to keep track when your child brushes their teeth! Have your child color in the Sun and the Moon every time they brush

| | |
|---|---|
| Availability: | All requesters |
| Suggested Grade: | Parents |
| Order Number: | not applicable |
| Format: | Downloadable Chart |

**Source: Orajel**
**World Wide Web URL:**
**http://www.orajel.com/products/toddler/brush_chart.htm**

## Do You Know the Health Risks of Being Overweight?

A guide to help you lose weight which also explains why, perhaps, you should.

| | |
|---|---|
| Availability: | All requesters |
| Suggested Grade: | 4-Adult |
| Order Number: | not applicable |
| Format: | Online Article; 10 pages |
| Special Notes: | Use the on-site search engine to easily find this title. You may request a printed copy mailed to you for a fee. |

# HEALTH--PERSONAL HEALTH AND HYGIENE

Source: Federal Citizen Information Center
World Wide Web URL: http://www.pueblo.gsa.gov/

## Goofy Over Dental Health

Learn about good dental hygiene from Goofy and Dr. Molar.

Availability:       Schools, libraries, and homeschoolers in the United States who serve the hearing impaired.
Suggested Grade:    K-4
Order Number:       25305
Production Date:    1991
Format:             Streaming Video
Special Notes:      Also available as live streaming video over the Internet.
Terms:     Sponsor pays all transportation costs. Return one week after receipt. Participation is limited to deaf or hard of hearing Americans, their parents, families, teachers, counselors, or others whose use would benefit a deaf or hard of hearing person. Only one person in the audience needs to be hearing impaired. You must register--which is free. These videos are all open-captioned--no special equipment is required for viewing.

Source: Described and Captioned Media Program
National Association of the Deaf
4211 Church Street Ext.
Roebuck, SC  29376
Phone: 1-800-237-6213
Fax: 1-800-538-5636
World Wide Web URL: http://www.dcmp.org

## Health Finder

A searchable database of health topics.

Availability:       All requesters
Suggested Grade:    All ages
Order Number:       not applicable
Format:             Web Site

Source: U. S. Department of Health & Human Services
World Wide Web URL: http://www.healthfinder.gov/

## Healthy Teeth

Provides information about teeth, gums, cavities, braces, and oral health habits.

Availability:       All requesters
Suggested Grade:    3-6
Order Number:       not applicable
Format:             Web Site

Source: Nova Scotia Dental Association
World Wide Web URL: http://www.healthyteeth.org/

## HeartPower! Online

A curriculum-based program for teaching about the heart and how to keep it healthy for a lifetime.

Availability:       All requesters
Suggested Grade:    preK-8
Languges:           English; Spanish
Order Number:       not applicable
Format:             Online Curriculum

Source: American Heart Association
World Wide Web URL: http://www.americanheart.org/
presenter.jhtml?identifier=3003357

## Heartpower

Teaches about the heart and how to keep it healthy.

Availability:       Librarians in the United States.
Suggested Grade:    preK
Order Number:       Kit No. 360
Production Date:    1996
Format:             Audiotape
Special Notes:      This kit includes posters, a sing-along music book, and much more. Produced by the American Heart Association.
Terms:     Borrower pays return postage. RETURN the day after scheduled use. Book at least 4 weeks in advance. Requests must include your name, phone, mail address, eligibility program, title, NAL number, show date, and a statement, "I have read the warning on copyright restrictions and accept full responsibility for compliance." One title per request.

Source: National Agricultural Library
Document Delivery Services Branch
4th Floor, Photo Lab
10301 Baltimore Avenue
Beltsville, MD  20705-2351
Phone: 1-301-504-5994
Fax: 1-301-504-5675
World Wide Web URL: http://www.nal.usda.gov/fnic
Email Address: lending@nal.usda.gov

## Heartpower

Teaches about the heart and how to keep it healthy.

Availability:       Staff at schools with NET, WIC, CSFP, FDPIR, CACFP, UMD or Child Nutrition Program food programs in the United States. Those not having such an affiliation should contact their library to place an interlibrary loan request.
Suggested Grade:    6-8
Order Number:       NAL Kit 359
Production Date:    1996
Format:             Set of 2 VHS videotapes
Special Notes:      Contains a number of supplementary teaching materials. From the American Heart Association
Terms:     Borrower pays return postage. RETURN the day after scheduled use. Book at least 4 weeks in advance. Requests must include your name, phone, mail address, eligibility program, title, NAL number, show date, and a statement, "I have read the warning on copyright restrictions and accept full responsibility for compliance." One title per request.

Source: National Agricultural Library
Document Delivery Services Branch
4th Floor, Photo Lab
10301 Baltimore Avenue
Beltsville, MD  20705-2351
Phone: 1-301-504-5994
Fax: 1-301-504-5675

*All materials listed in this 2018-2019 edition are **BRAND NEW!***

World Wide Web URL: http://www.nal.usda.gov/fnic
Email Address: lending@nal.usda.gov

## Hosford Muscle Tables, The: Skeletal Muscles of the Human Body
This site is an index containing detailed information about the skeletal muscles of the human body. Included is each muscle's origin, insertion, action, blood supply, and innervation.

Availability: All requesters
Suggested Grade: 9-12
Order Number: not applicable
Format: Web Site
Source: Hosford Web Service
World Wide Web URL: http://www.ptcentral.com/muscles/

## Laughing Out Loud to Good Health
Explores alternative methods to good health.

Availability: All requesters
Suggested Grade: 4-12
Order Number: not applicable
Format: Web Site
Special Notes: This URL will lead you to a subject page. Then click on the appropriate subject heading.
Source: ThinkQuest
World Wide Web URL:
http://www.thinkquest.org/pls/html/think.library

## Lifesteps: Weight Management
A program that helps participants develop new eating habits through behavior modification.

Availability: Staff at schools with NET, WIC, CSFP, FDPIR, CACFP, UMD or Child Nutrition Program food programs in the United States. Those not having such an affiliation should contact their library to place an interlibrary loan request.
Suggested Grade: 6-12
Order Number: NAL Kit 205
Production Date: 1994
Format: Set of 2 VHS videotapes
Special Notes: Includes a teacher's guide and many other supplemental teaching aids.
Terms: Borrower pays return postage. RETURN the day after scheduled use. Book at least 4 weeks in advance. Requests must include your name, phone, mail address, eligibility program, title, NAL number, show date, and a statement, "I have read the warning on copyright restrictions and accept full responsibility for compliance." One title per request.
Source: National Agricultural Library
Document Delivery Services Branch
4th Floor, Photo Lab
10301 Baltimore Avenue
Beltsville, MD 20705-2351
Phone: 1-301-504-5994
Fax: 1-301-504-5675
World Wide Web URL: http://www.nal.usda.gov/fnic
Email Address: lending@nal.usda.gov

## Live Healthier, Live Longer
Explains coronary heart disease and how to avoid it.
Availability: All requesters
Suggested Grade: 6-12
Order Number: not applicable
Format: Web Site
Source: National Institutes of Health
World Wide Web URL: http://rover.nhlbi.nih.gov/chd/

## Outdoor Allergens
Details what pollen and molds are and tells how to avoid them so allergies don't flare up.
Availability: Limit of one copy to non-profit schools, libraries, and homeschoolers world-wide.
Suggested Grade: 7-Adult
Languages: English; Spanish
Order Number: order by title
Format: Brochure
Special Notes: Requests must be made via web site or email ONLY.
Source: American Academy of Allergy, Asthma & Immunology
Attn: Membership Assistant
555 East Wells Street, Suite 1100
Milwaukee, WI 53202
World Wide Web URL: http://www.aaaai.org
Email Address: info@aaaai.org

## Protecting Kids from the Sun
Why, and how, to protect children from the sun's harmful rays.
Availability: Limit of 49 copies to schools, libraries, and homeschoolers world-wide.
Suggested Grade: 4-Adult
Order Number: order by title
Format: Brochure
Special Notes: May also be downloaded from the Web site. Quantities in excess of 50 are available from Federal Trade Commission, Distribution Office, 600 Pennsylvania Avenue, NW, Washington, D. C. 20580-0001 or fax to: 1-703-739-0991.
Source: Federal Trade Commission
Consumer Response Center
600 Pennsylvania, N. W., Room H-130
Washington, DC 20580
World Wide Web URL:
http://www.ftc.gov/bcp/consumer.shtm

## Rx for Survival
Anchored by a six-hour PBS television series, this site offers all sorts of games, experiments, resources, and more to supplement health, biology, and general science classes.
Availability: All requesters
Suggested Grade: 7-Adult
Order Number: not applicable
Format: Web Site

# HEALTH--PERSONAL HEALTH AND HYGIENE

Source: WGBH Educational Foundation and Vulcan
Productions, Inc.
World Wide Web URL:
http://www.pbs.org/wgbh/rxforsurvival/

## Seal Out Tooth Decay
Explains what sealants are and how they are applied.
Availability: Limit of 50 copies to schools, libraries, and homeschoolers in the United States and Canada.
Suggested Grade: All ages
Languages: English; Spanish
Order Number: English NIH Pub. No. 07-489; Spanish NIH Pub. No. 04-489S
Production Date: 2007
Format: Brochure
Source: National Institute of Dental and Craniofacial Research
National Oral Health Information Clearinghouse
1 NOHIC Way
Bethesda, MD 20892-3500
Phone: 1-301-232-4528
Fax: 1-301-480-4098
World Wide Web URL: http://www.nidcr.nih.gov
Email Address: nidcrinfo@mail.nih.gov

## Setting Goals for Weight Loss
Tells how to set realistic goals for losing weight.
Availability: Limit of 49 copies to schools, libraries, and homeschoolers world-wide.
Suggested Grade: 6-Adult
Order Number: order by title
Format: Brochure
Special Notes: May also be downloaded from the Web site. Quantities in excess of 50 are available from Federal Trade Commission, Distribution Office, 600 Pennsylvania Avenue, NW, Washington, D. C. 20580-0001 or fax to: 1-703-739-0991.
Source: Federal Trade Commission
Consumer Response Center
600 Pennsylvania, N. W., Room H-130
Washington, DC 20580
World Wide Web URL:
http://www.ftc.gov/bcp/consumer.shtm

## Simple Steps to Better Dental Health
Information for people of all ages, speaking many different languages, about how to care for your teeth.
Availability: All requesters
Suggested Grade: All ages
Order Number: not applicable
Format: Web Site
Source: Aetna Company
World Wide Web URL:
http://www.simplestepsdental.com/SS/ihtSS/
r.WSIHW000/st.31819/pr.3.html

## Sunscreens and Sun-Protective Clothing
How to select sunscreens--and why it is important to wear them.
Availability: Limit of 49 copies to schools, libraries, and homeschoolers world-wide.
Suggested Grade: 6-Adult
Order Number: order by title
Format: Brochure
Special Notes: May also be downloaded from the Web site. Quantities in excess of 50 are available from Federal Trade Commission, Distribution Office, 600 Pennsylvania Avenue, NW, Washington, D. C. 20580-0001 or fax to: 1-703-739-0991.
Source: Federal Trade Commission
Consumer Response Center
600 Pennsylvania, N. W., Room H-130
Washington, DC 20580
World Wide Web URL:
http://www.ftc.gov/bcp/consumer.shtm

## SunSmart
Students will learn how to protect themselves from the dangers of the sun.
Availability: All requesters
Suggested Grade: K-1
Order Number: not applicable
Format: Online Lesson Plan
Source: Bo Campbell
World Wide Web URL:
http://www.eduref.org/Virtual/Lessons/Health/
Safety/SFY0200.html

## Traveling with Allergies and Asthma
Tips on how to make sure your allergy doesn't ruin your trip.
Availability: Limit of one copy to non-profit schools, libraries, and homeschoolers world-wide.
Suggested Grade: 7-Adult
Languages: English; Spanish
Order Number: order by title
Format: Brochure
Special Notes: Requests must be made via web site or email ONLY.
Source: American Academy of Allergy, Asthma & Immunology
Attn: Membership Assistant
555 East Wells Street, Suite 1100
Milwaukee, WI 53202
World Wide Web URL: http://www.aaaai.org
Email Address: info@aaaai.org

## Using Live Insects in Elementary Classrooms
A program dedicated to introducing health topics to children in kindergarten through third grade. The result is a printable collection of twenty integrated lessons with science and math activities that use live insects.

Availability:        All requesters
Suggested Grade:     K-3
Languages:           English; Spanish
Order Number:        not applicable
Format:              Online Lesson Plans
Special Notes:       Printed copies may be ordered for $11 each.
**Source: University of Arizona, Center for Insect Science**
**World Wide Web URL: http://insected.arizona.edu/uli.htm**

## Weight Loss for Life

Information to help you learn how to lose weight safely and stay healthy.

Availability:        All requesters
Suggested Grade:     4-Adult
Order Number:        not applicable
Production Date:     1998
Format:              Online Article; 20 pages
Special Notes:       Use the on-site search engine to easily find this title. You may request a printed copy mailed to you for a fee.
**Source: Federal Citizen Information Center**
**World Wide Web URL: http://www.pueblo.gsa.gov/**

## What Is an Allergic Reaction?

Contains specific information on how and why the body responds to certain substances.

Availability:        Limit of one copy to non-profit schools, libraries, and homeschoolers world-wide.
Suggested Grade:     7-Adult
Languages:           English; Spanish
Order Number:        order by title
Format:              Brochure
Special Notes:       Requests must be made via web site or email ONLY.
**Source: American Academy of Allergy, Asthma & Immunology**
**Attn: Membership Assistant**
**555 East Wells Street, Suite 1100**
**Milwaukee, WI 53202**
**World Wide Web URL: http://www.aaaai.org**
**Email Address: info@aaaai.org**

## You're in Charge: Teens With Asthma

Teens talk about their experiences with asthma and the use of peak flow meters as well as prescribed medications. Animated graphics illustrate how asthma acts in the body.

Availability:        Schools, libraries, and homeschoolers in Connecticut, Maine, Massachusetts, New Hampshire, Rhode Island, and Vermont.
Suggested Grade:     4-12
Order Number:        VID 167
Format:              VHS videotape
Terms:               Borrower pays return postage. Return within three weeks of receipt. If the tape you request is available, it will be mailed within 5 business days. If not, you will be notified that this video is already out on loan. No more than three titles may be borrowed by one requestor at a time. No reservations for a specific date will be accepted. It is most efficient to order via the web site.
**Source: U. S. Environmental Protection Agency, Region 1**
**Customer Service Center**
**One Congress Street, Suite 1100**
**Boston, MA 02214**
**World Wide Web URL:**
**http://yosemite.epa.gov/r1/videolen.nsf/**

## Black Water

Study of effects of water pollution on the maritime community of Bahai in Brazil.

Availability: Schools, libraries, and nursing homes in the United States.
Suggested Grade: 6-12
Order Number: GEBRA10-video
Production Date: 1990
Format: VHS videotape
Terms: Borrowers must have a User's Agreement on file with this source--available by mail or via the Internet. Return postage is paid by borrower; return 12 days after showing. Book at least three weeks in advance. All borrowers are limited to a total of ten items per semester.

**Source: Latin American Resource Center**
**Stone Center for Latin American Studies**
**Tulane University**
**100 Jones Hall**
**New Orleans, LA 70118**
**Phone: 1-504-862-3143**
**Fax: 1-504-865-6719**
**World Wide Web URL:**
**http://stonecenter.tulane.edu/pages/detail/48/**
**Lending-Library**
**Email Address: crcrts@tulane.edu**

## Bright Sparks: Water, Water Everywhere

Cartoon characters travel over the Earth to learn that water is a very important resource. What we do with water, how we use it, and the attitudes that we have towards conservation are discussed. Solutions to shortages, polluted drinking water, arid areas of the planet, and flooding are explored. Water can provide for all, so long as we all learn how to use, enjoy, and share it.

Availability: Schools, libraries, homeschoolers, and nursing homes in the United States.
Suggested Grade: 1-8
Order Number: order by title
Format: VHS videotape
Terms: Borrower pays return postage. Return the day after scheduled showing, via UPS or Priority Mail, insured for $100.00. Book 4 weeks in advance and include an alternate date. Order should include name of person responsible for handling the video, and complete mailing address. Please mention this Guide when ordering. Tapes may not be duplicated, edited or exhibited for a fee.

**Source: Church World Service**
**Film & Video Library**
**28606 Phillips Street, P. O. Box 968**
**Elkhart, IN 46515**
**Phone: 1-800-297-1516, ext. 338**
**Fax: 1-574-262-0966**
**World Wide Web URL: http://www.churchworldservice.org**
**Email Address: videos@churchworldservice.org**

## Challenge of Global Warming, The

Scientifically looks at ways to dispose of air polluting carbon.

Availability: Schools, libraries, homeschoolers, and nursing homes in Connecticut (except Fairfield County), Maine, Massachusetts, New Hampshire, Rhode Island, and Vermont.
Suggested Grade: 6-12
Order Number: 557
Format: VHS videotape
Terms: Borrower pays return postage, including insurance. Return two weeks after receipt.

**Source: Consulate General of Japan, Boston**
**Federal Reserve Plaza, 14th Floor**
**600 Atlantic Avenue**
**Boston, MA 02210**
**Phone: 1-617-973-9772**
**Fax: 1-617-542-1329**
**World Wide Web URL:**
**http://www.boston.us.emb-japan.go.jp**
**Email Address: infocul@cgjbos.org**

## Challenge of Global Warming, The

Scientifically looks at ways to dispose of air polluting carbon.

Availability: Schools, libraries, and nursing homes in Hawaii.
Suggested Grade: 6-12
Order Number: NA-29
Format: VHS videotape
Terms: Borrower pays return postage. A maximum of 3 videos may be borrowed per person. Return within one week of date borrowed.

**Source: Consulate General of Japan, Honolulu**
**1742 Nuuanu Avenue**
**Honolulu, HI 96817-3294**
**Phone: 1-808-543-3111**
**Fax: 1-808-543-3170**
**World Wide Web URL:**
**http://www.honolulu.us.emb-japan.go.jp**

## Choices

Where does our trash go? Real people tell how their lives have been impacted by the problem of solid waste disposal. Air and ground water contamination, explosions from methane accumulation, and the spread of disease and vermin are discussed.

Availability: Schools, libraries, homeschoolers, and nursing homes in the United States.
Suggested Grade: 5-Adult
Order Number: order by title
Format: VHS videotape
Terms: Borrower pays return postage. Return the day after scheduled showing, via UPS or Priority Mail, insured for $100.00. Book 4 weeks in advance and include an alternate date. Order should include name of person responsible for handling the video, and complete mailing address. Please mention this Guide when ordering. Tapes may not be duplicated, edited or exhibited for a fee.

*All materials listed in this 2018-2019 edition are BRAND NEW!*

Source: Church World Service
Film & Video Library
28606 Phillips Street, P. O. Box 968
Elkhart, IN 46515
Phone: 1-800-297-1516, ext. 338
Fax: 1-574-262-0966
World Wide Web URL: http://www.churchworldservice.org
Email Address: videos@churchworldservice.org

## Earth Force

Invites children to make a difference in the quality of the environment in their communities by presenting things they can do themselves.

Availability:       All requesters
Suggested Grade:   K-8
Order Number:      not applicable
Format:            Web Site

Source: Earth Force
World Wide Web URL: http://www.earthforce.org/

## Environmental Dog

Ralphie the Dog, poisoned when he snacks on powdered cleanser, becomes Environmental Dog, and teaches his human family to be careful with the energy and materials they use. This program makes learning about environmental issues fun.

Availability:       Schools, libraries, homeschoolers, and nursing homes in the United States.
Suggested Grade:   2-8
Order Number:      order by title
Production Date:   1990
Format:            VHS videotape
Terms:  Borrower pays return postage. Return the day after scheduled showing, via UPS or Priority Mail, insured for $100.00. Book 4 weeks in advance and include an alternate date. Order should include name of person responsible for handling the video, and complete mailing address. Please mention this Guide when ordering. Tapes may not be duplicated, edited or exhibited for a fee.

Source: Church World Service
Film & Video Library
28606 Phillips Street, P. O. Box 968
Elkhart, IN 46515
Phone: 1-800-297-1516, ext. 338
Fax: 1-574-262-0966
World Wide Web URL: http://www.churchworldservice.org
Email Address: videos@churchworldservice.org

## Environmental Kids Club

Emphasizes the role of good citizens in maintaining the environment.

Availability:       All requesters
Suggested Grade:   K-6
Order Number:      not applicable
Format:            Web Site

Source: Environmental Protection Agency
World Wide Web URL: http://www.epa.gov/kids/

## Fit and Healthy: Earth and Me

Explores the relationship between the Earth's health and our own.

Availability:       All requesters
Suggested Grade:   6-12
Order Number:      not applicable
Format:            Web Site
Special Notes:      This URL will lead you to a subject page. Then click on the appropriate subject heading.

Source: ThinkQuest
World Wide Web URL:
http://www.thinkquest.org/pls/html/think.library

## How the Waste Was Won

Explains how to conquer waste disposal problems.

Availability:       Schools, libraries, and homeschoolers in Connecticut, Maine, Massachusetts, New Hampshire, Rhode Island, and Vermont.
Suggested Grade:   All ages
Order Number:      RL 29
Production Date:   1990
Format:            VHS videotape
Terms:  Borrower pays return postage. Return within three weeks of receipt. If the tape you request is available, it will be mailed within 5 business days. If not, you will be notified that this video is already out on loan. No more than three titles may be borrowed by one requestor at a time. No reservations for a specific date will be accepted. It is most efficient to order via the web site.

Source: U. S. Environmental Protection Agency, Region 1
Customer Service Center
One Congress Street, Suite 1100
Boston, MA 02214
World Wide Web URL:
http://yosemite.epa.gov/r1/videolen.nsf/

## I Need the Earth and the Earth Needs Me

This video presents a group of 4th grade children and their understanding of the Earth's valuable resources and demonstrates steps that each one can take in keeping the environment clean and vital for the present and future generations.

Availability:       Schools, libraries, and homeschoolers in Connecticut, Maine, Massachusetts, New Hampshire, Rhode Island, and Vermont.
Suggested Grade:   K-6
Order Number:      VID 017
Production Date:   1990
Format:            VHS videotape
Terms:  Borrower pays return postage. Return within three weeks of receipt. If the tape you request is available, it will be mailed within 5 business days. If not, you will be notified that this video is already out on loan. No more than three titles may be borrowed by one requestor at a time. No reservations for a specific date will be accepted. It is most efficient to order via the web site.

Source:  U. S. Environmental Protection Agency, Region 1
Customer Service Center
One Congress Street, Suite 1100
Boston, MA   02214
World Wide Web URL:
http://yosemite.epa.gov/r1/videolen.nsf/

## In Partnership with Earth

Late singer John Denver hosts this informative program on pollution and its effect on our earth.  We learn that the future looks more promising as we begin to generate less pollution.

Availability:  Schools, libraries, homeschoolers, and nursing homes in the United States.
Suggested Grade:  6-Adult
Order Number:  order by title
Production Date:  1990
Format:  VHS videotape
Terms:  Borrower pays return postage.  Return the day after scheduled showing, via UPS or Priority Mail, insured for $100.00.  Book 4 weeks in advance and include an alternate date.  Order should include name of person responsible for handling the video, and complete mailing address.  Please mention this Guide when ordering.  Tapes may not be duplicated, edited or exhibited for a fee.

Source:  Church World Service
Film & Video Library
28606 Phillips Street, P. O. Box 968
Elkhart, IN   46515
Phone:  1-800-297-1516, ext. 338
Fax:  1-574-262-0966
World Wide Web URL:  http://www.churchworldservice.org
Email Address:  videos@churchworldservice.org

## Kids by the Bay

Featuring an upbeat score highlighted by the Otis Redding classic "Sittin' on the Dock of the Bay," this video shows how much fun it is to pitch in and restore the environment.  From the simple clean-up of trash to the planting of native plants; from island habitat restoration to the rescue and care of wild animals; we see youngsters having a real impact on the natural world around them.

Availability:  All requesters through interlibrary loan.
Suggested Grade:  4-Adult
Order Number:  557(276) K5272 1997 VIDEOC
Production Date:  1997
Format:  VHS videotape
Terms:  These videotapes are available through interlibrary loan only.  Simply request the specific video by name and number at your local public library, university library, or company library.  The librarian will submit your request using an ALA interlibrary loan form, and the videos will be mailed to your library for your use.  Interlibrary loans are limited to two videos at a time.  The address listed below is for the ALA loan form only--your librarian must submit requests to this address.

Source:  U. S. Geological Survey Library
345 Middlefield Road, MS 955
Menlo Park, CA   94025

## Lead in School Drinking Water

What you can do about lead in your school drinking water.

Availability:  Schools, libraries, and homeschoolers in Connecticut, Maine, Massachusetts, New Hampshire, Rhode Island, and Vermont.
Suggested Grade:  7-12
Order Number:  VID 156
Production Date:  1990
Format:  VHS videotape
Terms:  Borrower pays return postage.  Return within three weeks of receipt.  If the tape you request is available, it will be mailed within 5 business days.  If not, you will be notified that this video is already out on loan.  No more than three titles may be borrowed by one requestor at a time.  No reservations for a specific date will be accepted.  It is most efficient to order via the web site.

Source:  U. S. Environmental Protection Agency, Region 1
Customer Service Center
One Congress Street, Suite 1100
Boston, MA   02214
World Wide Web URL:
http://yosemite.epa.gov/r1/videolen.nsf/

## Lead--The Hidden Poison

A father is awakened to the dangers of lead by his daughter.

Availability:  Schools, libraries, and homeschoolers in Connecticut, Maine, Massachusetts, New Hampshire, Rhode Island, and Vermont.
Suggested Grade:  5-Adult
Order Number:  VID 385
Production Date:  1993
Format:  VHS videotape
Terms:  Borrower pays return postage.  Return within three weeks of receipt.  If the tape you request is available, it will be mailed within 5 business days.  If not, you will be notified that this video is already out on loan.  No more than three titles may be borrowed by one requestor at a time.  No reservations for a specific date will be accepted.  It is most efficient to order via the web site.

Source:  U. S. Environmental Protection Agency, Region 1
Customer Service Center
One Congress Street, Suite 1100
Boston, MA   02214
World Wide Web URL:
http://yosemite.epa.gov/r1/videolen.nsf/

## Pointless Pollution Kit

A collection of interactive lessons, hands-on activities, and information about nonpoint source pollution, the number one cause of water pollution.

Availability:  Single copies to schools, libraries, and homeschoolers world-wide.
Suggested Grade:  3-12
Order Number:  order by title
Format:  Booklet

*All materials listed in this 2018-2019 edition are **BRAND NEW!***

Special Notes:    May also be downloaded from the web site.

**Source: Clean Ocean Action**
**18 Hartshorne Drive, Suite 2**
**Sandy Hook, NJ 07732**
**Phone: 1-732-872-0111**
**Fax: 1-732-872-8041**
**World Wide Web URL: http://www.cleanoceanaction.org**
**Email Address: education@cleanoceanaction.org**

## Preserving Our Environmental Heritage

Introduces Japan's methods for combating high levels of pollution and improving public awareness of environmental conservation.

Availability:    Schools, libraries, and nursing homes in Connecticut (except Fairfield county), Maine, Massachusetts, New Hampshire, Rhode Island, and Vermont.
Suggested Grade:    9-Adult
Order Number:    order by title
Format:    16mm film
Terms:    Borrower pays return postage, including insurance. Return two weeks after receipt.

**Source: Consulate General of Japan, Boston**
**Federal Reserve Plaza, 14th Floor**
**600 Atlantic Avenue**
**Boston, MA 02210**
**Phone: 1-617-973-9772**
**Fax: 1-617-542-1329**
**World Wide Web URL:**
**http://www.boston.us.emb-japan.go.jp**
**Email Address: infocul@cgjbos.org**

## Preserving the Global Environment

Depicts the ecological efforts being made in modern Japan to preserve the environment for future generations.

Availability:    Schools, libraries, and nursing homes in Connecticut (except Fairfield county), Maine, Massachusetts, New Hampshire, Rhode Island, and Vermont.
Suggested Grade:    9-Adult
Order Number:    order by title
Format:    16mm film
Terms:    Borrower pays return postage, including insurance. Return two weeks after receipt.

**Source: Consulate General of Japan, Boston**
**Federal Reserve Plaza, 14th Floor**
**600 Atlantic Avenue**
**Boston, MA 02210**
**Phone: 1-617-973-9772**
**Fax: 1-617-542-1329**
**World Wide Web URL:**
**http://www.boston.us.emb-japan.go.jp**
**Email Address: infocul@cgjbos.org**

## Recycle This! Rock 'n Roll & Recycling

Set to rock and roll music, this video emphasizes that recycling helps protect the environment, save energy, reduce waste, and conserve resources.

Availability:    Schools, libraries, and homeschoolers in Connecticut, Maine, Massachusetts, New Hampshire, Rhode Island, and Vermont.
Suggested Grade:    1-5
Order Number:    VID 079
Format:    VHS videotape
Special Notes:    Produced by the Dow Chemical Company.
Terms:    Borrower pays return postage. Return within three weeks of receipt. If the tape you request is available, it will be mailed within 5 business days. If not, you will be notified that this video is already out on loan. No more than three titles may be borrowed by one requestor at a time. No reservations for a specific date will be accepted. It is most efficient to order via the web site.

**Source: U. S. Environmental Protection Agency, Region 1**
**Customer Service Center**
**One Congress Street, Suite 1100**
**Boston, MA 02214**
**World Wide Web URL:**
**http://yosemite.epa.gov/r1/videolen.nsf/**

## Reduce, Reuse, Recycle: The Bottom Line

Representatives of a few companies teach businesses how to reuse materials, source, and recycle.

Availability:    Schools, libraries, and homeschoolers in Connecticut, Maine, Massachusetts, New Hampshire, Rhode Island, and Vermont.
Suggested Grade:    9-Adult
Order Number:    VID RL48
Production Date:    1992
Format:    VHS videotape
Terms:    Borrower pays return postage. Return within three weeks of receipt. If the tape you request is available, it will be mailed within 5 business days. If not, you will be notified that this video is already out on loan. No more than three titles may be borrowed by one requestor at a time. No reservations for a specific date will be accepted. It is most efficient to order via the web site.

**Source: U. S. Environmental Protection Agency, Region 1**
**Customer Service Center**
**One Congress Street, Suite 1100**
**Boston, MA 02214**
**World Wide Web URL:**
**http://yosemite.epa.gov/r1/videolen.nsf/**

## Save the Rainforest

Provides a virtual tour of the rainforest and lots of information about why we need them and why they are becoming endangered ecosystems.

Availability:    All requesters
Suggested Grade:    All ages
Order Number:    not applicable
Format:    Web Site

**Source: Save the Rainforest.org**
**World Wide Web URL: http://www.savetherainforest.org/**

## Stepan Chemical: The Poisoning of a Mexican Community

A moving account of the people of Matamoros, Mexico,

and their struggle for a clean environment. The Chicago-based Stepan plant has dumped xylene, a toxic solvent linked to birth defects, into open canals near their homes. Faced with this deadly pollution, the Sanchez family and their neighbors decide to fight back. With help from the U. S. based Coalition for Justice in the Maguiladoras, community leaders demand an end to the contamination and a full accounting from Stepan and environmental agencies in the U. S. and Mexico.

Availability: Schools, libraries, homeschoolers, and nursing homes in the United States.
Suggested Grade: 9-Adult
Order Number: order by title
Format: VHS videotape
Terms: Borrower pays return postage. Return the day after scheduled showing, via UPS or Priority Mail, insured for $100.00. Book 4 weeks in advance and include an alternate date. Order should include name of person responsible for handling the video, and complete mailing address. Please mention this Guide when ordering. Tapes may not be duplicated, edited or exhibited for a fee.

Source: Church World Service
Film & Video Library, 28606 Phillips Street, P. O. Box 968
Elkhart, IN 46515
Phone: 1-800-297-1516, ext. 338
Fax: 1-574-262-0966
World Wide Web URL: http://www.churchworldservice.org
Email Address: videos@churchworldservice.org

## Storm Drain Stenciling Instruction Cards
Designed to improve the quality of our ocean waters through reduction of pointless pollution and develop leadership among the participants in the campaign. Instructions how to organize a local storm drain stenciling campaign.

Availability: Single copies to schools, libraries, and homeschoolers world-wide.
Suggested Grade: 3-12
Order Number: order by title
Format: Cards

Source: Clean Ocean Action
18 Hartshorne Drive, Suite 2
Sandy Hook, NJ 07732
Phone: 1-732-872-0111
Fax: 1-732-872-8041
World Wide Web URL: http://www.cleanoceanaction.org
Email Address: education@cleanoceanaction.org

## Turning the Tide Part 4: Into Deep Water
Why is clean drinking water becoming scarce even in the richest countries in the world? On a trip down the Thames River, David Bellamy encounters pesticides, nitrates, and heavy metals, problems for outmoded water and sewage works. He also tackles acid rain and polluted beaches. We know how to clean up these polluted areas. Why don't we do it?

Availability: Schools, libraries, homeschoolers, and nursing homes in the United States.
Suggested Grade: 6-Adult
Order Number: order by title
Production Date: 1988
Format: VHS videotape
Terms: Borrower pays return postage. Return the day after scheduled showing, via UPS or Priority Mail, insured for $100.00. Book 4 weeks in advance and include an alternate date. Order should include name of person responsible for handling the video, and complete mailing address. Please mention this Guide when ordering. Tapes may not be duplicated, edited or exhibited for a fee.

Source: Church World Service
Film & Video Library
28606 Phillips Street, P. O. Box 968
Elkhart, IN 46515
Phone: 1-800-297-1516, ext. 338
Fax: 1-574-262-0966
World Wide Web URL: http://www.churchworldservice.org
Email Address: videos@churchworldservice.org

## Water Conservation Lesson Plan
Students will learn the importance of water in everyday living, how we use it, and how to conserve it.

Availability: All requesters
Suggested Grade: 3
Order Number: not applicable
Format: Online Lesson Plan

Source: Hope Wenzel
World Wide Web URL:
http://sfr.psu.edu/youth/sftrc/lesson-plans/
water/k-5/conservation-2

## World In Our Backyard, A
Shows the beauty of wetlands and explains how teachers can convey the need to conserve these lands.

Availability: Schools, libraries, and homeschoolers in Connecticut, Maine, Massachusetts, New Hampshire, Rhode Island, and Vermont.
Suggested Grade: 4-12
Order Number: VID 101
Production Date: 1993
Format: VHS videotape
Terms: Borrower pays return postage. Return within three weeks of receipt. If the tape you request is available, it will be mailed within 5 business days. If not, you will be notified that this video is already out on loan. No more than three titles may be borrowed by one requestor at a time. No reservations for a specific date will be accepted. It is most efficient to order via the web site.

Source: U. S. Environmental Protection Agency, Region 1
Customer Service Center
One Congress Street, Suite 1100
Boston, MA 02214
World Wide Web URL:
http://yosemite.epa.gov/r1/videolen.nsf/

**You Can't Grow Home Again**
Pre-teen takes viewers on a trip to the Costa Rican rainforest to examine issues of preservation.

Availability: Schools and libraries in Iowa, Illinois, Michigan, Minnesota, and Wisconsin.
Suggested Grade: 6-12
Order Number: ENVRFY8VHS
Production Date: 1990
Format: VHS videotape
Terms: Borrower pays return postage. Return 8 days after showing. Book 2 weeks in advance. Order may also be picked up for those near the Center.
**Source: Center for Latin American and Caribbean Studies**
**UW-Milwaukee**
**P. O. Box 413**
**Milwaukee, WI 53201**
**Phone: 1-414-229-5987**
**World Wide Web URL: http://www.uwm.edu/Dept/CLACS**
**Email Address: audvis@usm.edu**

**You Can't Grow Home Again**
Pre-teen takes viewers on a trip to the Costa Rican rainforest to examine issues of preservation.

Availability: Schools, libraries, and nursing homes in the United States.
Suggested Grade: 6-12
Order Number: GELA12-video
Production Date: 1990
Format: VHS videotape
Terms: Borrowers must have a User's Agreement on file with this source--available by mail or via the Internet. Return postage is paid by borrower; return 12 days after showing. Book at least three weeks in advance. All borrowers are limited to a total of ten items per semester.
**Source: Latin American Resource Center**
**Stone Center for Latin American Studies**
**Tulane University**
**100 Jones Hall**
**New Orleans, LA 70118**
**Phone: 1-504-862-3143**
**Fax: 1-504-865-6719**
**World Wide Web URL:**
**http://stonecenter.tulane.edu/pages/detail/48/**
**Lending-Library**
**Email Address: crcrts@tulane.edu**

# HEALTH--SAFETY AND FIRST AID

## Air Bags and Children
Discusses the dangers of air bags interacting with unrestrained or improperly restrained children riding in motor vehicles.

| | |
|---|---|
| Availability: | Schools, libraries, and homeschoolers in KANSAS only. |
| Suggested Grade: | 6-Adult |
| Order Number: | 2-0485 |
| Production Date: | 1996 |
| Format: | VHS videotape |
| Terms: | Borrower pays return postage. Book three weeks in advance. Indicate if substitutions are acceptable. Return two days after showing via U. S. Mail. Available to KANSAS requesters only. |

**Source: School Bus Safety Education Unit**
**Kansas State Department of Education**
**Attn: Wilma Crabtree**
**120 S. E. 10th Street**
**Topeka, KS 66614**
**Phone: 1-785-296-3551**
**Fax: 1-785-296-6659**
**World Wide Web URL:**
**http://www.ksde.org/schoolbus/ksdevideocatlg.htm**
**Email Address: wcrabtree@ksde.org**

## Bikeability Checklist
Written for adult and child bicyclists to help them assess the conditions they encounter when biking.

| | |
|---|---|
| Availability: | |
| Suggested Grade: | 4-Adult |
| Order Number: | not applicable |
| Format: | Downloadable Brochure |

**Source: National Highway Traffic Safety Administration**
**World Wide Web URL: http://www.nhtsa.dot.gov/**

## Broken Glass
Examines common rationalizations for not using seat belts, and shows how flimsy these excuses are when compared with the dangers of not wearing them.

| | |
|---|---|
| Availability: | Schools, libraries, and homeschoolers in KANSAS only. |
| Suggested Grade: | 8-12 |
| Order Number: | 2-0174 |
| Format: | VHS videotape |
| Terms: | Borrower pays return postage. Book three weeks in advance. Indicate if substitutions are acceptable. Return two days after showing via U. S. Mail. Available to KANSAS requesters only. |

**Source: School Bus Safety Education Unit**
**Kansas State Department of Education**
**Attn: Wilma Crabtree**
**120 S. E. 10th Street**
**Topeka, KS 66614**
**Phone: 1-785-296-3551**
**Fax: 1-785-296-6659**
**World Wide Web URL:**
**http://www.ksde.org/schoolbus/ksdevideocatlg.htm**
**Email Address: wcrabtree@ksde.org**

## Common Sense About Kids and Guns
This site offers common sense solutions for reducing gun-related injuries and deaths to children and teens.

| | |
|---|---|
| Availability: | All requesters |
| Suggested Grade: | All ages |
| Order Number: | not applicable |
| Format: | Web Site |

**Source: Common Sense About Kids and Guns**
**World Wide Web URL: http://www.kidsandguns.org/**

## Education: Bike Safety and Bicycle Helmets
A number of articles about bicycling safety and the effectiveness of bicycle helmets.

| | |
|---|---|
| Availability: | All requesters |
| Suggested Grade: | All ages |
| Order Number: | not applicable |
| Format: | Online Articles |

**Source: International Bicycle Fund**
**World Wide Web URL:**
**http://www.ibike.org/education/index.htm**

## Energy Safety
Tips from Smarty the Dog's Electric Safety coloring book.

| | |
|---|---|
| Availability: | All requesters |
| Suggested Grade: | preK-3 |
| Order Number: | not applicable |
| Format: | Downloadable Coloring Book |

**Source: California Energy Commission**
**World Wide Web URL: http://www.energyquest.ca.gov/**

## Fire and Fire Prevention: A Thematic Unit Plan
The purpose of this interdisciplinary unit is to educate students about fire, fire prevention, and to provide them with the essential skills they will need if a fire actually occurs.

| | |
|---|---|
| Availability: | All requesters |
| Suggested Grade: | 2-3 |
| Order Number: | not applicable |
| Format: | Online Lesson Plan |

**Source: Melissa Himberger**
**World Wide Web URL:**
**http://www.eduref.org/Virtual/Lessons/Health/Safety/**
**SFY0012.html**

## Firearms Responsibility in the Home
Explains the responsibilities all firearms users must accept when they bring a gun into the home.

| | |
|---|---|
| Availability: | Limit of 100 copies to schools, libraries, and homeschoolers in the United States and Canada. Make request on official stationery. |
| Suggested Grade: | 6-Adult |
| Order Number: | 080 |
| Format: | Leaflet |

**Source: National Shooting Sports Foundation**
**Council for Wildlife Conservation and Education**
**11 Mile Hill Road**
**Newtown, CT 06470-2359**
**Phone: 1-203-426-1320**

Fax: 1-203-426-1245
World Wide Web URL: http://www.nssf.org
Email Address: literature@nssf.org

## Fire Safety for Young Children

Students will learn about the role of a fire fighter along with important fire safety tips.

Availability:     All requesters
Suggested Grade:  preK-K
Order Number:     not applicable
Format:           Online Lesson Plan
Source: Sue Bouchard and Claire Gerin Buell
World Wide Web URL:
http://www.eduref.org/Virtual/Lessons/Health/Safety/
SFY0201.html

## Fire Safety WebQuest

Help a youngster overcome his fear that his house is not safe from a fire.

Availability:     All requesters
Suggested Grade:  2-5
Order Number:     not applicable
Format:           WebQuest
Source: Joanne Groff and Bev Crouch
World Wide Web URL:
http://www.hobart.k12.in.us/bcrouch/fire2/FSintro.html

## First Aid

Find out how to react in an emergency.

Availability:     All requesters
Suggested Grade:  5-Adult
Order Number:     not applicable
Format:           Online Course
Source: BBC Learning
World Wide Web URL:
http://www.bbc.co.uk/health/first_aid_action/

## First Aid Kit

Teaches children about the contents of a first aid kit and how to use each item.

Availability:     All requesters
Suggested Grade:  3-6
Order Number:     not applicable
Format:           Online Lesson Plan
Source: Marlana Marasco
World Wide Web URL:
http://www.eduref.org/Virtual/Lessons/Health/Safety/
SFY0016.html

## Food Safety Fact Sheets

Fact sheets on safe food handling and more.

Availability:     All requesters
Suggested Grade:  4-12
Order Number:     not applicable
Format:           Downloadable Fact Sheets
Source: U. S. Department of Agriculture, Food Safety and
Inspection Service
World Wide Web URL: http://www.fsis.usda.gov/factsheets/

## For Kids Sake, Think Toy Safety

Explains why, and how, to make sure a child's toys are not hazardous to them.

Availability:      Limit of 50 copies to schools, libraries, and homeschoolers in the United States and Canada. May be copied.
Suggested Grade:   Adult
Languages:         English; Spanish
Order Number:      English 281; Spanish 281S
Format:            Sheet of Paper
Special Notes:     May also be downloaded from the web site.
Source: U. S. Consumer Product Safety Commission
Order by email or web site
World Wide Web URL: http://www.cpsc.gov
Email Address: info@cpsc.gov

## Great American Home Safety Check

Gives important tips to help stop slips/falls, poisoning, and fire or burns--the leading causes of home safety issues in the United States.

Availability:      All requesters
Suggested Grade:   4-Adult
Order Number:      not applicable
Production Date:   2003
Format:            Online Article; 4 pages
Special Notes:     Use the on-site search engine to easily find this title. You may request a printed copy mailed to you for a fee.
Source: Federal Citizen Information Center
World Wide Web URL: http://www.pueblo.gsa.gov/

## Heart Healthy: Getting Personal and Changing Habits

This program on heart health presents information on risks to the heart and how to avoid these risks. Cholesterol, HDL, and LDL are described and the lifestyle required for promoting heart health is discussed. The importance of diet and exercise in promoting cardiovascular health is emphasized.

Availability:      Staff at schools with NET, WIC, CSFP, FDPIR, CACFP, UMD or Child Nutrition Program food programs in the United States. Those not having such an affiliation should contact their library to place an interlibrary loan request.
Suggested Grade:   9-Adult
Order Number:      NAL Video 577
Production Date:   1988
Format:            VHS videotape
Terms:             Borrower pays return postage. RETURN the day after scheduled use. Book at least 4 weeks in advance. Requests must include your name, phone, mail address, eligibility program, title, NAL number, show date, and a statement, "I have read the warning on copyright restrictions and accept full responsibility for compliance." One title per request.
Source: National Agricultural Library
Document Delivery Services Branch
4th Floor, Photo Lab, 10301 Baltimore Avenue
Beltsville, MD  20705-2351

*All materials listed in this 2018-2019 edition are BRAND NEW!*

Phone: 1-301-504-5994
Fax: 1-301-504-5675
World Wide Web URL: http://www.nal.usda.gov/fnic
Email Address: lending@nal.usda.gov

## How to Not Get Hit by Cars

A very extensive article on how to bike safely.

| | |
|---|---|
| Availability: | All requesters |
| Suggested Grade: | All ages |
| Order Number: | not applicable |
| Format: | Online Article |

**Source:  Michael Bluejay**
World Wide Web URL: http://bicyclesafe.com/

## Introduction to Diabetes:  The Game Plan

Explains managing diabetes through lifestyle changes--better nutrition, daily medication, regular exercise, and monitoring blood sugar levels.

| | |
|---|---|
| Availability: | Staff at schools with NET, WIC, CSFP, FDPIR, CACFP, UMD or Child Nutrition Program food programs in the United States. Those not having such an affiliation should contact their library to place an interlibrary loan request. |
| Suggested Grade: | 9-12 |
| Order Number: | NAL Video 1875 |
| Production Date: | 1994 |
| Format: | VHS videotape |
| Terms: | Borrower pays return postage.  RETURN the day after scheduled use.  Book at least 4 weeks in advance. Requests must include your name, phone, mail address, eligibility program, title, NAL number, show date, and a statement, "I have read the warning on copyright restrictions and accept full responsibility for compliance."  One title per request. |

**Source:  National Agricultural Library**
**Document Delivery Services Branch**
**4th Floor, Photo Lab**
**10301 Baltimore Avenue**
**Beltsville, MD  20705-2351**
Phone:  1-301-504-5994
Fax:  1-301-504-5675
World Wide Web URL:  http://www.nal.usda.gov/fnic
Email Address:  lending@nal.usda.gov

## It's Your Call:  Playing It Safe Around Guns; McCruff the Crime Dog on Gun Safety; Firearms Safety Depends on You

Three educational programs on one DVD to help people of all ages learn gun safety.

| | |
|---|---|
| Availability: | Limit of one copy to schools and homeschoolers in the United States and Canada. |
| Suggested Grade: | 5-9 |
| Order Number: | order by title |
| Format: | DVD |
| Special Notes: | May be retained permanently.  Includes a teacher's guide. |

Source:  National Shooting Sports Foundation
11 Mile Hill Road
Newtown, CT  06470-2359
Phone:  1-203-426-1320
World Wide Web URL:  http://www.nssf.org/safety
Email Address:  literature@nssf.org

## Knowing My 8 Rules for Safety:  Multilingual Child Safety and Prevention Tips

Lists eight safety tips for children to follow in several languages.

| | |
|---|---|
| Availability: | Limit of 50 copies to schools, libraries, and homeschoolers world-wide. |
| Suggested Grade: | 4-12 |
| Languages: | Twenty-three different languages in same book |
| Order Number: | 69 |
| Production Date: | 1999 |
| Format: | Book; 32 pages |
| Special Notes: | Additional copies are $3.00 each. |

**Source:  National Center for Missing & Exploited Children**
**Administrative Services**
**Charles B. Wang International Children's Building**
**699 Prince Street**
**Alexandria, VA  22314-3175**
Phone:  1-703-274-3900
Fax:  1-703-274-2200
World Wide Web URL:  http://www.missingkids.com

## Know the Rules...For Child Safety in Amusement or Theme Parks

A list of rules to follow for children in this situation.

| | |
|---|---|
| Availability: | Limit of 50 copies to schools, libraries, and homeschoolers world-wide. |
| Suggested Grade: | 4-12 |
| Languages: | English; Spanish |
| Order Number: | English 33; Spanish 145 |
| Production Date: | 2000 |
| Format: | Brochure |
| Special Notes: | Additional copies are 10 cents each. |

**Source:  National Center for Missing & Exploited Children**
**Administrative Services**
**Charles B. Wang International Children's Building**
**699 Prince Street**
**Alexandria, VA  22314-3175**
Phone:  1-703-274-3900
Fax:  1-703-274-2200
World Wide Web URL:  http://www.missingkids.com

## Know the Rules...For Child Safety in Youth Sports

A list of rules to follow for children in this situation.

| | |
|---|---|
| Availability: | Limit of 50 copies to schools, libraries, and homeschoolers world-wide. |
| Suggested Grade: | 4-12 |
| Languages: | English; Spanish |
| Order Number: | English 34; Spanish 146 |
| Production Date: | 2000 |
| Format: | Brochure |
| Special Notes: | Additional copies are 10 cents each. |

*All materials listed in this 2018-2019 edition are **BRAND NEW!***

Source: National Center for Missing & Exploited Children
Administrative Services
Charles B. Wang International Children's Building
699 Prince Street
Alexandria, VA 22314-3175
Phone: 1-703-274-3900
Fax: 1-703-274-2200
World Wide Web URL: http://www.missingkids.com

## Know the Rules...For Going To and From School More Safely

Ten tips for traveling to and from school more safely.

| | |
|---|---|
| Availability: | Limit of 50 copies to schools, libraries, and homeschoolers world-wide. |
| Suggested Grade: | Parents |
| Languages: | English; Spanish |
| Order Number: | English 91; Spanish 150 |
| Production Date: | 2002 |
| Format: | Brochure |
| Special Notes: | Additional copies are 10 cents each. |

Source: National Center for Missing & Exploited Children
Administrative Services
Charles B. Wang International Children's Building
699 Prince Street
Alexandria, VA 22314-3175
Phone: 1-703-274-3900
Fax: 1-703-274-2200
World Wide Web URL: http://www.missingkids.com

## Ladders, Lifting and Falls

Students will learn how to properly use and ladder as well as how to lift properly to avoid injury.

| | |
|---|---|
| Availability: | All requesters |
| Suggested Grade: | 6-Adult |
| Order Number: | not applicable |
| Format: | Online Lesson Plan |

Source: Dawna L. Cyr and Steven B. Johnson
World Wide Web URL:
http://nasdonline.org/document/1032/d000826/
ladders-lifting-and-falls.html

## Making Your Home Safe from Fire and Carbon Monoxide

Tips on preventing fires, creating an emergency exit plan, what types of safety equipment you should have, and more.

| | |
|---|---|
| Availability: | All requesters |
| Suggested Grade: | 4-Adult |
| Order Number: | not applicable |
| Format: | Online Article; 6 pages |
| Special Notes: | Use the on-site search engine to easily find this title. You may request a printed copy mailed to you for a fee. |

Source: Federal Citizen Information Center
World Wide Web URL: http://www.pueblo.gsa.gov/

## Natural Gas Safety World

Features information, experiments, games, and activities to teach students natural gas science and safety principles.

| | |
|---|---|
| Availability: | All requesters |
| Suggested Grade: | K-8 |
| Order Number: | not applicable |
| Format: | Web Site |

Source: Wisconsin Public Service
World Wide Web URL:
http://www.wisconsinpublicservice.com/
safetyforkids/landing.html

## New Neighborhood Safety Tips Brochure

Tips to follow when moving into a new neighborhood.

| | |
|---|---|
| Availability: | Limit of 50 copies to schools, libraries, and homeschoolers world-wide. |
| Suggested Grade: | 4-12 |
| Order Number: | 23 |
| Production Date: | 1998 |
| Format: | Brochure |
| Special Notes: | Additional copies are 10 cents each. |

Source: National Center for Missing & Exploited Children
Administrative Services
Charles B. Wang International Children's Building
699 Prince Street
Alexandria, VA 22314-3175
Phone: 1-703-274-3900
Fax: 1-703-274-2200
World Wide Web URL: http://www.missingkids.com

## Operation Lifesaver Lesson Plans

Lessons plans for teaching railroad safety--reinforces the theme, "Stay Off! Stay Away! Stay Alive!"

| | |
|---|---|
| Availability: | All requesters |
| Suggested Grade: | K-5; 6-8; 9-12 |
| Order Number: | not applicable |
| Format: | Online Lesson Plans |

Source: Operation Lifesaver, Inc.
World Wide Web URL: http://www.oli.org/

## OSHA Fact Sheets

Lots of fact sheets pertaining to workplace safety.

| | |
|---|---|
| Availability: | All requesters |
| Suggested Grade: | 6-Adult |
| Order Number: | not applicable |
| Format: | Downloadable Fact Sheets |

Source: United States Department of Labor, OSHA
World Wide Web URL:
http://www.osha.gov/OshDoc/toc_fact.html

## Plants That Poison

Indicates which plants are poisonous when ingested.

| | |
|---|---|
| Availability: | Single copies to schools, libraries, and homeschoolers in the United States and Canada. Send a stamped, self-addressed envelope for reply. |
| Suggested Grade: | All ages |
| Order Number: | order by title |
| Format: | Brochure |

# HEALTH--SAFETY AND FIRST AID

Source: Bronson Methodist Hospital Pharmacy
Attn: Nancy
601 John Street, 56
Kalamazoo, MI 49007

## Play it Safe: Rural Safety Program for Kids
A safety awareness program designed to educate young people about safety precautions in a rural environment.
Availability:      All requesters
Suggested Grade: 5-6
Order Number:   not applicable
Format:            Online Slide Show
Source: University of Vermont Extension System Farm Safety Program
World Wide Web URL:
http://nasdonline.org/document/2170/d000803/
play-it-safe-rural-safety-program-for-kids.html

## Product Safety Publications
Here are a number of articles about accident prevention when using certain items.
Availability:      All requesters
Suggested Grade: All ages
Order Number:   not applicable
Format:            Online Articles
Source: Consumer Product Safety Commission
World Wide Web URL:
http://www.cpsc.gov/cpscpub/pubs/pub_idx.html

## Safety & Health Fact Sheets
Lots of fact sheets covering weather safety, driving safety, agricultural safety, and safety inside and outside the home.
Availability:      All requesters
Suggested Grade: 4-Adult
Order Number:   not applicable
Format:            Downloadable Fact Sheets
Source: National Safety Council
World Wide Web URL:
http://www.nsc.org/news_resources/Resources/Pages/
SafetyHealthFactsheets.aspx

## Safety in the Laboratory
These safety rules apply to all laboratory activities.
Availability:      All requesters
Suggested Grade: 6-Adult
Order Number:   not applicable
Format:            Web Site
Source: Gwen Sibert
World Wide Web URL:
http://www.files.chem.vt.edu/RVGS/ACT/lab/
safety_rules.html

## Sparky the Fire Dog
Young children will learn about fire education and other safety issues with Sparky as their guide.
Availability:      All requesters
Suggested Grade: K-5
Order Number:   not applicable

Format:            Web Site
Source: National Fire Protection Association
World Wide Web URL:
http://www.sparky.orghttp://www.sparky.org

## SunWise: Sun Safety Program K-8
An environmental and health education program that aims to teach children and their caregivers how to protect themselves from overexposure to the sun. This video describes the program itself which is a free program.
Availability:      Schools, libraries, and homeschoolers in Connecticut, Maine, Massachusetts, New Hampshire, Rhode Island, and Vermont.
Suggested Grade: Teacher Reference
Languages:       English; Spanish
Order Number:   English VID 396; Spanish VID 397
Production Date: 2003
Format:            VHS videotape
Terms:   Borrower pays return postage. Return within three weeks of receipt. If the tape you request is available, it will be mailed within 5 business days. If not, you will be notified that this video is already out on loan. No more than three titles may be borrowed by one requestor at a time. No reservations for a specific date will be accepted. It is most efficient to order via the web site.
Source: U. S. Environmental Protection Agency, Region 1
Customer Service Center
One Congress Street, Suite 1100
Boston, MA 02214
World Wide Web URL:
http://yosemite.epa.gov/r1/videolen.nsf/

## Teaching Elementary Students About Fire Safety
A lesson plan for teaching about environmental health and fire safety.
Availability:      All requesters
Suggested Grade: 2-3
Order Number:   not applicable
Format:            Online Lesson Plan
Source: Brian F. Geiger
World Wide Web URL:
http://www.eduref.org/Virtual/Lessons/Health/Safety/
SFY0013.html

## Water and Canal Safety with Otto Otter
This lively and entertaining presentation was developed to encourage young people, as well as older people, to be aware of the danger around canals, canal structures, swimming areas, boats, etc. and large bodies of water.
Availability:      Schools, libraries, homeschoolers, nursing homes, and others in the United States and Canada.
Suggested Grade: All ages
Order Number:   order by title
Production Date: 1996
Format:            VHS videotape
Special Notes:   May be copied for permanent retention. Cleared for TV broadcast with advance permission.

*All materials listed in this 2018-2019 edition are **BRAND NEW!***

Terms:    Borrowers pay return postage. <u>Return 30 days after scheduled showing</u>, via U.S. Mail. Book 30 days in advance. Up to 2 videos will be sent out to one customer at a time. Your next order will be mailed as soon as you return previously borrowed tapes.

**Source:  Bureau of Reclamation**
**U.S. Department of the Interior**
**Attn:  Kristi Thompson, Library, 84-21320**
**6th Avenue & Kipling Street, Building 67**
**Denver, CO   80225-0007**
**Phone:  1-303-445-2039**
**Fax:  1-303-445-6303**
**World Wide Web URL:  http://www.usbr.gov/library**
**Email Address:  library@do.usbr.gov**

## Adolescent & School Health

Visitors to this site will find the latest research on student health as well as information on school health strategies. Designed to improve the physical fitness of young people.

Availability: All requesters
Suggested Grade: All ages
Order Number: not applicable
Format: Web Site

Source: Adolescent and School Health
World Wide Web URL:
http://www.cdc.gov/nccdphp/dash/index.htm

## Athletic Experiences of Ethnically Diverse Girls, The

Discusses how race and ethnicity, socioeconomic status, and area of residence impact on girls' sports experiences.

Availability: All requesters
Suggested Grade: Teacher Reference
Order Number: not applicable
Production Date: 1998
Format: Online Article

Source: Jeanne Weiler
World Wide Web URL:
http://www.ericdigests.org/1998-2/athletic.htm

## Ball/Barrel Attack

Students throw balls at a designated target (a cageball, barrel, or box, for example) to make it move toward a goal line.

Availability: All requesters
Suggested Grade: 3-8
Order Number: not applicable
Production Date: 2007
Format: Online Lesson Plan

Source: Charles Milliren
World Wide Web URL:
http://www.educationworld.com/a_tsl/archives/
07-1/lesson017.shtml

## Ball Monster

A great indoor activity using basketballs.

Availability: All requesters
Suggested Grade: 5-7
Order Number: not applicable
Format: Online Lesson Plan

Source: Kim Winters
World Wide Web URL:
http://www.pecentral.org/lessonideas/
ViewLesson.asp?ID=4986

## Beanbag Freeze Tag

An exercise using swim noodles.

Availability: All requesters
Suggested Grade: 6-8
Order Number: not applicable
Format: Online Lesson Plan

Source: Nick Jurman
World Wide Web URL: http://www.pecentral.org/
lessonideas/ViewLesson.asp?ID=5347

## Best Bones Forever!

Information for girls on how to develop lifelong bone-healthy habits for a healthier future.

Availability: All requesters
Suggested Grade: 3-8
Order Number: not applicable
Format: Web Site

Source: Centers for Disease Control and Prevention
World Wide Web URL: http://www.bestbonesforever.gov/

## Budo Sai: The Spirit of the Samurai

Filmed live at the Budo Sai festival, this film brings together twelve of the world's top martial arts masters who demonstrate their awesome powers. Masters of Kendo, Yui Shin Kai, Karate, and Aikido display their stunning skills.

Availability: Schools, libraries, and nursing homes in the United States and Canada.
Suggested Grade: 6-Adult
Order Number: JV063
Format: VHS videotape
Terms: Borrower pays return postage. Return with 14 days after scheduled showing, via UPS or U. S. Mail. All requests must included an educational institution affiliation, a current address, and phone number. Order through web site only.

Source: Cornell University East Asia Program
World Wide Web URL:
http://www.einaudi.cornell.edu/eastasia/outreach/video.asp
Email Address: east_asia1@cornell.edu

## Budo: The Martial Arts/The Art of Karate

Introduces the art and philosophy of the representative martial arts of Japan: Judo, Karate, and Aikido.

Availability: Schools, libraries, homeschoolers, and nursing homes in Connecticut (except Fairfield County), Maine, Massachusetts, New Hampshire, Rhode Island, and Vermont.
Suggested Grade: 6-Adult
Order Number: 138
Production Date: 1982
Format: VHS videotape
Terms: Borrower pays return postage, including insurance. Return two weeks after receipt.

Source: Consulate General of Japan, Boston
Federal Reserve Plaza, 14th Floor
600 Atlantic Avenue
Boston, MA 02210
Phone: 1-617-973-9772
Fax: 1-617-542-1329
World Wide Web URL:
http://www.boston.us.emb-japan.go.jp
Email Address: infocul@cgjbos.org

## Building Leadership Skills in Middle School Girls Through Interscholastic Athletics

Discusses this issue.

Availability: All requesters
Suggested Grade: Teacher Reference

Order Number: not applicable
Production Date: 2003
Format: Online Article
**Source: Lawrence Hart et al.**
**World Wide Web URL:**
**http://www.ericdigests.org/2005-2/girls.html**

## Christian Laettner: The Power Forward

This basketball play shows how to play the power forward position. He reveals his conditioning program and positive mental approach to the game.

Availability: Schools, libraries, and homeschoolers in the United States who serve the hearing impaired.
Suggested Grade: Adult
Order Number: 10826
Production Date: 1998
Format: DVD
Special Notes: Also available as live streaming video over the Internet.
Terms: Sponsor pays all transportation costs. Return one week after receipt. Participation is limited to deaf or hard of hearing Americans, their parents, families, teachers, counselors, or others whose use would benefit a deaf or hard of hearing person. Only one person in the audience needs to be hearing impaired. You must register--which is free. These videos are all open-captioned--no special equipment is required for viewing.
**Source: Described and Captioned Media Program**
**National Association of the Deaf**
**4211 Church Street Ext.**
**Roebuck, SC 29376**
**Phone: 1-800-237-6213**
**Fax: 1-800-538-5636**
**World Wide Web URL: http://www.dcmp.org**

## Competition Without Medals--Folk Sports in Taiwan

Taiwan is home to many diverse cultures, each with its own forms of physical recreation and athletic competition. These activities are not mere exercise, however, but sophisticated manifestations of each culture's experience. This film captures many facets of the subtle strength and grace of Taiwan folk sports.

Availability: Schools and libraries in Connecticut, New Jersey, New York, and Pennsylvania.
Suggested Grade: 7-12
Order Number: order by title
Production Date: 2003
Format: VHS videotape
Terms: Borrower pays return postage. Return 7 days after showing. Book at least 21 days in advance and provide alternate showing date.
**Source: Taipei Economic and Cultural Office in New York**
**Press Division**
**1 East 42nd Street, 11th Floor**
**New York, NY 10017**
**Phone: 1-212-317-7343**
**Fax: 1-212-557-3043**
**World Wide Web URL: http://www.taipei.org**
**Email Address: roctaiwan@taipei.org**

## Covert Bailey's Fit or Fat

A series of programs on fitness and how to get fit.

Availability: Staff at schools with NET, WIC, CSFP, FDPIR, CACFP, UMD or Child Nutrition Program food programs in the United States. Those not having such an affiliation should contact their library to place an interlibrary loan request.
Suggested Grade: 4-12
Order Number: NAL Video 1757
Production Date: 1993
Format: Set of 4 VHS videotapes
Terms: Borrower pays return postage. RETURN the day after scheduled use. Book at least 4 weeks in advance. Requests must include your name, phone, mail address, eligibility program, title, NAL number, show date, and a statement, "I have read the warning on copyright restrictions and accept full responsibility for compliance." One title per request.
**Source: National Agricultural Library**
**Document Delivery Services Branch**
**4th Floor, Photo Lab**
**10301 Baltimore Avenue**
**Beltsville, MD 20705-2351**
**Phone: 1-301-504-5994**
**Fax: 1-301-504-5675**
**World Wide Web URL: http://www.nal.usda.gov/fnic**
**Email Address: lending@nal.usda.gov**

## Exercise-Induced Asthma

Tells what types of exercise are best for those with asthma.

Availability: Limit of one copy to non-profit schools, libraries, and homeschoolers world-wide.
Suggested Grade: 7-Adult
Languages: English; Spanish
Order Number: order by title
Format: Brochure
Special Notes: Requests must be made via web site or email ONLY.
**Source: American Academy of Allergy, Asthma &**
**Immunology**
**Attn: Membership Assistant**
**555 East Wells Street, Suite 1100**
**Milwaukee, WI 53202**
**World Wide Web URL: http://www.aaaai.org**
**Email Address: info@aaaai.org**

## Exercise: It's Good for You!

Explains why exercise is important for a healthy body, how a balanced diet and staying active are beneficial, and that bathing and getting plenty of rest are good for you.

Availability: Schools, libraries, and homeschoolers in the United States who serve the hearing impaired.
Suggested Grade: 1-4
Order Number: 11140
Production Date: 2003
Format: DVD
Special Notes: Also available as live streaming video over the Internet.

Terms:    Sponsor pays all transportation costs. Return one week after receipt. Participation is limited to deaf or hard of hearing Americans, their parents, families, teachers, counselors, or others whose use would benefit a deaf or hard of hearing person. Only one person in the audience needs to be hearing impaired. You must register--which is free. These videos are all open-captioned--no special equipment is required for viewing.

**Source: Described and Captioned Media Program**
**National Association of the Deaf**
**4211 Church Street Ext.**
**Roebuck, SC 29376**
**Phone: 1-800-237-6213**
**Fax: 1-800-538-5636**
**World Wide Web URL: http://www.dcmp.org**

## Field Day Games for Whole-Class Fun
Lots of fun games for field day.
Availability:    All requesters
Suggested Grade:    preK-8
Order Number:    not applicable
Format:    Online Lesson Plan
**Source: Gary Hopkins**
**World Wide Web URL:**
**http://www.educationworld.com/a_lesson/03/lp315-03.shtml**

## 15 Relays for Field Days
Relay races can be a fun part of any field day--here are fifteen different ones.
Availability:    All requesters
Suggested Grade:    preK-8
Order Number:    not applicable
Format:    Online Lesson Plan
**Source: Gary Hopkins**
**World Wide Web URL:**
**http://www.educationworld.com/a_lesson/03/lp315-02.shtml**

## Fitness for Youth
Offers lots of information and helpful ideas for implementing and running physical fitness programs for children.
Availability:    All requesters
Suggested Grade:    preK-8
Order Number:    not applicable
Format:    Web Site
**Source: University of Michigan and Blue Cross Blue Shield**
**World Wide Web URL:**
**http://www.fitnessforyouth.umich.edu/**

## Fitness Jumpsite
Lots of information about physical fitness.
Availability:    All requesters
Suggested Grade:    6-12
Order Number:    not applicable
Format:    Web Site
**Source: Vicki Pierson and Renee Cloe**
**World Wide Web URL:**
**http://primusweb.com/fitnesspartner**

## GoGirlGo Secondary
This unique education program utilizes four characters to educate high school girls about health risk behaviors and life lessons such as body image, bullying, diversity, smoking, drugs, and stress. Designed for girls' sports and physical
Availability:    Schools and libraries in the United States.
Suggested Grade:    9-12
Order Number:    order by title
Production Date:    2004
Format:    Curriculum
Special Notes:    May also be downloaded from the web site.
**Source: Women's Sports Foundation**
**Phone: 1-800-227-3988**
**World Wide Web URL: http://www.gogirlgo.com/**

## Help Keep Your Classmates Healthy
Help design a game that will keep your classmates in good physical condition.
Availability:    All requesters
Suggested Grade:    K-2
Order Number:    not applicable
Format:    WebQuest
**Source: David Ascolani**
**World Wide Web URL:**
**http://www.yorkville.k12.il.us/webquests/**
**webqascolani/webqsascolani.html**

## KidsRunning.Com
A site devoted to help kids and their parents learn more about exercise--how to as well as the benefits.
Availability:    All requesters
Suggested Grade:    preK-6
Order Number:    not applicable
Format:    Web Site
**Source: Carol Goodrow**
**World Wide Web URL: http://www.kidsrunning.com/**

## Log It
An online program that allows 4th grade aged students and higher (as well as individuals) to record their physical activity steps and miles to encourage more activity.
Availability:    All requesters
Suggested Grade:    4-Adult
Order Number:    not applicable
Format:    Web Site
Special Notes:    Schools must register, but registration is free.
**Source: PE Central and New Lifestyles**
**World Wide Web URL: http://www.peclogit.org/logit.asp**

## Magic Rope Curl-Ups
This activity will help make all young children more successful in doing a crunch or curl-up using proper form.
Availability:    All requesters
Suggested Grade:    K-3
Order Number:    not applicable
Format:    Online Lesson Plan

*All materials listed in this 2018-2019 edition are **BRAND NEW!***

Source: Shelley Peterson
World Wide Web URL: http://www.pecentral.org/
lessonideas/ViewLesson.asp?ID=5271

## Marathon Challenge

Explore what it takes-physically and mentally-for novice runners to make it through a classic test of endurance.

| | |
|---|---|
| Availability: | All requesters |
| Suggested Grade: | 7-Adult |
| Order Number: | not applicable |
| Production Date: | 2007 |
| Format: | Streaming Video |

Source: NOVA
World Wide Web URL:
http://www.pbs.org/wgbh/nova/programs/index.html

## Naginata

In the Middle Ages, the "naginata," a long-handled sword, was the weapon of the infantry. Interestingly, this martial art is practiced today mainly by women. This video shows more about this sport.

| | |
|---|---|
| Availability: | Schools, libraries, and nursing homes in Hawaii. |
| Suggested Grade: | 6-Adult |
| Order Number: | SP-11 |
| Production Date: | 1999 |
| Format: | VHS videotape |
| Terms: | Borrower pays return postage. A maximum of 3 videos may be borrowed per person. Return within one week of date borrowed. |

Source: Consulate General of Japan, Honolulu
1742 Nuuanu Avenue
Honolulu, HI 96817-3294
Phone: 1-808-543-3111
Fax: 1-808-543-3170
World Wide Web URL:
http://www.honolulu.us.emb-japan.go.jp

## Naginata

In the Middle Ages, the "naginata," a long-handled sword, was the weapon of the infantry. Interestingly, this martial art is practiced today mainly by women. This video shows more about this sport.

| | |
|---|---|
| Availability: | Schools, libraries, homeschoolers, and nursing homes in OREGON AND SOUTHERN IDAHO ONLY. Please make requests via the web site. |
| Suggested Grade: | 6-Adult |
| Order Number: | 444 |
| Production Date: | 1999 |
| Format: | VHS videotape |
| Terms: | Borrower pays return postage. Return within three weeks after scheduled showing date. Book one month in advance if possible. Rewind the video and wrap securely for return. Be certain to indicate video number, date needed, name of your organization, and address to which video should be sent, along with phone number. Audience report enclosed with the video must be completed and returned. |

Source: Consulate General of Japan, Oregon
Attn: Tamara, Video Library
1300 S. W. Fifth Avenue, Suite 2700
Portland, OR 97201
Phone: 1-503-221-1811, ext. 17
World Wide Web URL:
http://www.portland.us.emb-japan.go.jp/en/index.html
Email Address: tamara@cgjpdx.org

## 99 Tips for Family Fitness Fun

Fitness can be fun as well as beneficial--find out how.

| | |
|---|---|
| Availability: | All requesters |
| Suggested Grade: | All ages |
| Order Number: | not applicable |
| Format: | Downloadable Brochure |

Source: National Association for Sports and Physical
Education and Shape Up America
World Wide Web URL:
http://www.shapeup.org/publications/
99.tips.for.family.fitness.fun/

## Posture

What is good posture? What does it tell the world about a person? Describes in detail the components of correct standing, sitting, and lying postures. Demonstrates and contrasts good and poor posture. Depicts how the line of gravity test is used to evaluate an individual's posture. Stresses the relationship between good posture and an individual's physical and mental well-being.

| | |
|---|---|
| Availability: | Schools, libraries, and homeschoolers in the United States who serve the hearing impaired. |
| Suggested Grade: | 3-6 |
| Order Number: | 2321 |
| Production Date: | 1987 |
| Format: | DVD |
| Special Notes: | Produced by New Dimension Media. |
| Terms: | Sponsor pays all transportation costs. Return one week after receipt. Participation is limited to deaf or hard of hearing Americans, their parents, families, teachers, counselors, or others whose use would benefit a deaf or hard of hearing person. Only one person in the audience needs to be hearing impaired. You must register--which is free. These videos are all open-captioned--no special equipment is required for viewing. |

Source: Described and Captioned Media Program
National Association of the Deaf
4211 Church Street Ext.
Roebuck, SC 29376
Phone: 1-800-237-6213
Fax: 1-800-538-5636
World Wide Web URL: http://www.dcmp.org

## Real Scoop About Diet and Exercise, The

Shows kids how to improve their health by diet and exercise.

| | |
|---|---|
| Availability: | Staff at schools with NET, WIC, CSFP, FDPIR, CACFP, UMD or Child Nutrition Program food programs in the United States. Those not having such an affiliation should |

contact their library to place an interlibrary loan request.

Suggested Grade:	4-12
Order Number:	NAL Video 2187
Production Date:	1995
Format:	VHS vidcotape
Special Notes:	Includes additional supplementary materials.
Terms:	Borrower pays return postage. RETURN the day after scheduled use. Book at least 4 weeks in advance. Requests must include your name, phone, mail address, eligibility program, title, NAL number, show date, and a statement, "I have read the warning on copyright restrictions and accept full responsibility for compliance." One title per request.

**Source: National Agricultural Library
Document Delivery Services Branch
4th Floor, Photo Lab
10301 Baltimore Avenue
Beltsville, MD 20705-2351
Phone: 1-301-504-5994
Fax: 1-301-504-5675
World Wide Web URL: http://www.nal.usda.gov/fnic
Email Address: lending@nal.usda.gov**

## RunStat 3

Enter the distance and time for your run and this program calculates your pace for your run.

Availability:	All requesters
Suggested Grade:	6-12
Platform:	Windows
Order Number:	not applicable
Format:	Downloadable FULL PROGRAM
Special Notes:	It is preferred that you download this program from the Web; if this does not work for you then you can send $5.00 to receive the program on disk.

**Source: Scott Diamond & Cats
World Wide Web URL:
http://ibiblio.org/drears/running/products/
software/runstat.html**

## Specific Sports Exercises

A number of exercises specific to certain sports.

Availability:	All requesters
Suggested Grade:	All ages
Order Number:	not applicable
Format:	Web Site

**Source: International Fitness Association
World Wide Web URL: http://www.ifafitness.com/sports/**

## Sumo

Reports on the popular and traditional Japanese sport of Sumo wrestling.

Availability:	Schools, libraries, and nursing homes in Hawaii.
Suggested Grade:	All ages
Order Number:	SP-6
Production Date:	1997
Format:	VHS videotape

Terms:	Borrower pays return postage. A maximum of 3 videos may be borrowed per person. Return within one week of date borrowed.

**Source: Consulate General of Japan, Honolulu
1742 Nuuanu Avenue
Honolulu, HI 96817-3294
Phone: 1-808-543-3111
Fax: 1-808-543-3170
World Wide Web URL:
http://www.honolulu.us.emb-japan.go.jp**

## Sumo

Reports on the popular and traditional Japanese sport of Sumo wrestling.

Availability:	Schools, libraries, homeschoolers, and nursing homes in OREGON AND SOUTHERN IDAHO ONLY. Please make requests via the web site.
Suggested Grade:	All ages
Order Number:	439
Production Date:	1997
Format:	VHS videotape
Terms:	Borrower pays return postage. Return within three weeks after scheduled showing date. Book one month in advance if possible. Rewind the video and wrap securely for return. Be certain to indicate video number, date needed, name of your organization, and address to which video should be sent, along with phone number. Audience report enclosed with the video must be completed and returned.

**Source: Consulate General of Japan, Oregon
Attn: Tamara, Video Library
1300 S. W. Fifth Avenue, Suite 2700
Portland, OR 97201
Phone: 1-503-221-1811, ext. 17
World Wide Web URL:
http://www.portland.us.emb-japan.go.jp/en/index.html
Email Address: tamara@cgjpdx.org**

## Super 6 Fitness Stations

A lesson plan utilizing pedometers which shows students how much activity they have done.

Availability:	All requesters
Suggested Grade:	3-5
Order Number:	not applicable
Format:	Online Lesson Plan

**Source: Sharon Welch
World Wide Web URL:
http://www.pecentral.org/lessonideas/
ViewLesson.asp?ID=1709**

## Tai Chi for Health

Five segments present the Yang Long Form from the beginner's level.

Availability:	Schools, libraries, homeschoolers, and nursing homes in the United States and Canada.
Suggested Grade:	6-12
Order Number:	order by title

*All materials listed in this 2018-2019 edition are **BRAND NEW!***

Format:          VHS videotape
Terms:    Postage is paid by borrower both ways--send $3.00 per tape to cover initial shipping to you--MONEY MUST BE SENT WITH REQUEST. Return 10 days after showing via U. S. Postal Service, library rate. Shipping is $5.00 to Canadian addresses.
> **Source: Center for Teaching About China**
> **Kathleen Trescott**
> **1214 West Schwartz**
> **Carbondale, IL  62901**
> **Phone: 1-618-549-1555**
> **Email Address: trescott@midwest.net**

## Tai Chi:  Healing Dance
Follow the 36 step training course to help obtain benefits to the mind and body.

Availability:    Schools, libraries, homeschoolers, and nursing homes in the United States and Canada.
Suggested Grade:   6-12
Order Number:     order by title
Production Date:   1995
Format:          VHS videotape
Terms:    Postage is paid by borrower both ways--send $3.00 per tape to cover initial shipping to you--MONEY MUST BE SENT WITH REQUEST. Return 10 days after showing via U. S. Postal Service, library rate. Shipping is $5.00 to Canadian addresses.
> **Source: Center for Teaching About China**
> **Kathleen Trescott**
> **1214 West Schwartz**
> **Carbondale, IL  62901**
> **Phone: 1-618-549-1555**
> **Email Address: trescott@midwest.net**

## Traditional Japanese Sports:  Judo
Reports on the popular and traditional Japanese sport of Judo.

Availability:    Schools, libraries, homeschoolers, and nursing homes in Connecticut (except Fairfield County), Maine, Massachusetts, New Hampshire, Rhode Island, and Vermont.
Suggested Grade:   All ages
Order Number:     597
Format:          VHS videotape
Terms:    Borrower pays return postage, including insurance. Return two weeks after receipt.
> **Source: Consulate General of Japan, Boston**
> **Federal Reserve Plaza, 14th Floor, 600 Atlantic Avenue**
> **Boston, MA  02210**
> **Phone: 1-617-973-9772**
> **Fax: 1-617-542-1329**
> **World Wide Web URL:**
> **http://www.boston.us.emb-japan.go.jp**
> **Email Address: infocul@cgjbos.org**

## Traditional Japanese Sports:  Judo
Reports on the popular and traditional Japanese sport of Judo.

Availability:    Schools, libraries, homeschoolers, and nursing homes in Connecticut, Delaware, Maryland, New Jersey, New York, Pennsylvania, and West Virginia.
Suggested Grade:   All ages
Order Number:     order by title
Format:          VHS videotape
Terms:    Send a blank videotape to this source and they will dub the program you desire onto it for permanent retention. You must send a self-addressed, stamped envelope with sufficient postage for return.
> **Source: Consulate General of Japan, New York**
> **Audio Video Dept.**
> **299 Park Avenue, 18th Floor**
> **New York, NY  10171**
> **Phone: 1-212-371-8222**
> **Fax: 1-212-319-6357**
> **World Wide Web URL: http://www.ny.us.emb-japan.go.jp**

## Traditional Japanese Sports:  Kendo
History of martial arts leading to the present-day Kendo, with scenes of training and contests, as well as the moral instruction that accompanies this art.

Availability:    Schools, libraries, homeschoolers, and nursing homes in Connecticut (except Fairfield County), Maine, Massachusetts, New Hampshire, Rhode Island, and Vermont.
Suggested Grade:   All ages
Order Number:     598
Production Date:   1997
Format:          VHS videotape
Terms:    Borrower pays return postage, including insurance. Return two weeks after receipt.
> **Source: Consulate General of Japan, Boston**
> **Federal Reserve Plaza, 14th Floor**
> **600 Atlantic Avenue**
> **Boston, MA  02210**
> **Phone: 1-617-973-9772**
> **Fax: 1-617-542-1329**
> **World Wide Web URL:**
> **http://www.boston.us.emb-japan.go.jp**
> **Email Address: infocul@cgjbos.org**

## Traditional Japanese Sports:  Kendo
History of martial arts leading to the present-day Kendo, with scenes of training and contests, as well as the moral instruction that accompanies this art.

Availability:    Schools, libraries, homeschoolers, and nursing homes in Connecticut, Delaware, Maryland, New Jersey, New York, Pennsylvania, and West Virginia.
Suggested Grade:   All ages
Order Number:     order by title
Production Date:   1997
Format:          VHS videotape
Terms:    Send a blank videotape to this source and they will dub the program you desire onto it for permanent retention. You must send a self-addressed, stamped envelope with sufficient postage for return.

# PHYSICAL EDUCATION

Source: Consulate General of Japan, New York
Audio Video Dept.
299 Park Avenue, 18th Floor
New York, NY  10171
Phone:  1-212-371-8222
Fax:  1-212-319-6357
World Wide Web URL:  http://www.ny.us.emb-japan.go.jp

## Traditional Japanese Sports:  Kendo

History of martial arts leading to the present-day Kendo, with scenes of training and contests, as well as the moral instruction that accompanies this art.

Availability:      Schools, libraries, homeschoolers, and nursing homes in OREGON AND SOUTHERN IDAHO ONLY.  Please make requests via the web site.
Suggested Grade:  All ages
Order Number:    216
Production Date:  1985
Format:             VHS videotape
Terms:    Borrower pays return postage.  Return within three weeks after scheduled showing date.  Book one month in advance if possible.  Rewind the video and wrap securely for return.  Be certain to indicate video number, date needed, name of your organization, and address to which video should be sent, along with phone number.  Audience report enclosed with the video must be completed and returned.

Source: Consulate General of Japan, Oregon
Attn: Tamara, Video Library
1300 S. W. Fifth Avenue, Suite 2700
Portland, OR  97201
Phone: 1-503-221-1811, ext. 17
World Wide Web URL:
http://www.portland.us.emb-japan.go.jp/en/index.html
Email Address:  tamara@cgjpdx.org

## 20 Field Day Activities Any Kid Can Do (And Do Well!)

Twenty great field day activities that emphasize fun over skill.

Availability:      All requesters
Suggested Grade:  preK-8
Order Number:    not applicable
Format:             Online Lesson Plan

Source:  Gary Hopkins
World Wide Web URL:
http://www.educationworld.com/a_lesson/03/lp315-01.shtml

## Why Assess in Physical Education?

Answers this question.

Availability:      All requesters
Suggested Grade:  Teacher Reference
Order Number:    not applicable
Format:             Online Article

Source:  Stephen Jefferies, Toni Jefferies, and Wendy Mustain
World Wide Web URL:
http://www.pecentral.org/assessment/assessmentresearch.html

*All materials listed in this 2018-2019 edition are **BRAND NEW!***

## Alex's Paper Airplanes
Lots of directions for making all sorts of paper airplanes.

| | |
|---|---|
| Availability: | All requesters |
| Suggested Grade: | All ages |
| Order Number: | not applicable |
| Format: | Web Site |

**Source: Alex Schultz**
**World Wide Web URL: http://www.paperairplanes.co.uk/**

## Appaloosa Coloring Pages
In addition to providing pages for coloring, these pages also display the versatility of the Appaloosa.

| | |
|---|---|
| Availability: | Classroom quantities to schools, libraries, and homeschoolers world-wide. |
| Suggested Grade: | preK-3 |
| Order Number: | order by title |
| Format: | Coloring Pages |

**Source: Appaloosa Horse Club, The**
**Attn: Marketing Department**
**2720 West Pullman Road**
**Moscow, ID 83843**
**Phone: 1-208-882-5578, ext. 229**
**Fax: 1-208-882-8150**
**World Wide Web URL: http://www.appaloosa.com**
**Email Address: promotions@appaloosa.com**

## Art of Karate, The
Presents the ancient oriental self-defense method of karate. Karate has now developed into a very popular sport in Japan and many other countries.

| | |
|---|---|
| Availability: | Schools, libraries, and nursing homes in Connecticut (except Fairfield county), Maine, Massachusetts, New Hampshire, Rhode Island, and Vermont. |
| Suggested Grade: | All ages |
| Order Number: | order by title |
| Format: | 16mm film |
| Terms: | Borrower pays return postage, including insurance. Return two weeks after receipt. |

**Source: Consulate General of Japan, Boston**
**Federal Reserve Plaza, 14th Floor**
**600 Atlantic Avenue**
**Boston, MA 02210**
**Phone: 1-617-973-9772**
**Fax: 1-617-542-1329**
**World Wide Web URL:**
**http://www.boston.us.emb-japan.go.jp**
**Email Address: infocul@cgjbos.org**

## Balloons
Animation and newsreel footage explore a brief history of balloons, airships, and dirigibles. Presents a balloon quiz at the end.

| | |
|---|---|
| Availability: | Schools, libraries, and homeschoolers in the United States who serve the hearing impaired. |
| Suggested Grade: | preK-4 |
| Order Number: | 12403 |
| Format: | DVD |

| | |
|---|---|
| Terms: | Sponsor pays all transportation costs. Return one week after receipt. Participation is limited to deaf or hard of hearing Americans, their parents, families, teachers, counselors, or others whose use would benefit a deaf or hard of hearing person. Only one person in the audience needs to be hearing impaired. You must register--which is free. These videos are all open-captioned--no special equipment is required for viewing. |

**Source: Described and Captioned Media Program**
**National Association of the Deaf**
**4211 Church Street Ext.**
**Roebuck, SC 29376**
**Phone: 1-800-237-6213**
**Fax: 1-800-538-5636**
**World Wide Web URL: http://www.dcmp.org**

## Baserunning for Softball: Skills and Drills
Presents a visual overview of the skills, fundamentals, and techniques involved in effective baserunning in this sport.

| | |
|---|---|
| Availability: | Schools, libraries, and homeschoolers in the United States who serve the hearing impaired. |
| Suggested Grade: | Adult |
| Order Number: | 12488 |
| Production Date: | 1997 |
| Format: | DVD |
| Terms: | Sponsor pays all transportation costs. Return one week after receipt. Participation is limited to deaf or hard of hearing Americans, their parents, families, teachers, counselors, or others whose use would benefit a deaf or hard of hearing person. Only one person in the audience needs to be hearing impaired. You must register--which is free. These videos are all open-captioned--no special equipment is required for viewing. |

**Source: Described and Captioned Media Program**
**National Association of the Deaf**
**4211 Church Street Ext.**
**Roebuck, SC 29376**
**Phone: 1-800-237-6213**
**Fax: 1-800-538-5636**
**World Wide Web URL: http://www.dcmp.org**

## Beginning Sewing Lessons
A complete and detailed book, available online, that teaches everything about sewing from a basic introduction to sewing darts and pleats.

| | |
|---|---|
| Availability: | All requesters |
| Suggested Grade: | 4-Adult |
| Order Number: | not applicable |
| Format: | Online Book |

**Source: CraftAndFabricLinks.com**
**World Wide Web URL:**
**http://craftandfabriclinks.com/sewingbook/sewbook.html**

## Bikesport
Information on cycling.

| | |
|---|---|
| Availability: | All requesters |
| Suggested Grade: | All ages |
| Order Number: | not applicable |
| Format: | Web Site |

Special Notes: This URL will lead you to a subject page. Then click on the appropriate subject heading.
**Source: ThinkQuest**
**World Wide Web URL:**
**http://www.thinkquest.org/pls/html/think.library**

## Caring for Your Pet Chihuahua

Covers Chihuahua history, personality, and much more to help you care for your dog.

Availability: Schools, libraries, and homeschoolers in the United States who serve the hearing impaired.
Suggested Grade: Adult
Order Number: 13635
Production Date: 1997
Format: DVD
Special Notes: Also available as live streaming video over the Internet.
Terms: Sponsor pays all transportation costs. Return one week after receipt. Participation is limited to deaf or hard of hearing Americans, their parents, families, teachers, counselors, or others whose use would benefit a deaf or hard of hearing person. Only one person in the audience needs to be hearing impaired. You must register--which is free. These videos are all open-captioned--no special equipment is required for viewing.
**Source: Described and Captioned Media Program**
**National Association of the Deaf**
**4211 Church Street Ext.**
**Roebuck, SC 29376**
**Phone: 1-800-237-6213**
**Fax: 1-800-538-5636**
**World Wide Web URL: http://www.dcmp.org**

## Caring for Your Pet Pomeranian

Tips on how to care for your Pomeranian along with information about the breed in general.

Availability: Schools, libraries, and homeschoolers in the United States who serve the hearing impaired.
Suggested Grade: Adult
Order Number: 24085
Production Date: 2000
Format: DVD
Special Notes: Also available as live streaming video over the Internet.
Terms: Sponsor pays all transportation costs. Return one week after receipt. Participation is limited to deaf or hard of hearing Americans, their parents, families, teachers, counselors, or others whose use would benefit a deaf or hard of hearing person. Only one person in the audience needs to be hearing impaired. You must register--which is free. These videos are all open-captioned--no special equipment is required for viewing.
**Source: Described and Captioned Media Program**
**National Association of the Deaf**
**4211 Church Street Ext.**
**Roebuck, SC 29376**
**Phone: 1-800-237-6213**
**Fax: 1-800-538-5636**
**World Wide Web URL: http://www.dcmp.org**

## CyberCycle

How to find the right bike, planning your ride, and a guide to trails in New England.

Availability: All requesters
Suggested Grade: 6-Adult
Order Number: not applicable
Format: Web Site
Special Notes: This URL will lead you to a subject page. Then click on the appropriate subject heading.
**Source: ThinkQuest**
**World Wide Web URL:**
**http://www.thinkquest.org/pls/html/think.library**

## Estes Educator Packet, The

Information for teaching model rocketry.

Availability: One packet to schools, libraries, and teachers in the United States.
Suggested Grade: 4-12
Order Number: order by title
Format: Teacher's Kit
**Source: Estes Rockets**
**Educational Services**
**1295 H Street, P. O. Box 227**
**Penrose, CO 81240**
**Phone: 1-800-820-0202**
**Fax: 1-800-820-0203**
**World Wide Web URL: http://www.esteseducator.com**
**Email Address: educator@estesrockets.com**

## Ethical Hunter, The

Explores all aspects of hunting ethics.

Availability: Limit of 100 copies to schools, libraries, and homeschoolers in the United States and Canada. Make request on official stationery.
Suggested Grade: 6-Adult
Order Number: 031
Format: Leaflet
**Source: National Shooting Sports Foundation**
**Council for Wildlife Conservation and Education**
**11 Mile Hill Road**
**Newtown, CT 06470-2359**
**Phone: 1-203-426-1320**
**Fax: 1-203-426-1245**
**World Wide Web URL: http://www.nssf.org**
**Email Address: literature@nssf.org**

## Fishing Is Fun for Everyone

Find out what equipment you need, what kind of bait to use, how to cast and tie knots, and more.

Availability: All requesters
Suggested Grade: All ages
Order Number: not applicable
Production Date: 1999
Format: Online Article; 11 pages
Special Notes: Use the on-site search engine to easily find this title. You may request a printed copy mailed to you for a fee.
**Source: Federal Citizen Information Center**
**World Wide Web URL: http://www.pueblo.gsa.gov/**

*All materials listed in this 2018-2019 edition are **BRAND NEW!***

## Fun at Recess

Here are the rules to many popular playground games.

Availability: All requesters
Suggested Grade: preK-6
Order Number: not applicable
Format: Web Site
Special Notes: This URL will lead you to a subject page. Then click on the appropriate subject heading.
**Source: ThinkQuest**
**World Wide Web URL:**
http://www.thinkquest.org/pls/html/think.library

## Game a Day, A

Literally thousands of games to keep you entertained for hours. There are educational games and games that are just plain fun.

Availability: All requesters
Suggested Grade: All ages
Order Number: not applicable
Format: Web Site
**Source: Game a Day.com, Inc.**
**World Wide Web URL: http://www.agameaday.com**

## Get Ready, Get Set, Grow!

The Brooklyn Children's Garden, where generations of children have gotten dirt under their fingernails, introduces students to the wonders of plant growth, and the basics of gardening, engendering respect for the natural world. After all, "Only plants can make food!"

Availability: Schools, libraries, homeschoolers, and nursing homes in the United States.
Suggested Grade: 1-8
Order Number: order by title
Production Date: 1986
Format: VHS videotape
Special Notes: Accompanied by information for children and adults on how to start a community garden.
Terms: Borrower pays return postage. Return the day after scheduled showing, via UPS or Priority Mail, insured for $100.00. Book 4 weeks in advance and include an alternate date. Order should include name of person responsible for handling the video, and complete mailing address. Please mention this Guide when ordering. Tapes may not be duplicated, edited or exhibited for a fee.
**Source: Church World Service**
**Film & Video Library**
**28606 Phillips Street, P. O. Box 968**
**Elkhart, IN 46515**
**Phone: 1-800-297-1516, ext. 338**
**Fax: 1-574-262-0966**
**World Wide Web URL: http://www.churchworldservice.org**
**Email Address: videos@churchworldservice.org**

## Ham Shack, The

Introduces the hobby of amateur radio, equipment and licensing needed, and what various terms mean.

Availability: All requesters
Suggested Grade: 6-12
Order Number: not applicable
Format: Web Site
Special Notes: This URL will lead you to a subject page. Then click on the appropriate subject heading.
**Source: ThinkQuest**
**World Wide Web URL:**
http://www.thinkquest.org/pls/html/think.library

## Judo

Demonstrates actual judo maneuvers.

Availability: Schools, libraries, and nursing homes in Connecticut (except Fairfield county), Maine, Massachusetts, New Hampshire, Rhode Island, and Vermont.
Suggested Grade: 7-12
Order Number: order by title
Format: 16mm film
Special Notes: Black and white.
Terms: Borrower pays return postage, including insurance. Return two weeks after receipt.
**Source: Consulate General of Japan, Boston**
**Federal Reserve Plaza, 14th Floor**
**600 Atlantic Avenue**
**Boston, MA 02210**
**Phone: 1-617-973-9772**
**Fax: 1-617-542-1329**
**World Wide Web URL:**
http://www.boston.us.emb-japan.go.jp
**Email Address: infocul@cgjbos.org**

## Karatedo

Illustrates "tamashi-wari," or a trial breaking of a concrete block with a bare hand, a feat which displays the tremendous power of Karate techniques, as well as the processes of Karate training.

Availability: Schools, libraries, and nursing homes in Illinois, Indiana, Iowa, Kansas, Minnesota, Missouri, Nebraska, North Dakota, South Dakota, and Wisconsin.
Suggested Grade: 6-12
Order Number: 18002
Production Date: 1994
Format: VHS videotape
Terms: Borrower pays return postage by U. S. Mail, UPS, or Federal Express, including insurance for "original" videos. Write, call, fax, or e-mail to request an application. An application form MUST be sent in one month in advance but not more than six months in advance. Include alternate titles and dates if provider can substitute titles. Send a SASE with request if you require confirmation. Return immediately after scheduled showing date. Videos may not be copied or broadcast without permission from the producer of the video. Borrower is responsible if video is lost or damaged.

Source: Consulate General of Japan at Chicago
Japan Information Center
Library
737 North Michigan Avenue, Suite 1000
Chicago, IL 60611
Phone: 1-312-280-0430
Fax: 1-312-280-6883
World Wide Web URL:
http://www.chicago.us.emb-japan.go.jp/jic.html
Email Address: jicchicago@webkddi.com

## Karatedo
The Japanese form of self-defense, Karatedo has developed into a major sport.

Availability:       Schools, libraries, and nursing homes in Hawaii.
Suggested Grade:    All ages
Order Number:       SP-4
Production Date:    1997
Format:             VHS videotape
Terms:    Borrower pays return postage. A maximum of 3 videos may be borrowed per person. Return within one week of date borrowed.

Source: Consulate General of Japan, Honolulu
1742 Nuuanu Avenue
Honolulu, HI 96817-3294
Phone: 1-808-543-3111
Fax: 1-808-543-3170
World Wide Web URL:
http://www.honolulu.us.emb-japan.go.jp

## Karatedo
The Japanese form of self-defense, Karatedo has developed into a major sport.

Availability:       Schools, libraries, homeschoolers, and nursing homes in OREGON AND SOUTHERN IDAHO ONLY. Please make requests via the web site.
Suggested Grade:    All ages
Order Number:       442
Production Date:    1997
Format:             VHS videotape
Terms:    Borrower pays return postage. Return within three weeks after scheduled showing date. Book one month in advance if possible. Rewind the video and wrap securely for return. Be certain to indicate video number, date needed, name of your organization, and address to which video should be sent, along with phone number. Audience report enclosed with the video must be completed and returned.

Source: Consulate General of Japan, Oregon
Attn: Tamara, Video Library
1300 S. W. Fifth Avenue, Suite 2700
Portland, OR 97201
Phone: 1-503-221-1811, ext. 17
World Wide Web URL:
http://www.portland.us.emb-japan.go.jp/en/index.html
Email Address: tamara@cgjpdx.org

## Kidsgardening.com
Lots of articles, stories, and activities about bringing the joy of gardening into the classroom.

Availability:       All requesters
Suggested Grade:    All ages
Order Number:       not applicable
Format:             Web Site

Source: Kidsgardening.com
World Wide Web URL: http://www.kidsgardening.com

## Kyudo
Kyudo is the Japanese sport of archery. This program looks at this sport in Japan.

Availability:       Schools, libraries, and nursing homes in Illinois, Indiana, Iowa, Kansas, Minnesota, Missouri, Nebraska, North Dakota, South Dakota, and Wisconsin.
Suggested Grade:    All ages
Order Number:       18004
Production Date:    1994
Format:             VHS videotape
Terms:    Borrower pays return postage by U. S. Mail, UPS, or Federal Express, including insurance for "original" videos. Write, call, fax, or e-mail to request an application. An application form MUST be sent in one month in advance but not more than six months in advance. Include alternate titles and dates if provider can substitute titles. Send a SASE with request if you require confirmation. Return immediately after scheduled showing date. Videos may not be copied or broadcast without permission from the producer of the video. Borrower is responsible if video is lost or damaged.

Source: Consulate General of Japan at Chicago
Japan Information Center
Library
737 North Michigan Avenue, Suite 1000
Chicago, IL 60611
Phone: 1-312-280-0430
Fax: 1-312-280-6883
World Wide Web URL:
http://www.chicago.us.emb-japan.go.jp/jic.html
Email Address: jicchicago@webkddi.com

## Lesson 29: Textured Pottery Using Self-Hardening Clay and Multicultural Designs
Learn how to create clay vessels that pay tribute to other cultures.

Availability:       All requesters
Suggested Grade:    Teacher Reference
Order Number:       not applicable
Format:             Online Lesson Plan

Source: American Art Clay Co., Inc.
Sales Support, 6060 Guion Road
Indianapolis, IN 46254
Phone: 1-800-374-1600
Fax: 1-317-248-9300
World Wide Web URL: http://www.amaco.com
Email Address: salessupport@amaco.com

## O' in Schools

Information, games, and teaching aids that will help students learn more about orienteering.

Availability:          All requesters
Suggested Grade:  All ages
Order Number:      not applicable
Format:                Online Newsletter; published 8 times a year

**Source: United States Orienteering Federation**
**World Wide Web URL: http://ocin.org/school/**

## Origami

Origami, the centuries-old Japanese art of paper-folding, still enjoys great popularity among the young and old alike. Parents encourage this pastime at home, guiding their offspring in creating a wide variety of intricate figures. It's an invaluable aid in developing the creative imaginations of youngsters.

Availability:          Schools, libraries, and nursing homes in Illinois, Indiana, Iowa, Kansas, Minnesota, Missouri, Nebraska, North Dakota, South Dakota, and Wisconsin.
Suggested Grade:  6-Adult
Order Number:      03403
Format:                VHS videotape
Terms:                 Borrower pays return postage by U. S. Mail, UPS, or Federal Express, including insurance for "original" videos. Write, call, fax, or e-mail to request an application. An application form MUST be sent in one month in advance but not more than six months in advance. Include alternate titles and dates if provider can substitute titles. Send a SASE with request if you require confirmation. Return immediately after scheduled showing date. Videos may not be copied or broadcast without permission from the producer of the video. Borrower is responsible if video is lost or damaged.

**Source: Consulate General of Japan at Chicago**
**Japan Information Center**
**Library**
**737 North Michigan Avenue, Suite 1000**
**Chicago, IL  60611**
**Phone: 1-312-280-0430**
**Fax: 1-312-280-6883**
**World Wide Web URL:**
**http://www.chicago.us.emb-japan.go.jp/jic.html**
**Email Address: jicchicago@webkddi.com**

## Origami--The Art of Paper Folding:  Part III & IV

Program consists of four parts, visually illustrating how to fold paper into a variety of familiar objects.  Excellent examples of sensitivity, creativity, and imagination of Japanese people.

Availability:          Schools, libraries, and nursing homes in Illinois, Indiana, Iowa, Kansas, Minnesota, Missouri, Nebraska, North Dakota, South Dakota, and Wisconsin.
Suggested Grade:  6-Adult
Order Number:      03401

Production Date:   1991
Format:                VHS videotape
Terms:                 Borrower pays return postage by U. S. Mail, UPS, or Federal Express, including insurance for "original" videos. Write, call, fax, or e-mail to request an application. An application form MUST be sent in one month in advance but not more than six months in advance. Include alternate titles and dates if provider can substitute titles. Send a SASE with request if you require confirmation. Return immediately after scheduled showing date. Videos may not be copied or broadcast without permission from the producer of the video. Borrower is responsible if video is lost or damaged.

**Source: Consulate General of Japan at Chicago**
**Japan Information Center**
**Library**
**737 North Michigan Avenue, Suite 1000**
**Chicago, IL  60611**
**Phone: 1-312-280-0430**
**Fax: 1-312-280-6883**
**World Wide Web URL:**
**http://www.chicago.us.emb-japan.go.jp/jic.html**
**Email Address: jicchicago@webkddi.com**

## Origami--The Art of Paper Folding:  Part III & IV

Program consists of four parts, visually illustrating how to fold paper into a variety of familiar objects.  Excellent examples of sensitivity, creativity, and imagination.

Availability:          Schools, libraries and homeschoolers in Alabama, Georgia, North Carolina, South Carolina, and Virginia.
Suggested Grade:  4-12
Order Number:      709
Production Date:   1991
Format:                VHS videotape
Terms:                 Borrower pays return postage.  Two tapes may be borrowed at a time.  Return within 7 days after receipt.  Reservations may be made by filling the application found on the web site.

**Source: Consulate General of Japan, Atlanta**
**Japan Information Center**
**One Alliance Center**
**3500 Lenox Road, Suite 1600**
**Atlanta, GA  30326**
**Phone: 1-404-365-9240**
**Fax: 1-404-240-4311**
**World Wide Web URL:**
**http://www.atlanta.us.emb-japan.go.jp**
**Email Address: info@cgjapanatlanta.org**

## Origami--The Art of Paper Folding:  Part III & IV

Program consists of four parts, visually illustrating how to fold paper into a variety of familiar objects.  Excellent examples of sensitivity, creativity, and imagination.

Availability:          Schools, libraries, homeschoolers, and nursing homes in Connecticut (except Fairfield County), Maine, Massachusetts, New Hampshire, Rhode Island, and Vermont.

Suggested Grade:   4-12
Order Number:   478
Production Date:   1991
Format:   VHS videotape
Terms:   Borrower pays return postage, including insurance. Return two weeks after receipt.
**Source:  Consulate General of Japan, Boston**
**Federal Reserve Plaza, 14th Floor**
**600 Atlantic Avenue**
**Boston, MA  02210**
**Phone:  1-617-973-9772**
**Fax:  1-617-542-1329**
**World Wide Web URL:**
**http://www.boston.us.emb-japan.go.jp**
**Email Address:  infocul@cgjbos.org**

## Origami--The Art of Paper Folding:  Part III & IV
Program consists of four parts, visually illustrating how to fold paper into a variety of familiar objects.  Excellent examples of sensitivity, creativity, and imagination.
Availability:   Schools, libraries, and  nursing homes in Hawaii.
Suggested Grade:   4-12
Order Number:   CU-40
Production Date:   1991
Format:   VHS videotape
Terms:   Borrower pays return postage.  A maximum of 3 videos may be borrowed per person.  Return within one week of date borrowed.
**Source:  Consulate General of Japan, Honolulu**
**1742 Nuuanu Avenue**
**Honolulu, HI  96817-3294**
**Phone:  1-808-543-3111**
**Fax:  1-808-543-3170**
**World Wide Web URL:**
**http://www.honolulu.us.emb-japan.go.jp**

## Origami--The Art of Paper Folding:  Part III & IV
Program consists of four parts, visually illustrating how to fold paper into a variety of familiar objects.  Excellent examples of sensitivity, creativity, and imagination.
Availability:   Schools,  libraries, homeschoolers, and nursing homes in Arizona and California (zipcodes beginning 900-931 and 935).
Suggested Grade:   4-12
Order Number:   169
Production Date:   1991
Format:   VHS videotape
Terms:   Borrower pays postage both ways; you may call the number below to learn how much postage costs.  Return within two weeks of date borrowed.  An individual may borrow 2 items at one time.  For non-profit and educational use only.
**Source:  Consulate General of Japan, Los Angeles**
**350 South Grand Avenue, Suite 1700**
**Los Angeles, CA  90071-3459**
**Phone:  1-213-617-6700**
**Fax:  1-213-617-6727**
**World Wide Web URL:  http://www.la.us.emb-japan.go.jp**

## Origami--The Art of Paper Folding:  Part III & IV
Program consists of four parts, visually illustrating how to fold paper into a variety of familiar objects.  Excellent examples of sensitivity, creativity, and imagination.
Availability:   Schools, libraries, homeschoolers, and nursing homes in OREGON AND SOUTHERN IDAHO ONLY.  Please make requests via the web site.
Suggested Grade:   4-12
Order Number:   179
Production Date:   1991
Format:   VHS videotape
Terms:   Borrower pays return postage.  Return within three weeks after scheduled showing date.  Book one month in advance if possible.  Rewind the video and wrap securely for return.  Be certain to indicate video number, date needed, name of your organization, and address to which video should be sent, along with phone number.  Audience report enclosed with the video must be completed and returned.
**Source:  Consulate General of Japan, Oregon**
**Attn:  Tamara, Video Library**
**1300 S. W. Fifth Avenue, Suite 2700**
**Portland, OR  97201**
**Phone:  1-503-221-1811, ext. 17**
**World Wide Web URL:**
**http://www.portland.us.emb-japan.go.jp/en/index.html**
**Email Address:  tamara@cgjpdx.org**

## Parent's Guide to Recreational Shooting for Youngsters, A
Answers parents most common questions about this topic.
Availability:   Limit of 100 copies to schools, libraries, and homeschoolers in the United States and Canada.  Make request on official stationery.
Suggested Grade:   Parents
Order Number:   002
Format:   Leaflet
**Source:  National Shooting Sports Foundation**
**Council for Wildlife Conservation and Education**
**11 Mile Hill Road**
**Newtown, CT  06470-2359**
**Phone:  1-203-426-1320**
**Fax:  1-203-426-1245**
**World Wide Web URL:  http://www.nssf.org**
**Email Address:  literature@nssf.org**

## Quilter's Ultimate Dictionary Online
Defines quilting terminology.
Availability:   All requesters
Suggested Grade:   6-Adult
Order Number:   not applicable
Format:   Online Dictionary
**Source:  Kimberly Crapsey**
**World Wide Web URL:**
**http://www.quiltpox.com/cgi-bin/glossary.pl**

## RulesCentral.com
Thousands of official rules for all types of sports and games.

| | |
|---|---|
| Availability: | All requesters |
| Suggested Grade: | All ages |
| Order Number: | not applicable |
| Format: | Web Site |

**Source: RulesCentral.com**
**World Wide Web URL: http://www.rulescentral.com**

## Salt Crystal Growth Directions
Instructions for growing salt crystals from table salt and other household ingredients. Also known as a "salt crystal garden" or a "depression garden." Excellent science project for rock/mineral units and for aiding in understanding evaporation.

| | |
|---|---|
| Availability: | One copy to schools, libraries, homeschoolers, and others in the United States and Canada. May be copied. |
| Suggested Grade: | K-12 |
| Order Number: | order by title |
| Format: | Flyer |
| Special Notes: | May also be downloaded from the web site. |

**Source: Mrs. Stewart's Bluing**
**P. O. Box 201405**
**Bloomington, MN 55420**
**Phone: 1-800-325-7785**
**Fax: 1-952-881-1873**
**World Wide Web URL: http://www.mrsstewart.com**
**Email Address: msb@mrsstewart.com**

## Set Net Fishing
Learn about this form of fishing.

| | |
|---|---|
| Availability: | All requesters |
| Suggested Grade: | 4-8 |
| Order Number: | not applicable |
| Format: | Web Site |
| Special Notes: | This URL will lead you to a subject page. Then click on the appropriate subject heading. |

**Source: ThinkQuest**
**World Wide Web URL:**
**http://www.thinkquest.org/pls/html/think.library**

## Sports for Everyday Living
Shows how everyday people enjoy some sort of sport throughout Japan--sports isn't just competitive activity.

| | |
|---|---|
| Availability: | Schools, libraries, and nursing homes in Connecticut (except Fairfield county), Maine, Massachusetts, New Hampshire, Rhode Island, and Vermont. |
| Suggested Grade: | 6-Adult |
| Order Number: | order by title |
| Format: | 16mm film |
| Terms: | Borrower pays return postage, including insurance. Return two weeks after receipt. |

**Source: Consulate General of Japan, Boston**
**Federal Reserve Plaza, 14th Floor, 600 Atlantic Avenue**
**Boston, MA 02210**

**Phone: 1-617-973-9772**
**Fax: 1-617-542-1329**
**World Wide Web URL:**
**http://www.boston.us.emb-japan.go.jp**
**Email Address: infocul@cgjbos.org**

## Tennis 101
Here are the rules of this game plus tips to help you improve.

| | |
|---|---|
| Availability: | All requesters |
| Suggested Grade: | All ages |
| Languages: | English; French; Spanish |
| Order Number: | not applicable |
| Format: | Web Site |
| Special Notes: | This URL will lead you to a subject page. Then click on the appropriate subject heading. |

**Source: ThinkQuest**
**World Wide Web URL:**
**http://www.thinkquest.org/pls/html/think.library**

## Traditional Japanese Sports: Kyudo
Kyudo is the Japanese sport of archery. This program looks at this sport in Japan.

| | |
|---|---|
| Availability: | Schools, libraries, homeschoolers, and nursing homes in Connecticut (except Fairfield County), Maine, Massachusetts, New Hampshire, Rhode Island, and Vermont. |
| Suggested Grade: | All ages |
| Order Number: | 600 |
| Production Date: | 1997 |
| Format: | VHS videotape |
| Terms: | Borrower pays return postage, including insurance. Return two weeks after receipt. |

**Source: Consulate General of Japan, Boston**
**Federal Reserve Plaza, 14th Floor**
**600 Atlantic Avenue**
**Boston, MA 02210**
**Phone: 1-617-973-9772**
**Fax: 1-617-542-1329**
**World Wide Web URL:**
**http://www.boston.us.emb-japan.go.jp**
**Email Address: infocul@cgjbos.org**

## Traditional Japanese Sports: Kyudo
Kyudo is the Japanese sport of archery. This program looks at this sport in Japan.

| | |
|---|---|
| Availability: | Schools, libraries, homeschoolers, and nursing homes in Connecticut, Delaware, Maryland, New Jersey, New York, Pennsylvania, and West Virginia. |
| Suggested Grade: | All ages |
| Order Number: | order by title |
| Production Date: | 1997 |
| Format: | VHS videotape |
| Terms: | Send a blank videotape to this source and they will dub the program you desire onto it for permanent retention. You must send a self-addressed, stamped envelope with sufficient postage for return. |

Source: Consulate General of Japan, New York
Audio Video Dept.
299 Park Avenue, 18th Floor
New York, NY  10171
Phone: 1-212-371-8222
Fax: 1-212-319-6357
World Wide Web URL: http://www.ny.us.emb-japan.go.jp

## Traditional Japanese Sports:  Kyudo

Kyudo is the Japanese sport of archery.  This program looks at this sport in Japan.

Availability:     Schools, libraries, homeschoolers, and nursing homes in OREGON AND SOUTHERN IDAHO ONLY.  Please make requests via the web site.

Suggested Grade:  All ages
Order Number:     443
Production Date:  1997
Format:           VHS videotape

Terms:   Borrower pays return postage.  Return within three weeks after scheduled showing date.  Book one month in advance if possible.  Rewind the video and wrap securely for return.  Be certain to indicate video number, date needed, name of your organization, and address to which video should be sent, along with phone number.  Audience report enclosed with the video must be completed and returned.

Source: Consulate General of Japan, Oregon
Attn: Tamara, Video Library
1300 S. W. Fifth Avenue, Suite 2700
Portland, OR  97201
Phone: 1-503-221-1811, ext. 17
World Wide Web URL:
http://www.portland.us.emb-japan.go.jp/en/index.html
Email Address: tamara@cgjpdx.org

## Wildlife for Tomorrow

Shows how wildlife managers work to prevent wildlife from becoming endangered and how regulated hunting fits into the overall conservation picture.

Availability:     Schools, libraries, homeschoolers, and nursing homes in the United States and Canada.

Suggested Grade:  4-7
Order Number:     502
Format:           VHS videotape
Special Notes:    May be retained permanently.  Cleared for TV broadcast.

Source: National Shooting Sports Foundation
11 Mile Hill Road
Newtown, CT  06470-2359
Phone: 1-203-426-1320
Fax: 1-203-426-1245 (ls)
World Wide Web URL:  http://www.nssf.org/safety
Email Address:  literature@nssf.org

## World of Stamps, The

A basic primer on how to start collecting stamps.

Availability:
Suggested Grade:  4-12
Order Number:     not applicable
Format:           Downloadable Pamphlet

Source:  American Philatelic Society
World Wide Web URL:  http://www.stamps.org

# TITLE INDEX

# TITLE INDEX

# TITLE INDEX

# SUBJECT INDEX

# SUBJECT INDEX

# SUBJECT INDEX

# SUBJECT INDEX

# SUBJECT INDEX

# SUBJECT INDEX

# SUBJECT INDEX

# SUBJECT INDEX

# SUBJECT INDEX

The SOURCE INDEX is an alphabetical list of the organizations from which the materials listed in the EDUCATORS GUIDE TO FREE HEALTH, PHYSICAL EDUCATION & RECREATION MATERIALS may be obtained. There are 165 sources listed in this Fifty-First Edition of the GUIDE, **of which 138 are new**. The numbers following each listing are the page numbers on which the materials from each source are annotated in the body of the GUIDE.

When requesting materials via mail or fax, please use a letter of request similar to the sample shown in the front part of the GUIDE. When requesting via telephone, please have the name of the material you desire in front of you (along with the order number if necessary). Please read each listing carefully to be certain that the material you are requesting is available via the method through which you choose to order.

**Bold type indicates a source that is new in the 2018-2019 edition**. Complete addresses for each source are found following the description of the material in the body of the GUIDE.

# SOURCE INDEX